Oh My Goddess!

あぁっ女神さまっ

1-555-GODDESS

PUBLISHER
Mike Richardson

SERIES EDITORS
Peet Janes & Greg Vest

COLLECTION EDITOR
Lynn Adair

COLLECTION DESIGNER
Julie Eggers Gassaway

COLLECTION DESIGN MANAGER
Brian Gogolin

English-language version produced by Studio Proteus
for Dark Horse Comics, Inc.

OH MY GODDESS! Volume I: 1-555-GODDESS

This book collects issues one through three of the Dark Horse comic book series *Oh My Goddess!
Part I* and issues three through five of the Dark Horse comic book series *Oh My Goddess! Part II.*

Published by
Dark Horse Comics, Inc.
10956 SE Main Street
Milwaukie, OR 97222

First edition: November 1996
ISBN: 1-56971-207-7

5 7 9 10 8 6
Printed in Canada

Oh My Goddess!

ああ女神さま

1-555-GODDESS

STORY AND ART BY

Kosuke Fujishima

TRANSLATION BY

Alan Gleason & Toren Smith

LETTERING AND TOUCH-UP BY

L. Lois Buhalis & Tom Orzechowski

DARK HORSE COMICS®

About the Creator

KOSUKE FUJISHIMA was born July 7, 1964 in the wilds of Chiba, Japan. It was soon determined that he was a human, with blood type B. He then proceeded to grow up and go to school. But let us draw a discreet curtain over those days.

After graduating from high school, Fujishima landed a job as an editor for *Puff*, a comics news magazine. While there, it is rumored he was responsible for the parody comic called "'X'-pa no Yoko-chan" that ran in *Puff.*

One of his jobs as editor was to interview Tatsuya Egawa, who was running his groundbreaking "Be Free!" serial in Kodansha's *Comic Morning* magazine at that time. After the interview, Fujishima mustered the nerve to ask Egawa if he needed an assistant. Egawa looked at Fujishima's work and said, "Sure!" Thus, our unsuspecting, young editor plunged into the abyss of comics-artist hell.

Fujishima generally dates his debut as a professional with the publication of a comics-style report he did for *Comic Morning* on the making of the 1986 live-action, theatrical-movie version of "Be Free!"

The fans loved his work, and *Morning* received a fan letter raving about the policewoman characters Fujishima had used in the *Making of Be Free!* report. He was inspired by this letter to create his first series, *You're Under Arrest!*, which began in *Morning Party Extra* in 1986.

In 1988, Fujishima did a four-panel gag cartoon that featured the characters from *You're Under Arrest!* praying to a goddess. This was part of a contest in which readers could win various *You're Under Arrest!* presents, such as T-shirts. In the cartoon, Miyuki and Natsumi were asking the goddess to please let them win the contest. Fujishima was so pleased with the way the goddess turned out that she became the basis for Belldandy and inspired the creation of the *Oh My Goddess!* series for *Afternoon* magazine.

So, as you can see, Fujishima's stories are often inspired by some minor characters he creates for another purpose entirely.

Fujishima has a ridiculous number of hobbies, including: playing electric guitar and with his new Mac, building plastic models and garage kits, and taking care of his numerous tropical fish. He also owns, rides, and repairs his seven (!) motorcycles and three cars. He listens to DMX — a digital, commercial-free radio service — while he works, and he likes classic American hard rock such as Van Halen and Bon Jovi. Fujishima also likes Japanese idol singers — in fact, there is a quite convincing rumor that the name "Morisato" (from *Oh My Goddess!*) comes from the name of the idol singer <u>Moritaka Chisato</u>. ❀

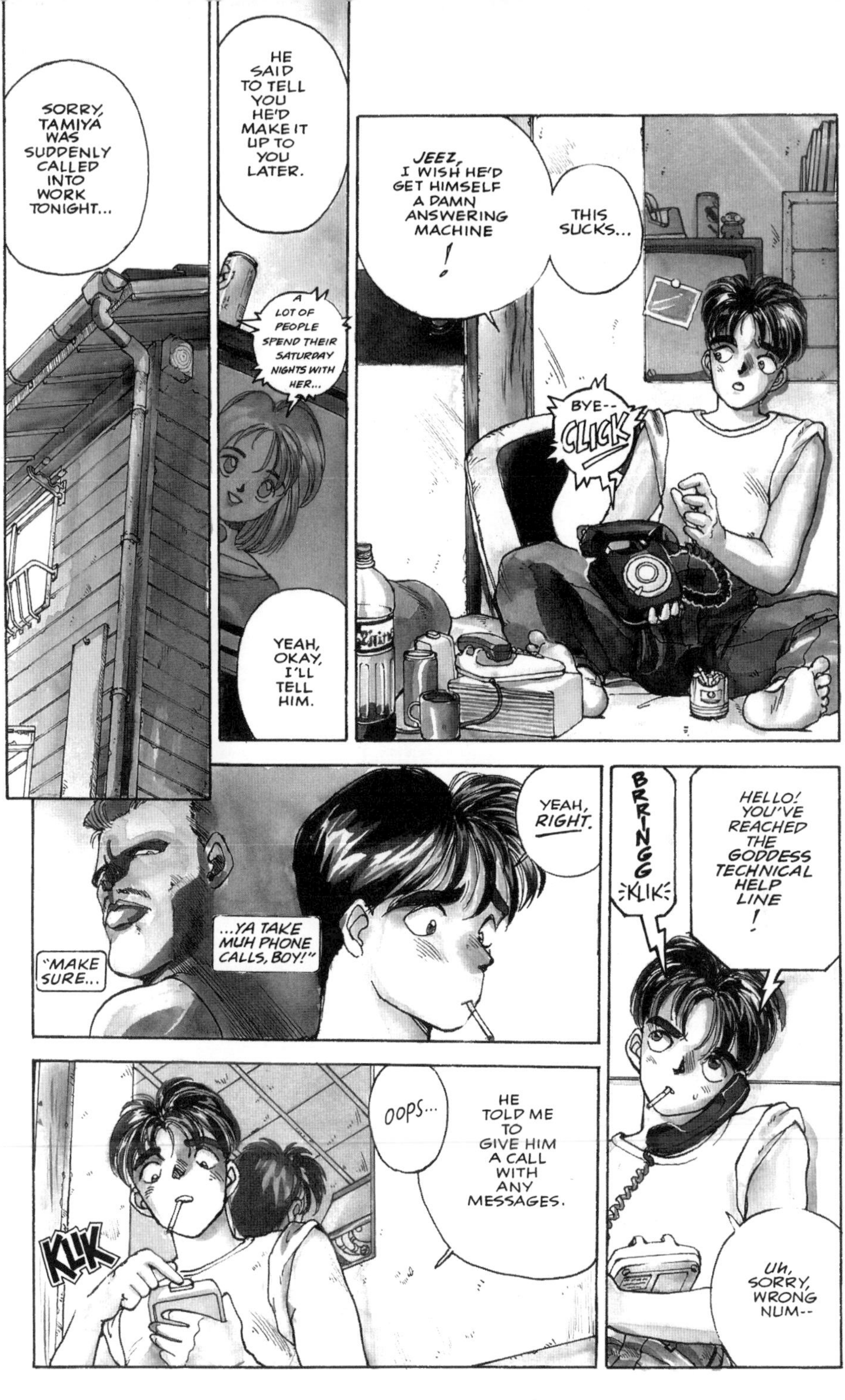
SORRY, TAMIYA WAS SUDDENLY CALLED INTO WORK TONIGHT...
HE SAID TO TELL YOU HE'D MAKE IT UP TO YOU LATER.
A LOT OF PEOPLE SPEND THEIR SATURDAY NIGHTS WITH HER...
YEAH, OKAY, I'LL TELL HIM.
JEEZ, I WISH HE'D GET HIMSELF A DAMN ANSWERING MACHINE!
THIS SUCKS...
BYE-- CLICK
"MAKE SURE...
...YA TAKE MUH PHONE CALLS, BOY!"
YEAH, RIGHT.
OOPS...
HE TOLD ME TO GIVE HIM A CALL WITH ANY MESSAGES.
KLIK
BRRINGG
KLIK
HELLO! YOU'VE REACHED THE GODDESS TECHNICAL HELP LINE!
UH, SORRY, WRONG NUM--

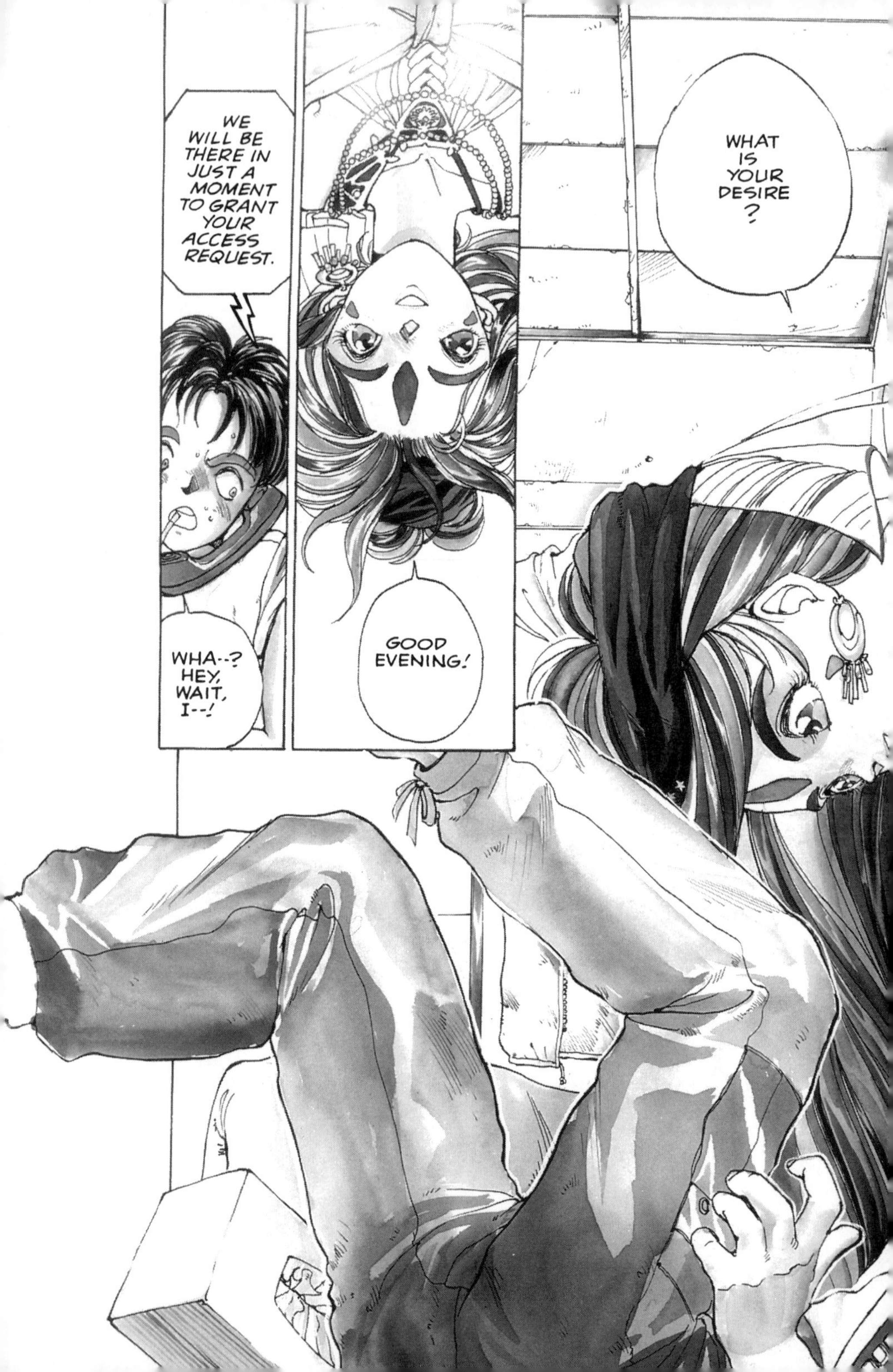
WE WILL BE THERE IN JUST A MOMENT TO GRANT YOUR ACCESS REQUEST.
WHA--? HEY, WAIT, I--!
GOOD EVENING!
WHAT IS YOUR DESIRE?

WRONG NUMBER

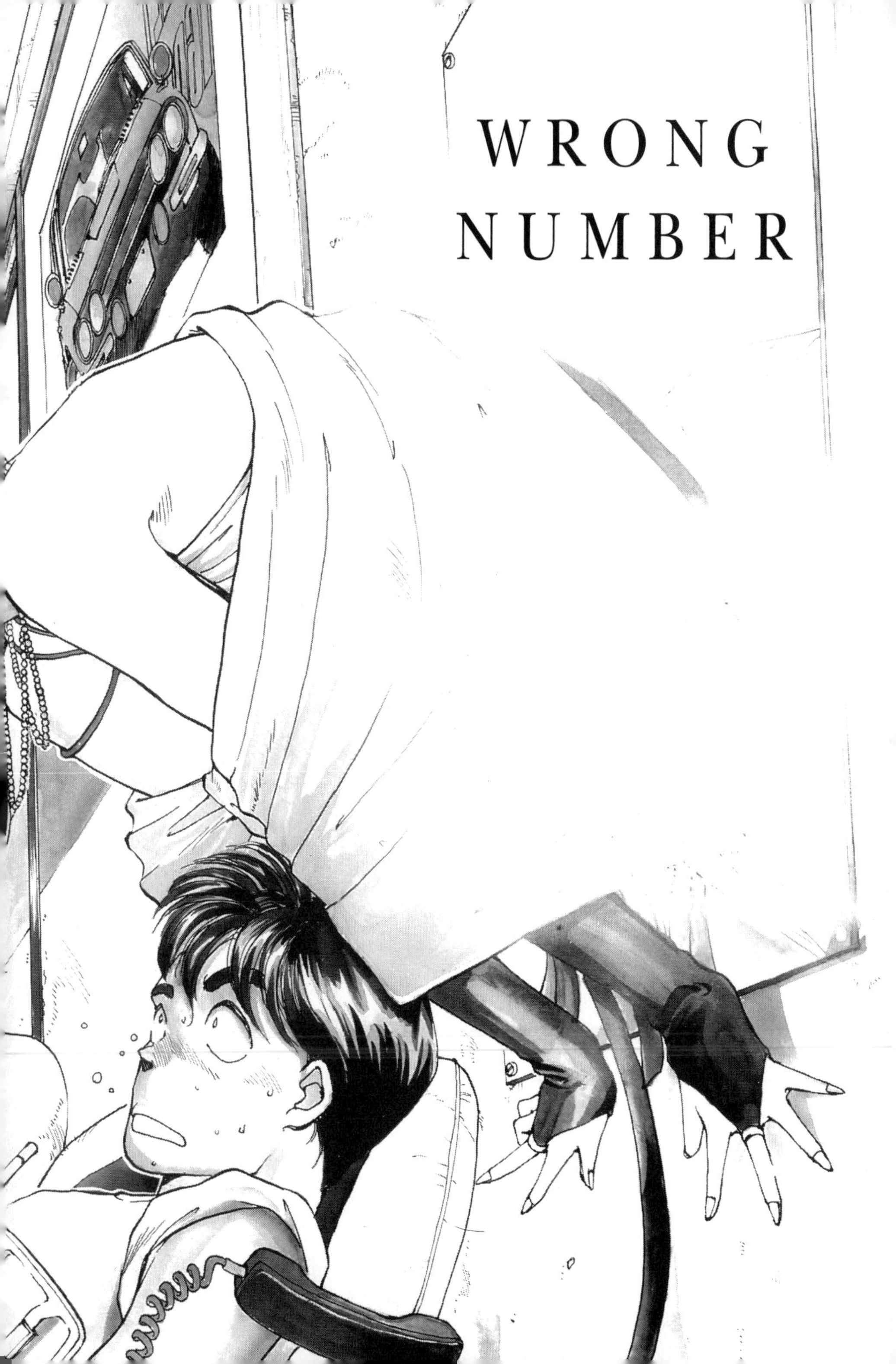

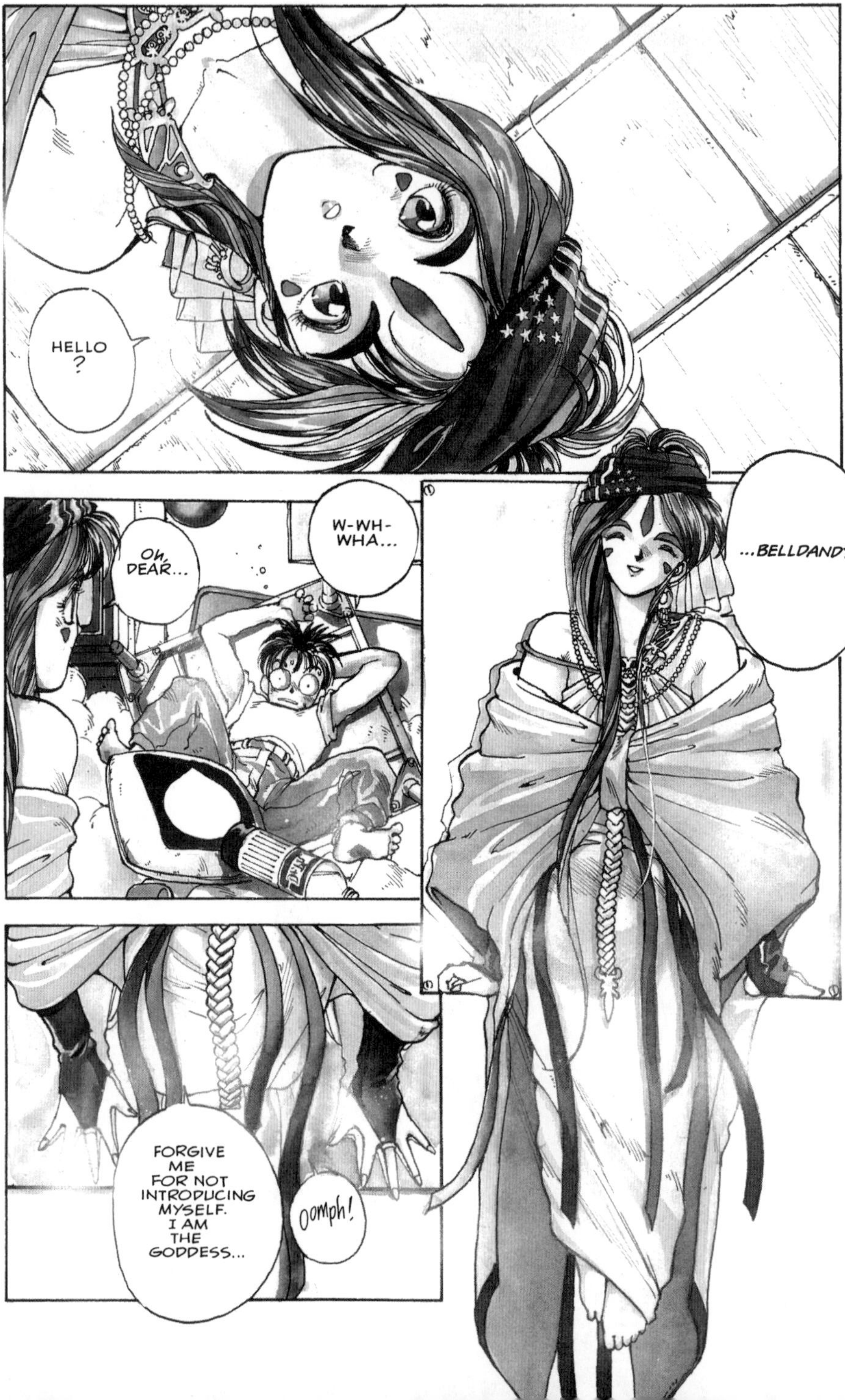
HELLO ?
Oh, DEAR...
W-WH- WHA...
FORGIVE ME FOR NOT INTRODUCING MYSELF. I AM THE GODDESS...
OOMPH!
...BELLDANDY.

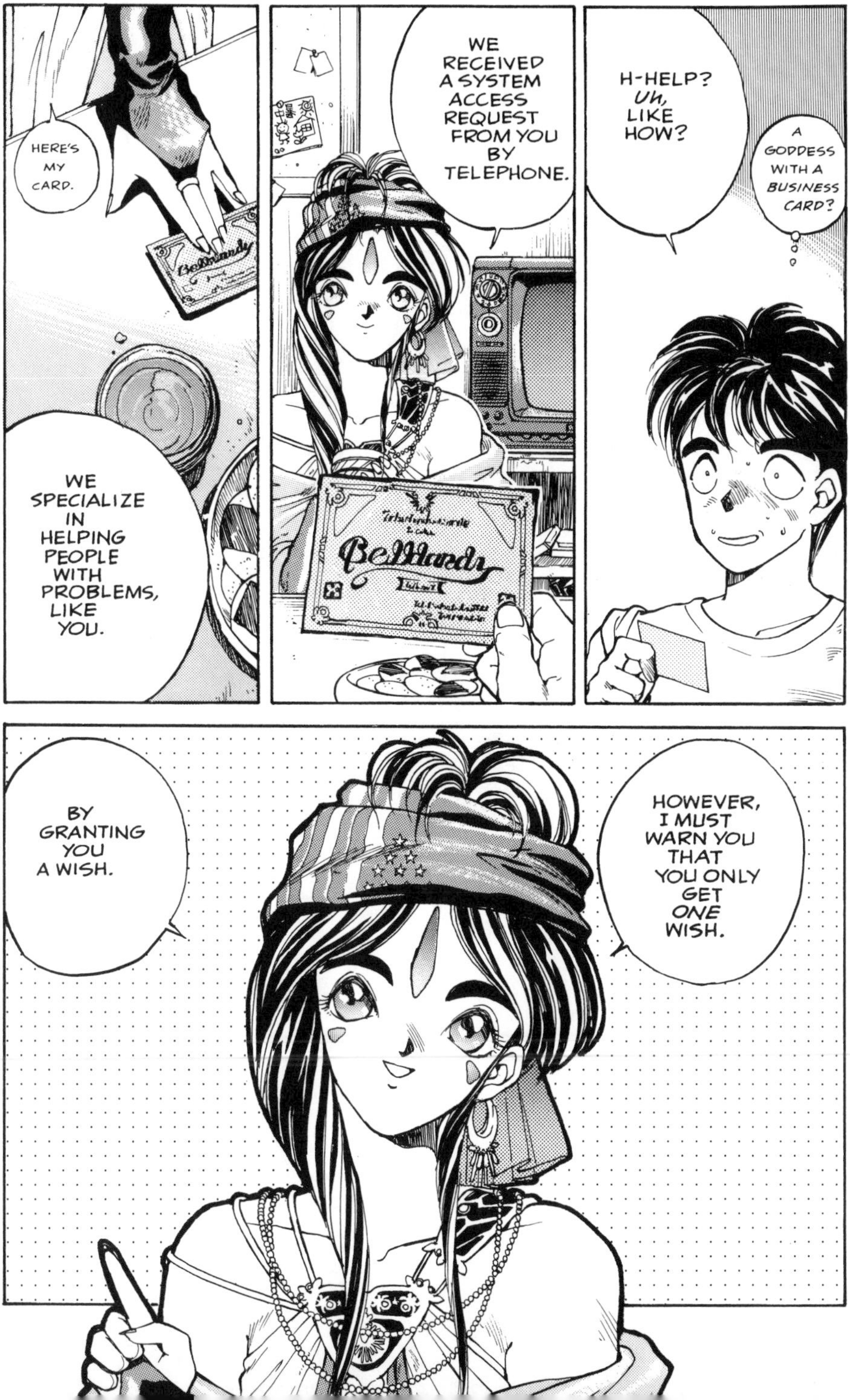
HERE'S MY CARD.
WE SPECIALIZE IN HELPING PEOPLE WITH PROBLEMS, LIKE YOU.
WE RECEIVED A SYSTEM ACCESS REQUEST FROM YOU BY TELEPHONE.
H-HELP? *UH,* LIKE HOW?
A GODDESS WITH A *BUSINESS* CARD?
BY GRANTING YOU A WISH.
HOWEVER, I MUST WARN YOU THAT YOU ONLY GET *ONE* WISH.

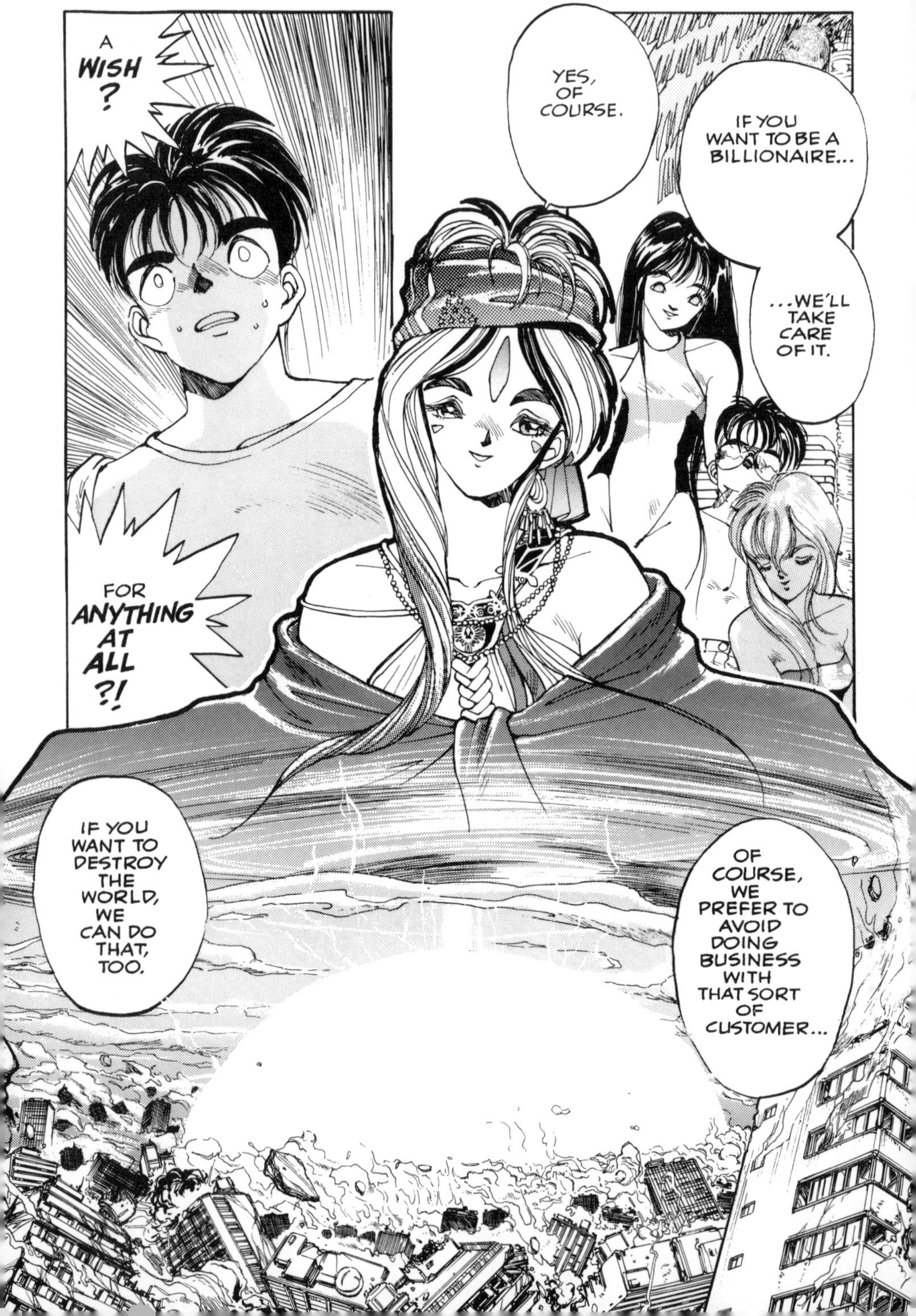
A WISH?
FOR ANYTHING AT ALL?!
YES, OF COURSE.
IF YOU WANT TO BE A BILLIONAIRE...
...WE'LL TAKE CARE OF IT.
IF YOU WANT TO DESTROY THE WORLD, WE CAN DO THAT, TOO.
OF COURSE, WE PREFER TO AVOID DOING BUSINESS WITH THAT SORT OF CUSTOMER...

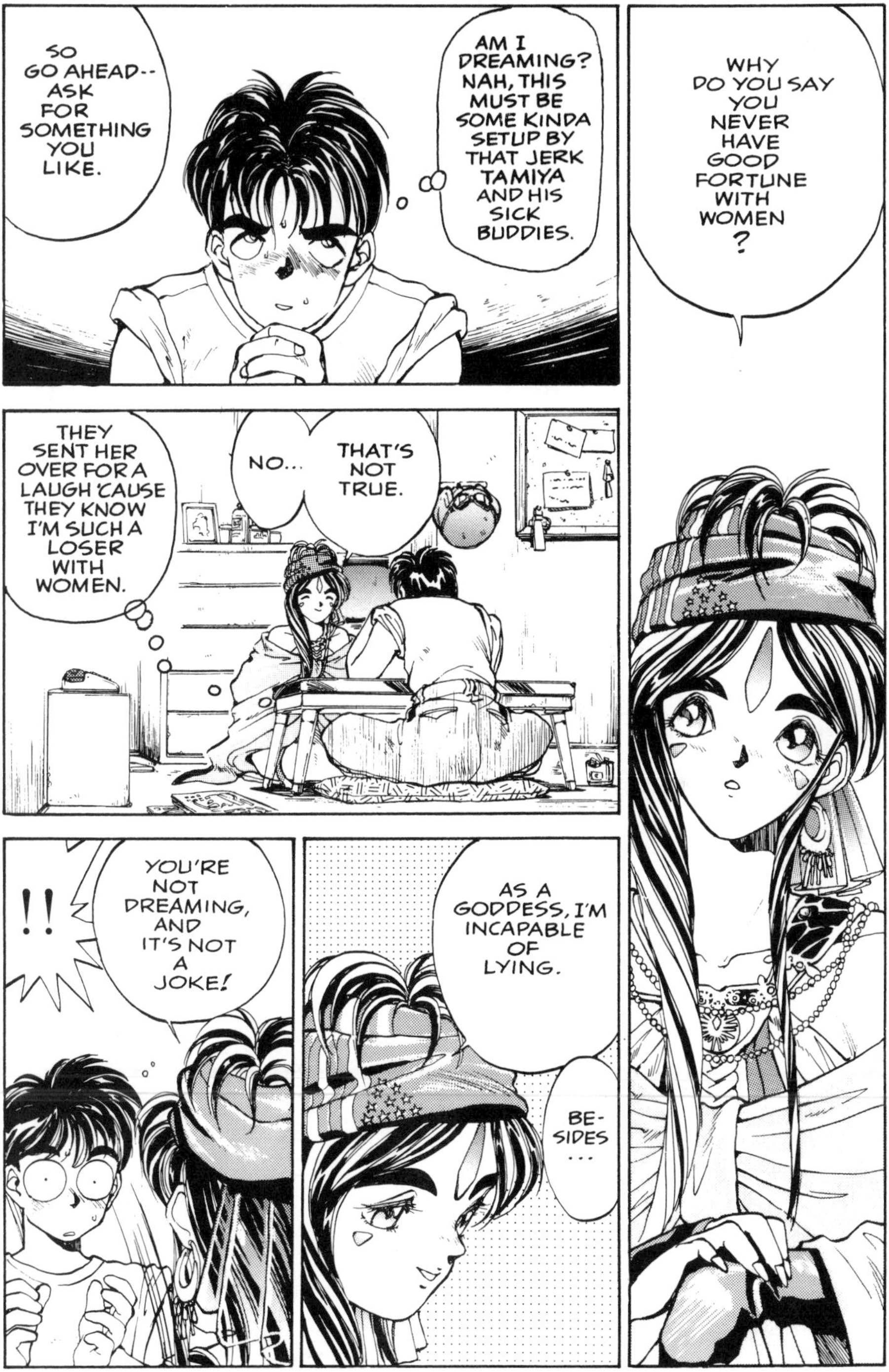
SO GO AHEAD-- ASK FOR SOMETHING YOU LIKE.
AM I DREAMING? NAH, THIS MUST BE SOME KINDA SETUP BY THAT JERK TAMIYA AND HIS SICK BUDDIES.
THEY SENT HER OVER FOR A LAUGH 'CAUSE THEY KNOW I'M SUCH A LOSER WITH WOMEN.
NO...
THAT'S NOT TRUE.
!!
YOU'RE NOT DREAMING, AND IT'S NOT A JOKE!
AS A GODDESS, I'M INCAPABLE OF LYING.
BE-SIDES...
WHY DO YOU SAY YOU NEVER HAVE GOOD FORTUNE WITH WOMEN?

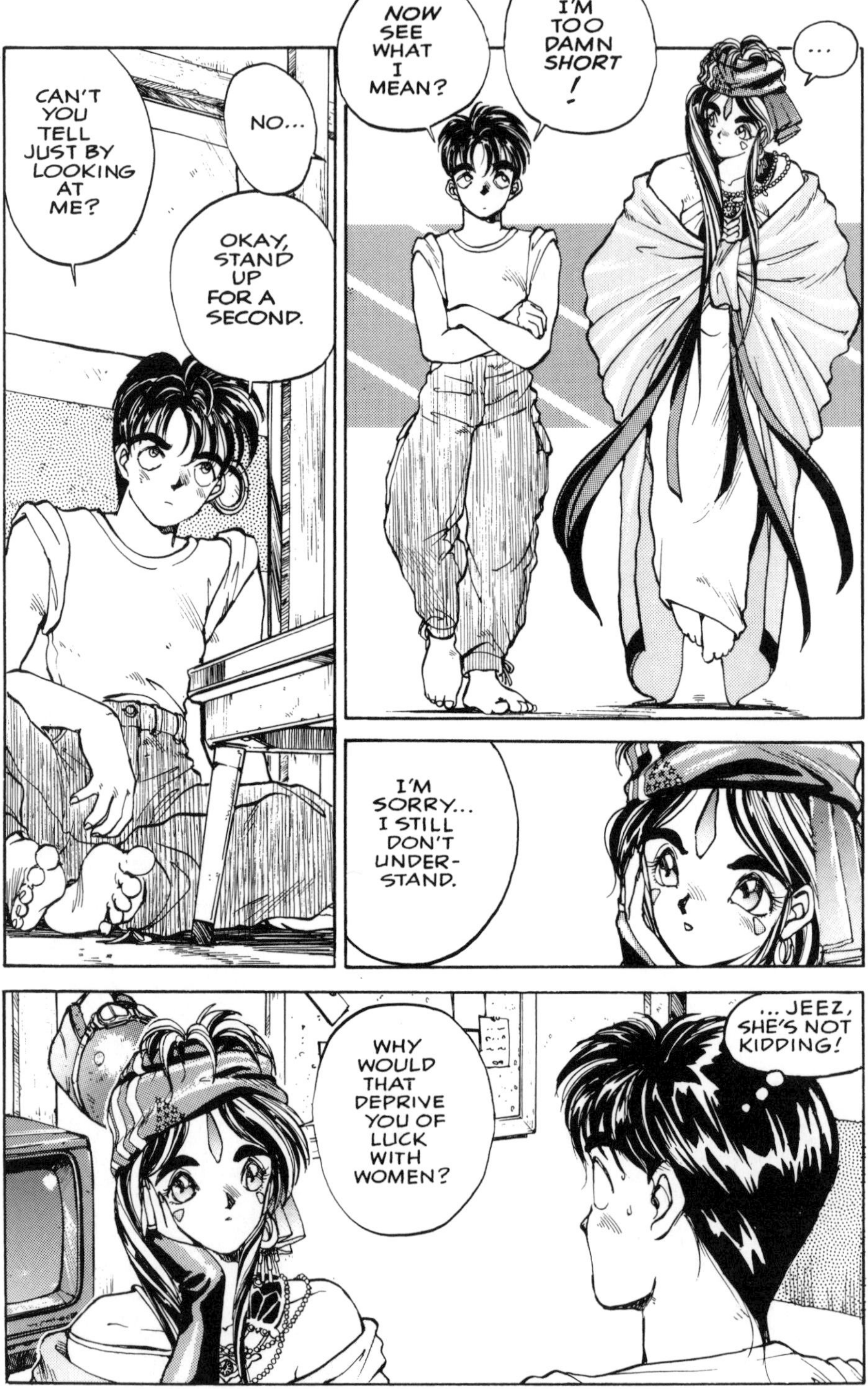
CAN'T YOU TELL JUST BY LOOKING AT ME?
NO...
OKAY, STAND UP FOR A SECOND.
NOW SEE WHAT I MEAN?
I'M TOO DAMN SHORT!
...
I'M SORRY... I STILL DON'T UNDER-STAND.
WHY WOULD THAT DEPRIVE YOU OF LUCK WITH WOMEN?
...JEEZ, SHE'S NOT KIDDING!

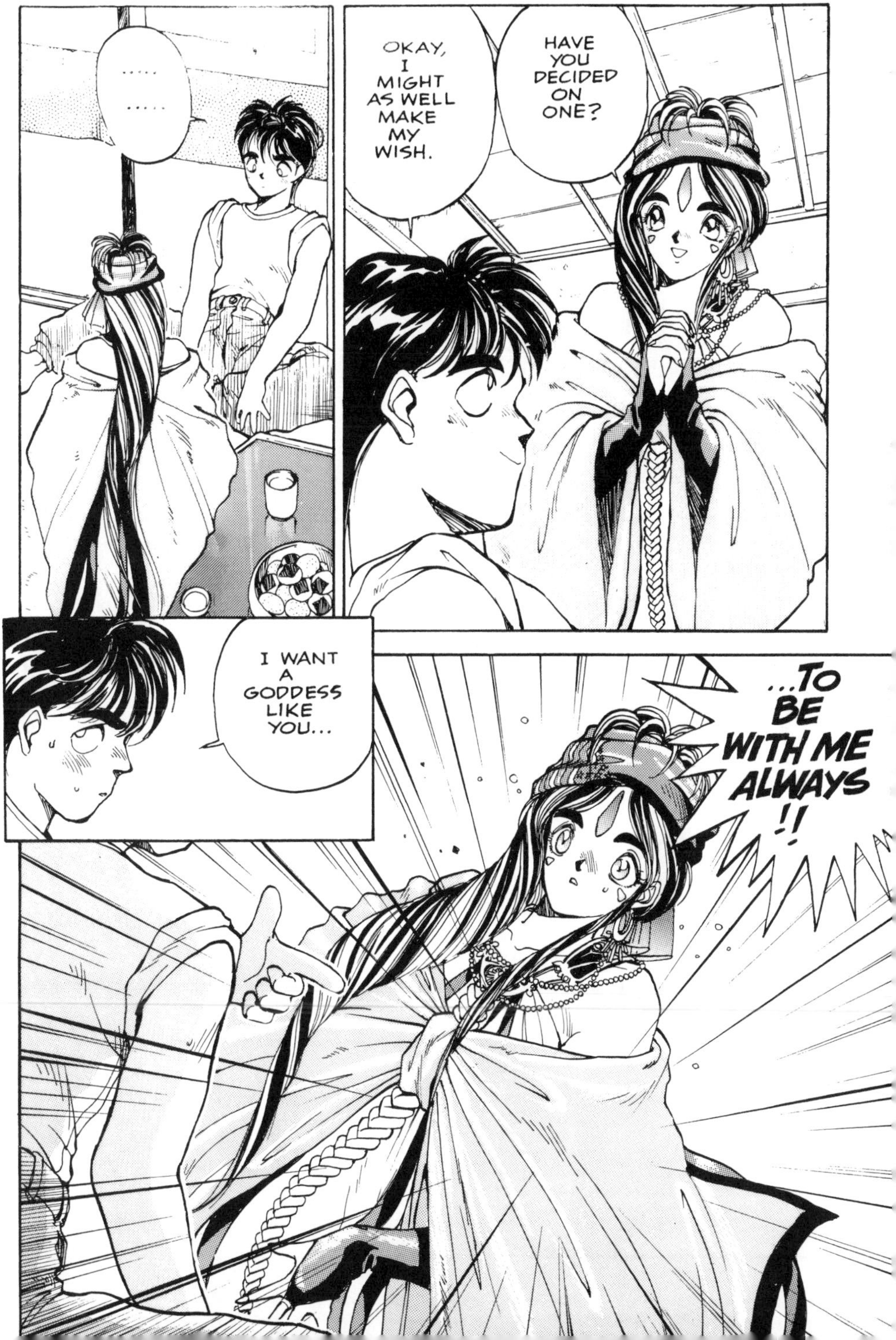

....
OKAY, I MIGHT AS WELL MAKE MY WISH.
HAVE YOU DECIDED ON ONE?
I WANT A GODDESS LIKE YOU...
...TO BE WITH ME ALWAYS !!

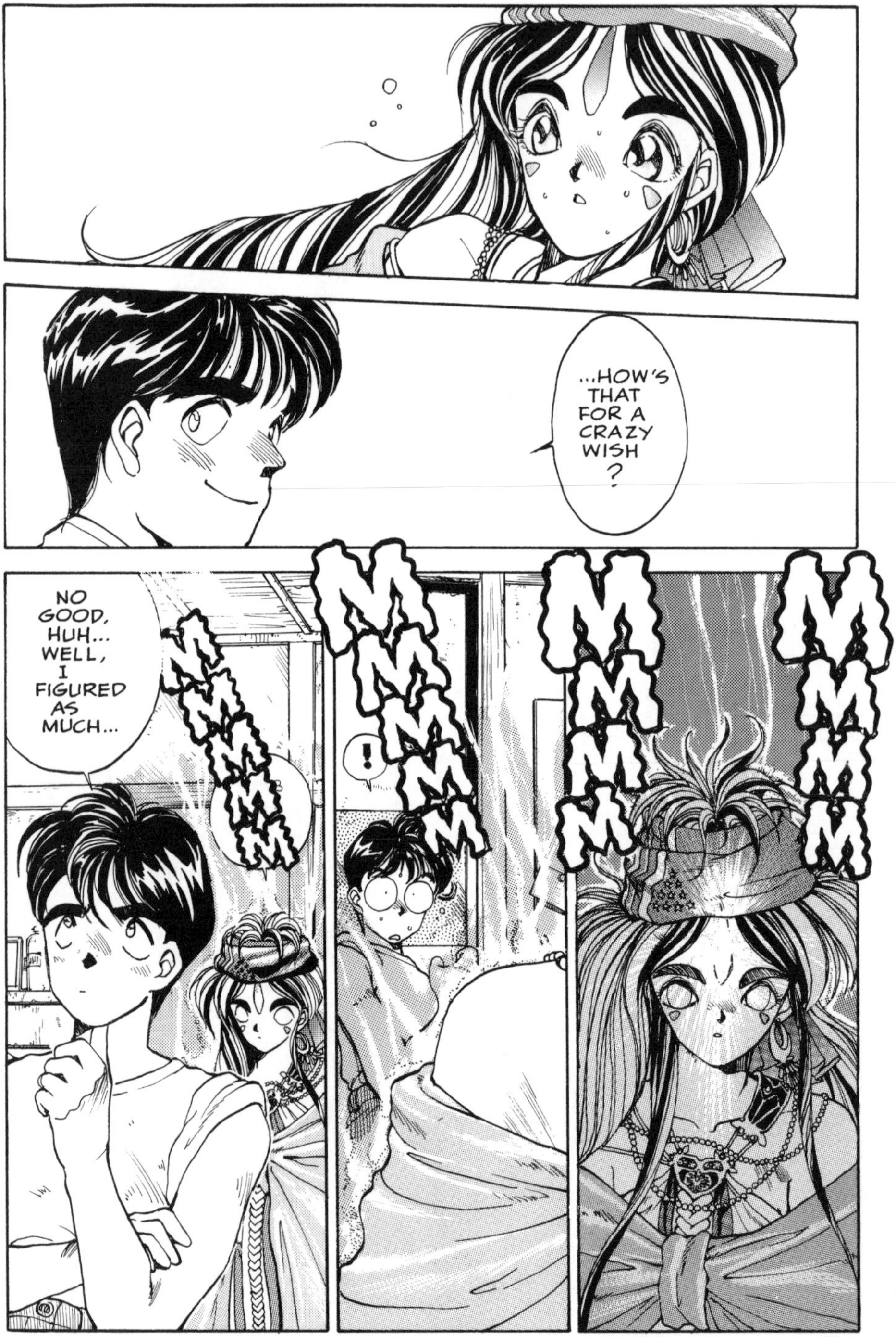
...HOW'S THAT FOR A CRAZY WISH ?
NO GOOD, HUH... WELL, I FIGURED AS MUCH...
MMMMMMM
!
MMMMMMM
MMMM
MMMMM

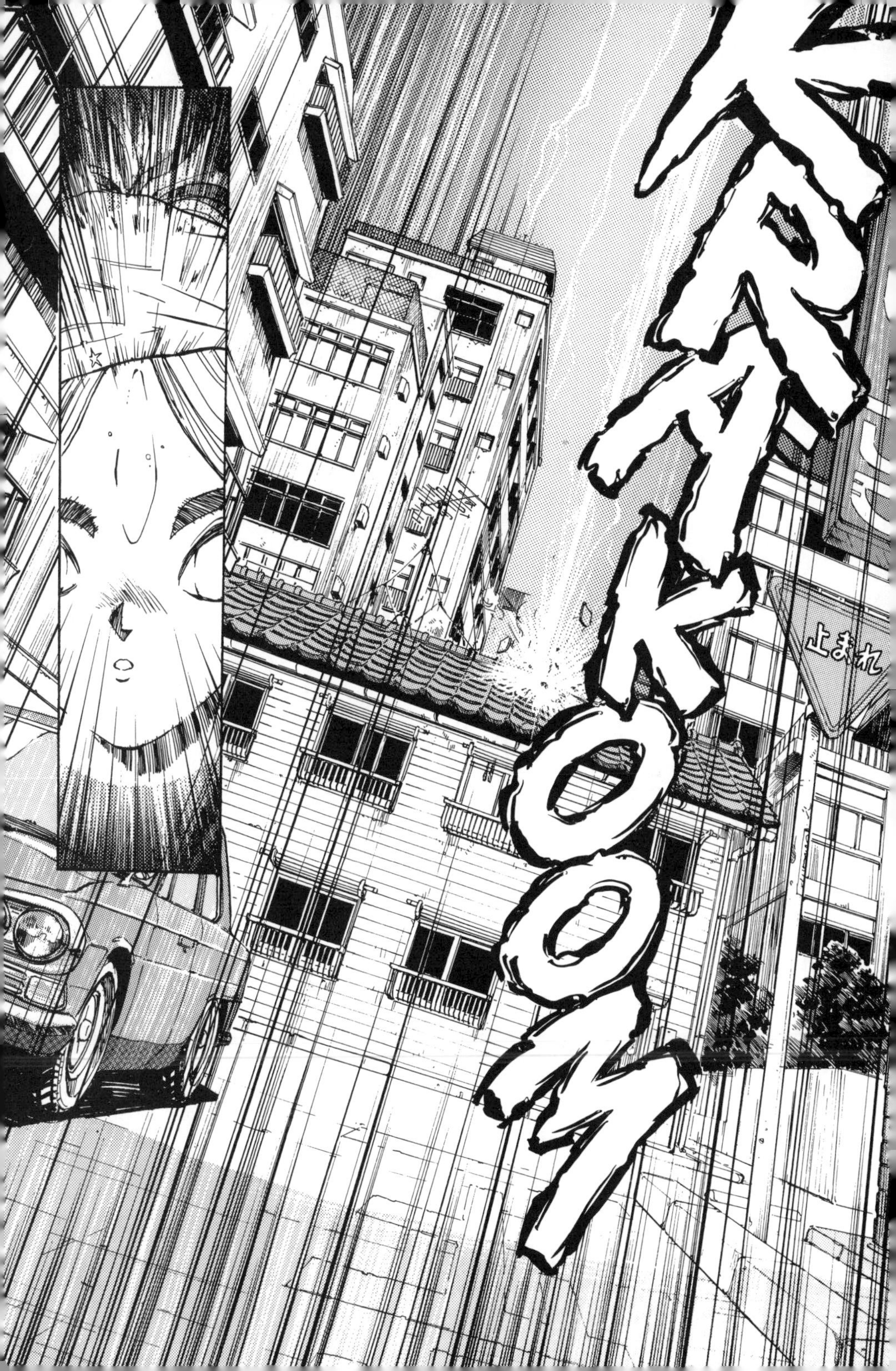
KRAKOOM
上まれ

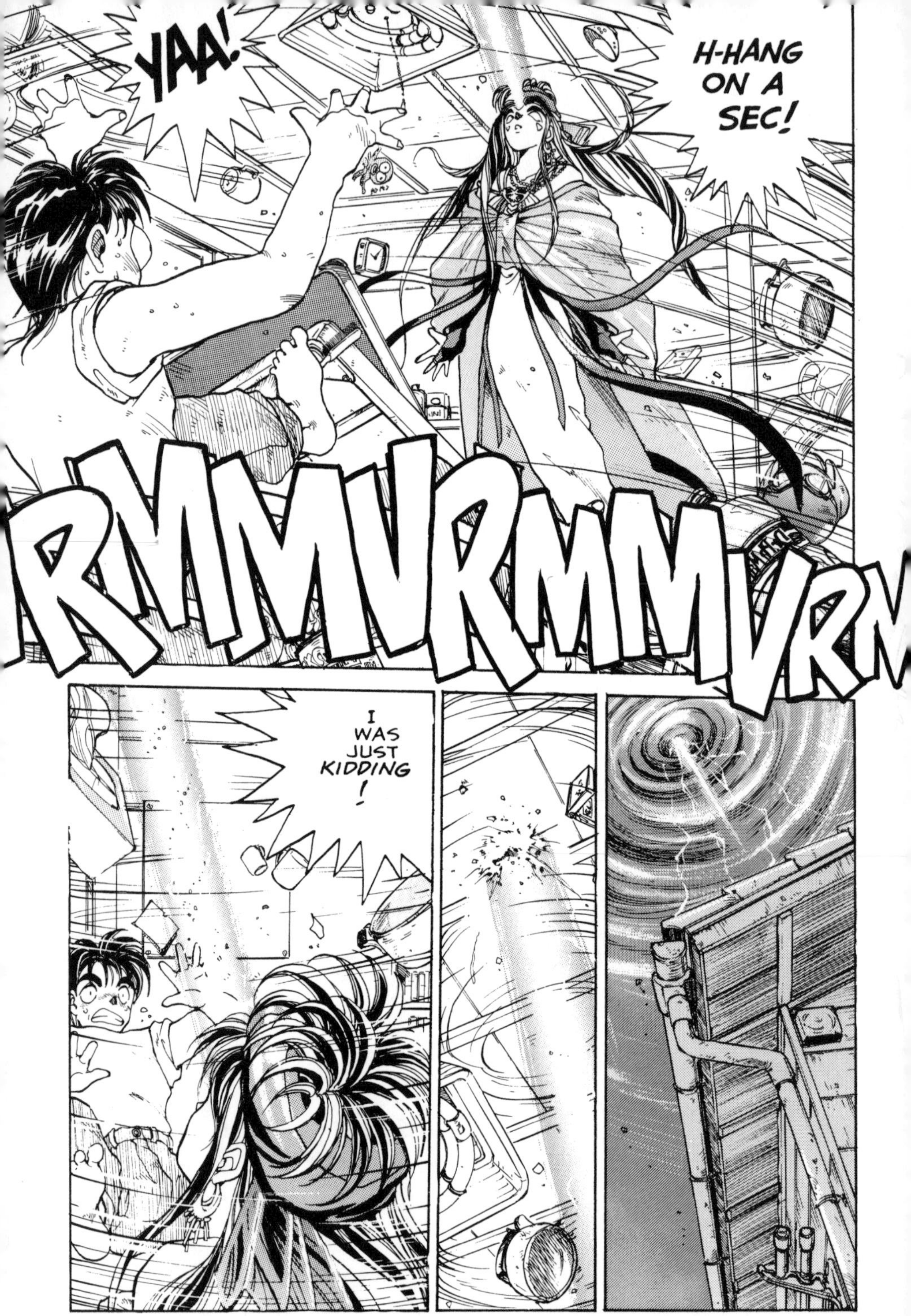
YAA!
H-HANG ON A SEC!
RMMVRMMMVRM
I WAS JUST KIDDING!

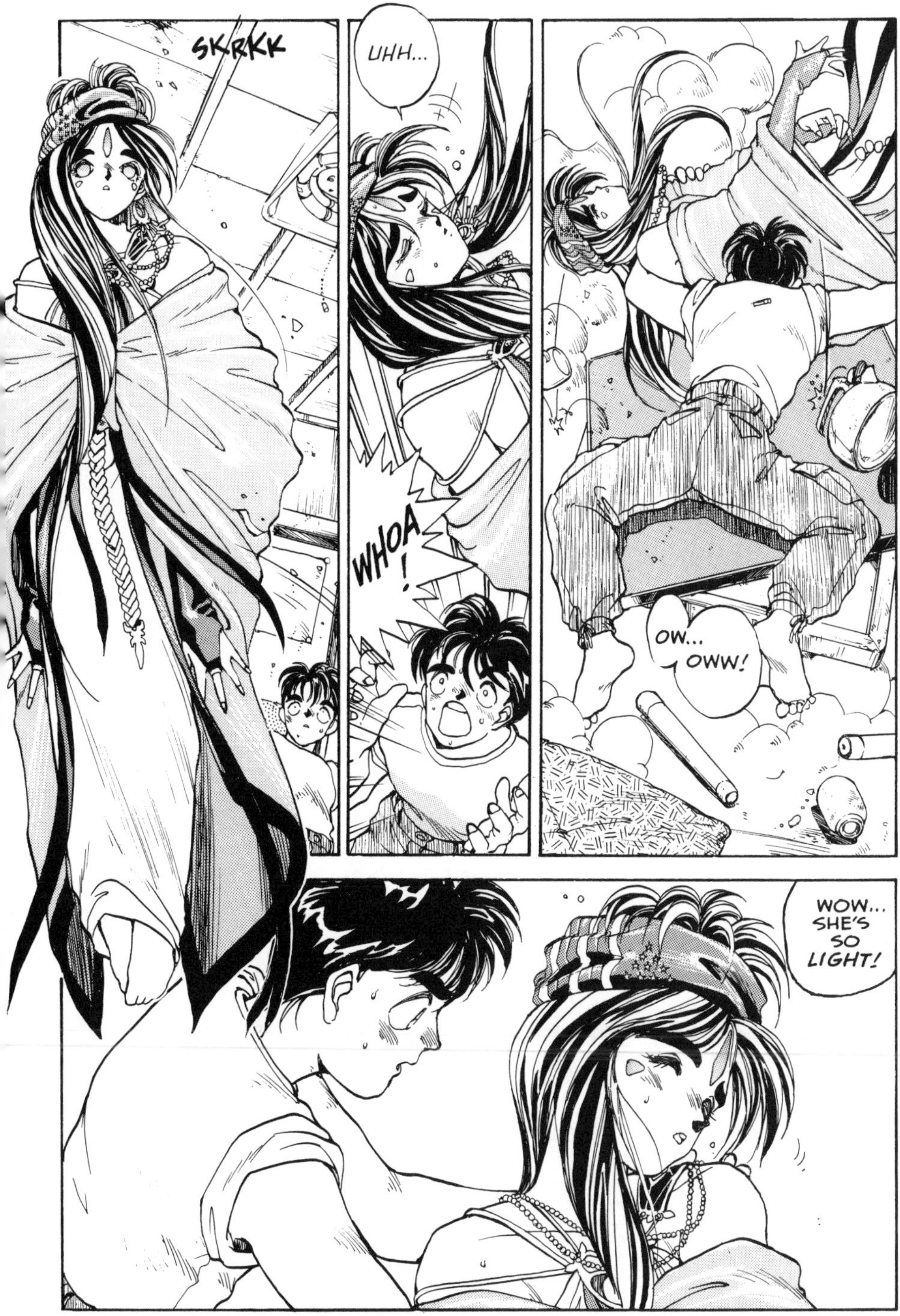
SKRKK
UHH...
WHOA!
OW... OWW!
WOW... SHE'S SO LIGHT!

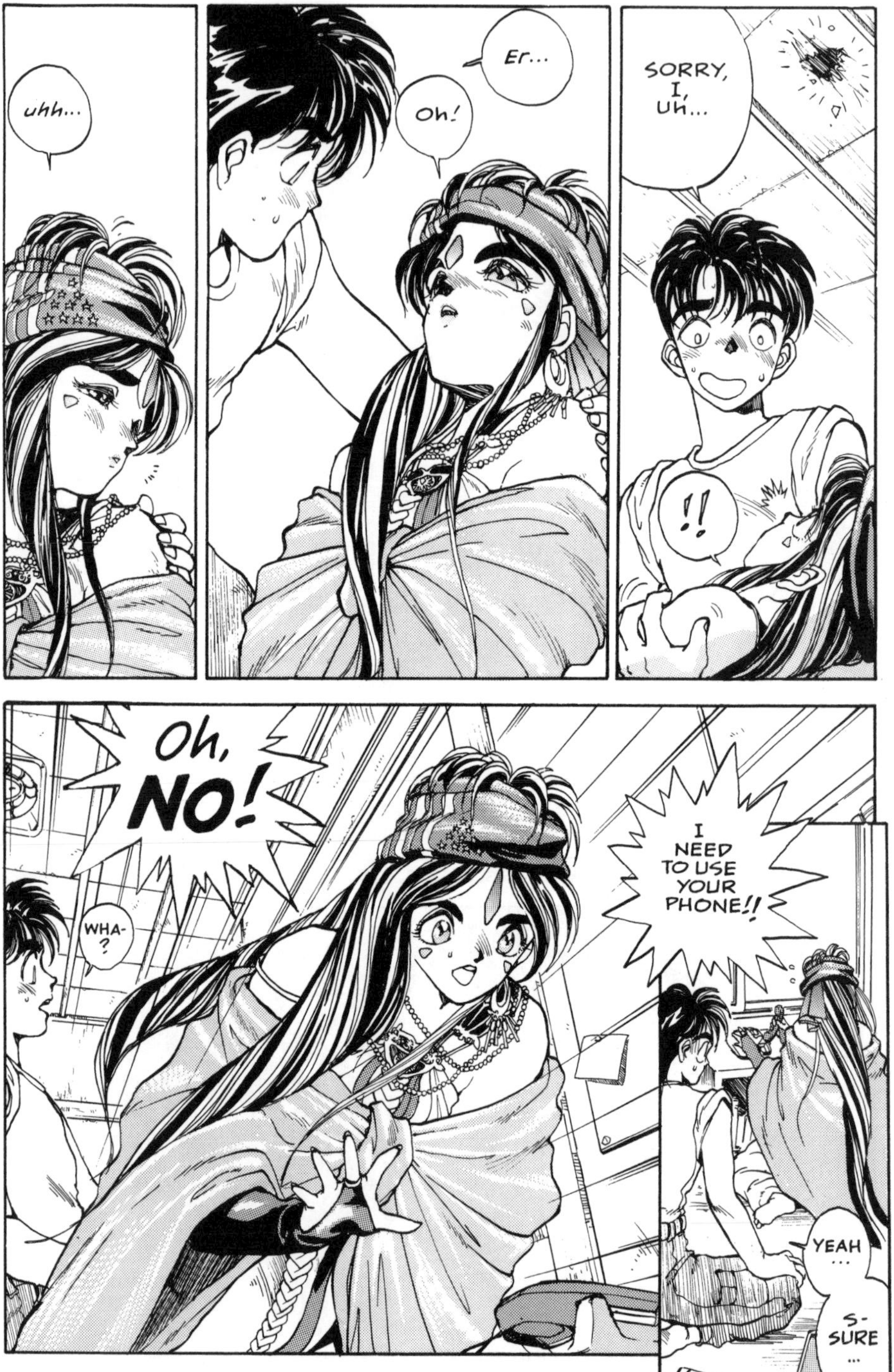
uhh...
Er...
Oh!
SORRY, I, UH...
!!
Oh, NO!
WHA-?
I NEED TO USE YOUR PHONE!!
YEAH ...
S-SURE ...

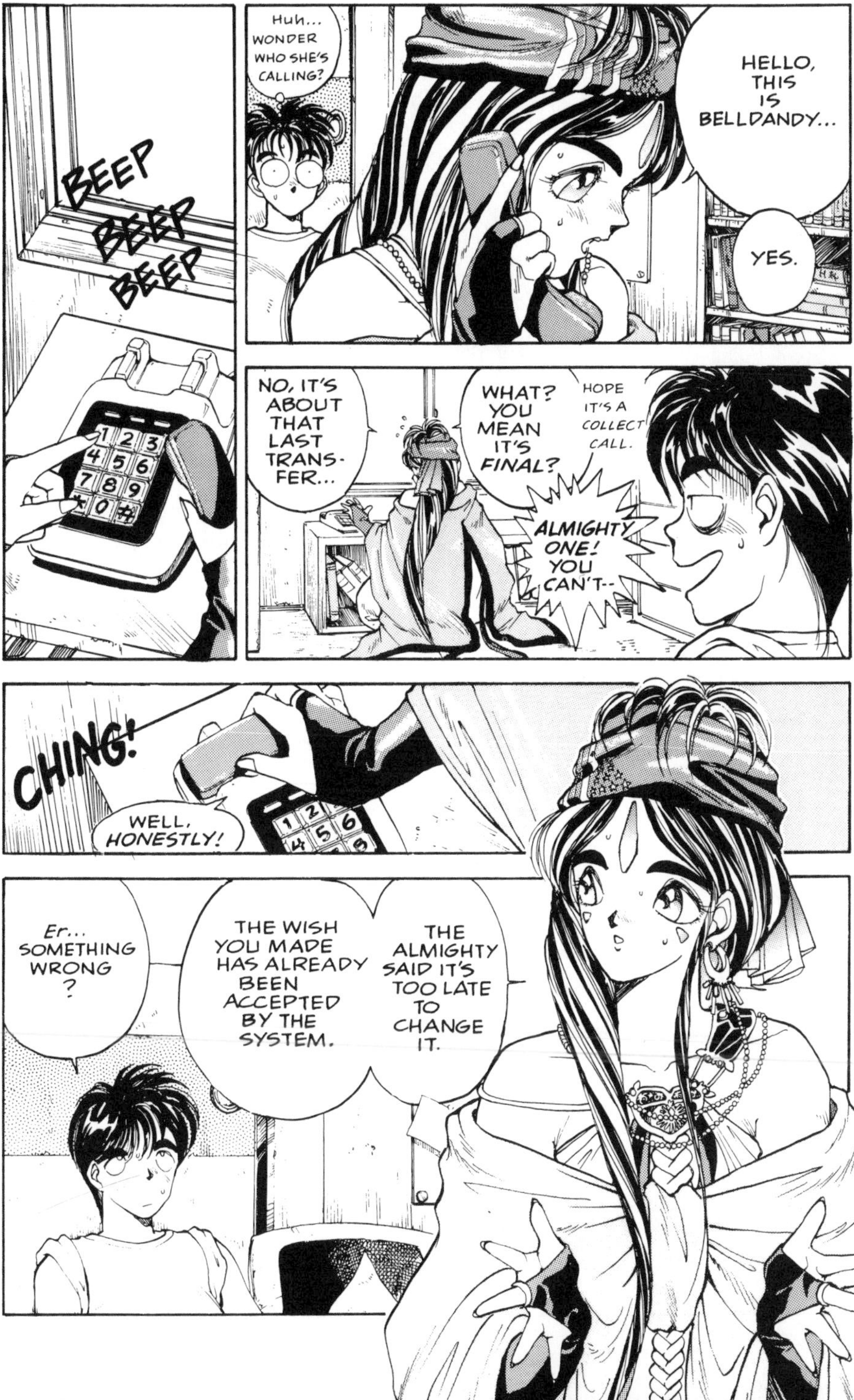
BEEP
BEEP
BEEP
Huh... WONDER WHO SHE'S CALLING?
HELLO, THIS IS BELLDANDY...
YES.
NO, IT'S ABOUT THAT LAST TRANSFER...
WHAT? YOU MEAN IT'S FINAL?
HOPE IT'S A COLLECT CALL.
ALMIGHTY ONE! YOU CAN'T--
CHING!
WELL, HONESTLY!
Er... SOMETHING WRONG?
THE WISH YOU MADE HAS ALREADY BEEN ACCEPTED BY THE SYSTEM.
THE ALMIGHTY SAID IT'S TOO LATE TO CHANGE IT.

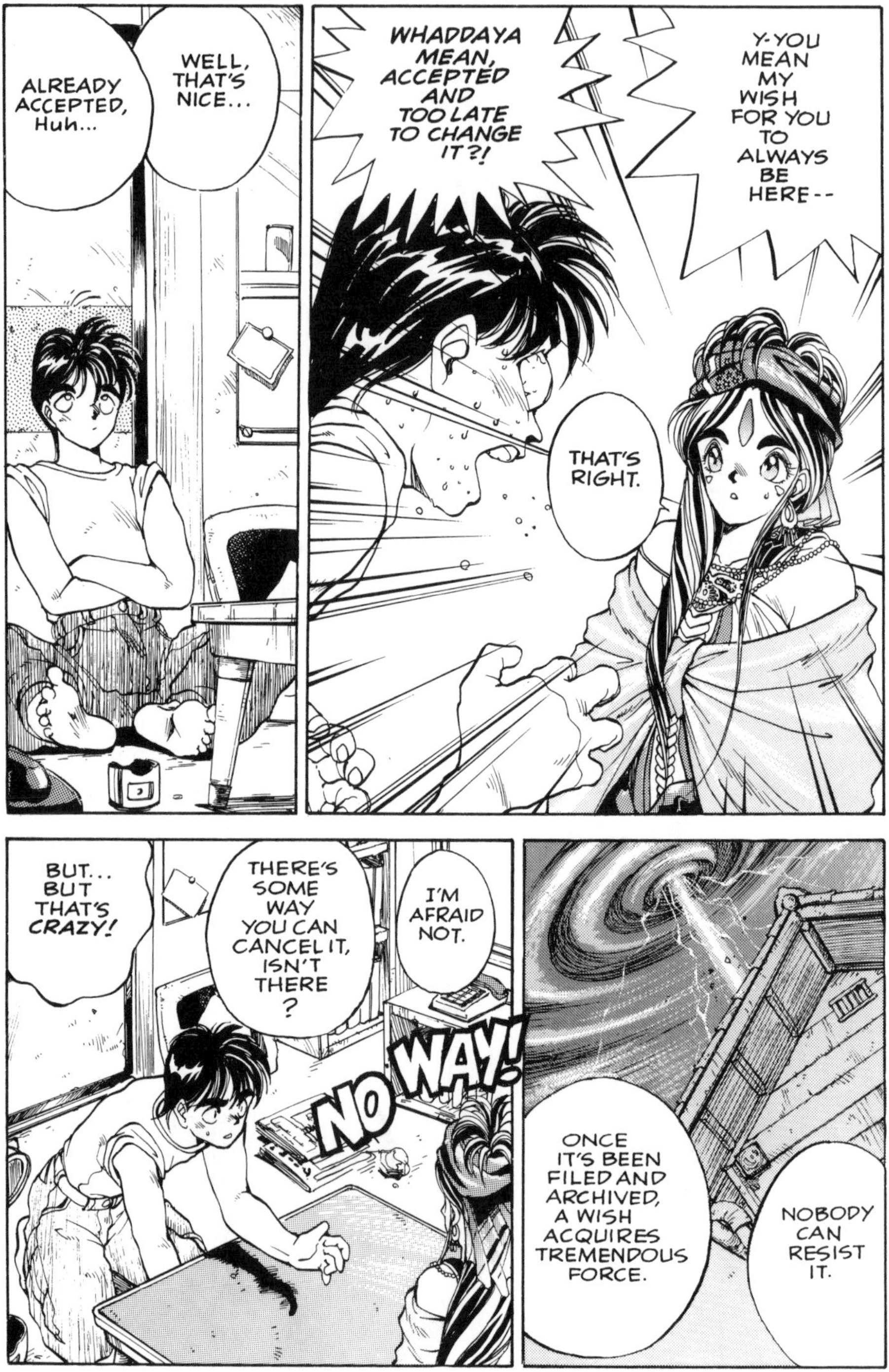
ALREADY ACCEPTED, Huh...
WELL, THAT'S NICE...
WHADDAYA MEAN, ACCEPTED AND TOO LATE TO CHANGE IT?!
Y-YOU MEAN MY WISH FOR YOU TO ALWAYS BE HERE--
THAT'S RIGHT.
BUT... BUT THAT'S CRAZY!
THERE'S SOME WAY YOU CAN CANCEL IT, ISN'T THERE?
I'M AFRAID NOT.
NO WAY!
ONCE IT'S BEEN FILED AND ARCHIVED, A WISH ACQUIRES TREMENDOUS FORCE.
NOBODY CAN RESIST IT.

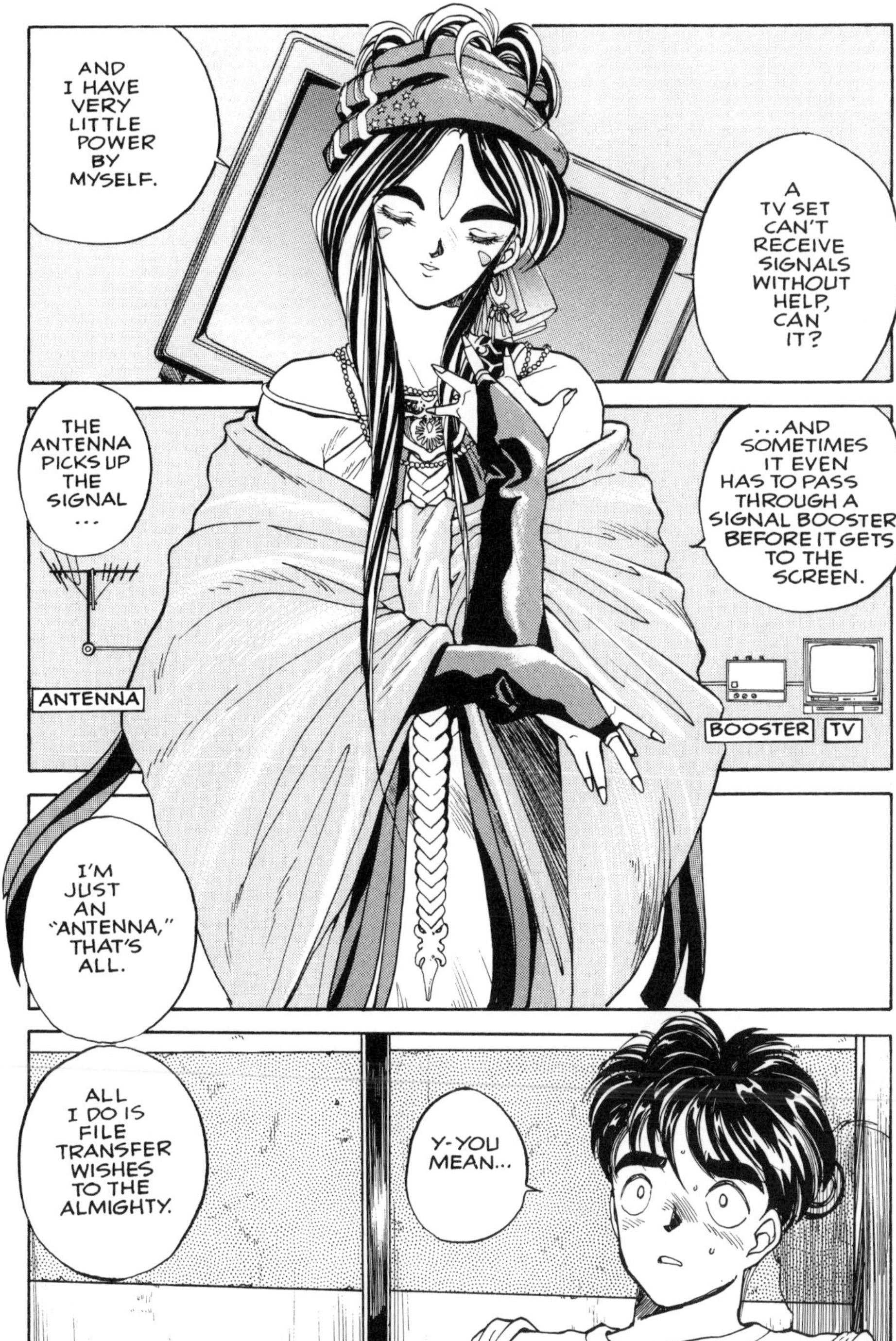
AND I HAVE VERY LITTLE POWER BY MYSELF.
A TV SET CAN'T RECEIVE SIGNALS WITHOUT HELP, CAN IT?
THE ANTENNA PICKS UP THE SIGNAL . . .
ANTENNA
. . .AND SOMETIMES IT EVEN HAS TO PASS THROUGH A SIGNAL BOOSTER BEFORE IT GETS TO THE SCREEN.
BOOSTER
TV
I'M JUST AN "ANTENNA," THAT'S ALL.
ALL I DO IS FILE TRANSFER WISHES TO THE ALMIGHTY.
Y-YOU MEAN...

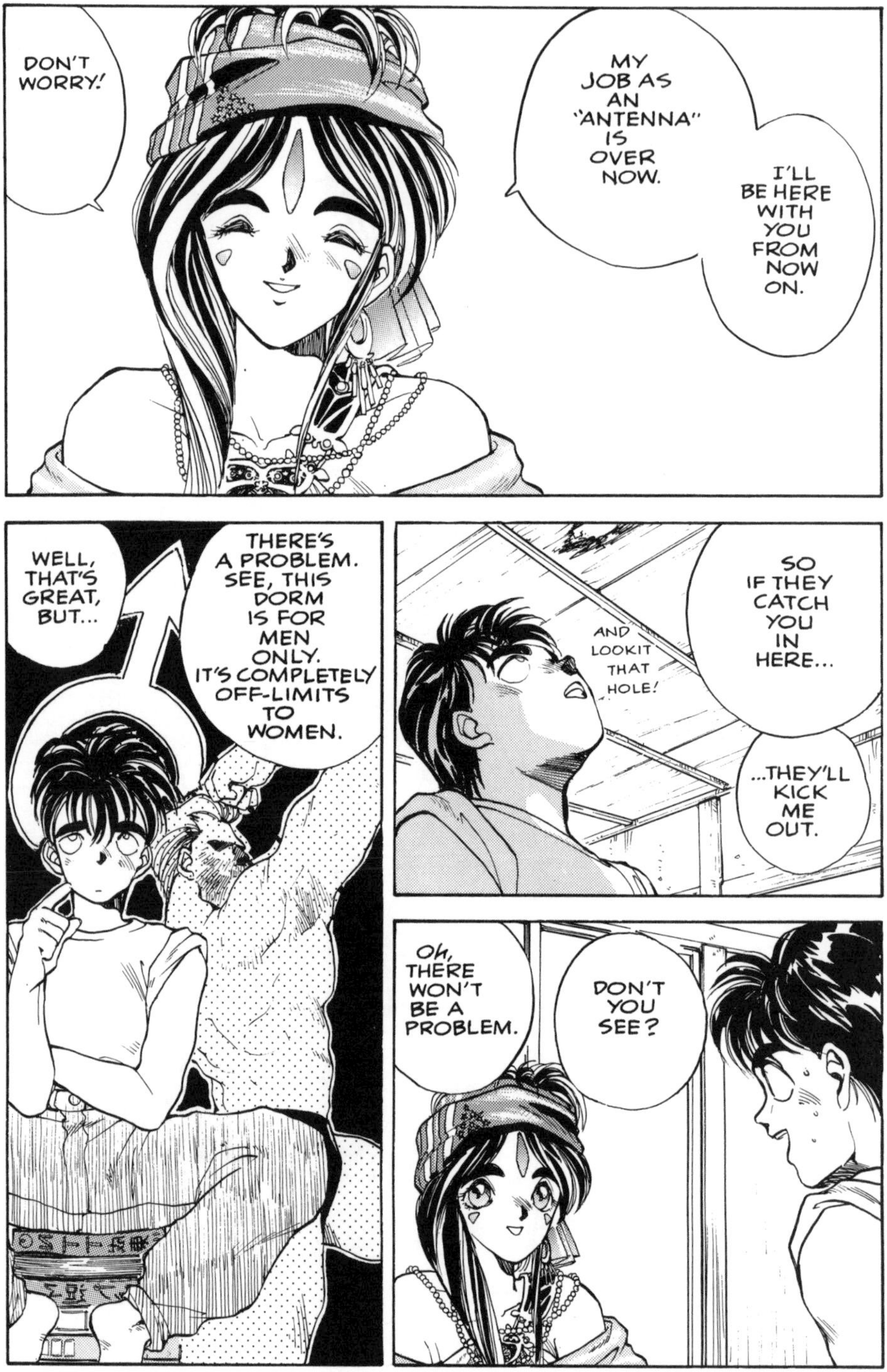
DON'T WORRY!
MY JOB AS AN "ANTENNA" IS OVER NOW.
I'LL BE HERE WITH YOU FROM NOW ON.
WELL, THAT'S GREAT, BUT...
THERE'S A PROBLEM. SEE, THIS DORM IS FOR MEN ONLY. IT'S COMPLETELY OFF-LIMITS TO WOMEN.
AND LOOKIT THAT HOLE!
SO IF THEY CATCH YOU IN HERE...
...THEY'LL KICK ME OUT.
Oh, THERE WON'T BE A PROBLEM.
DON'T YOU SEE?

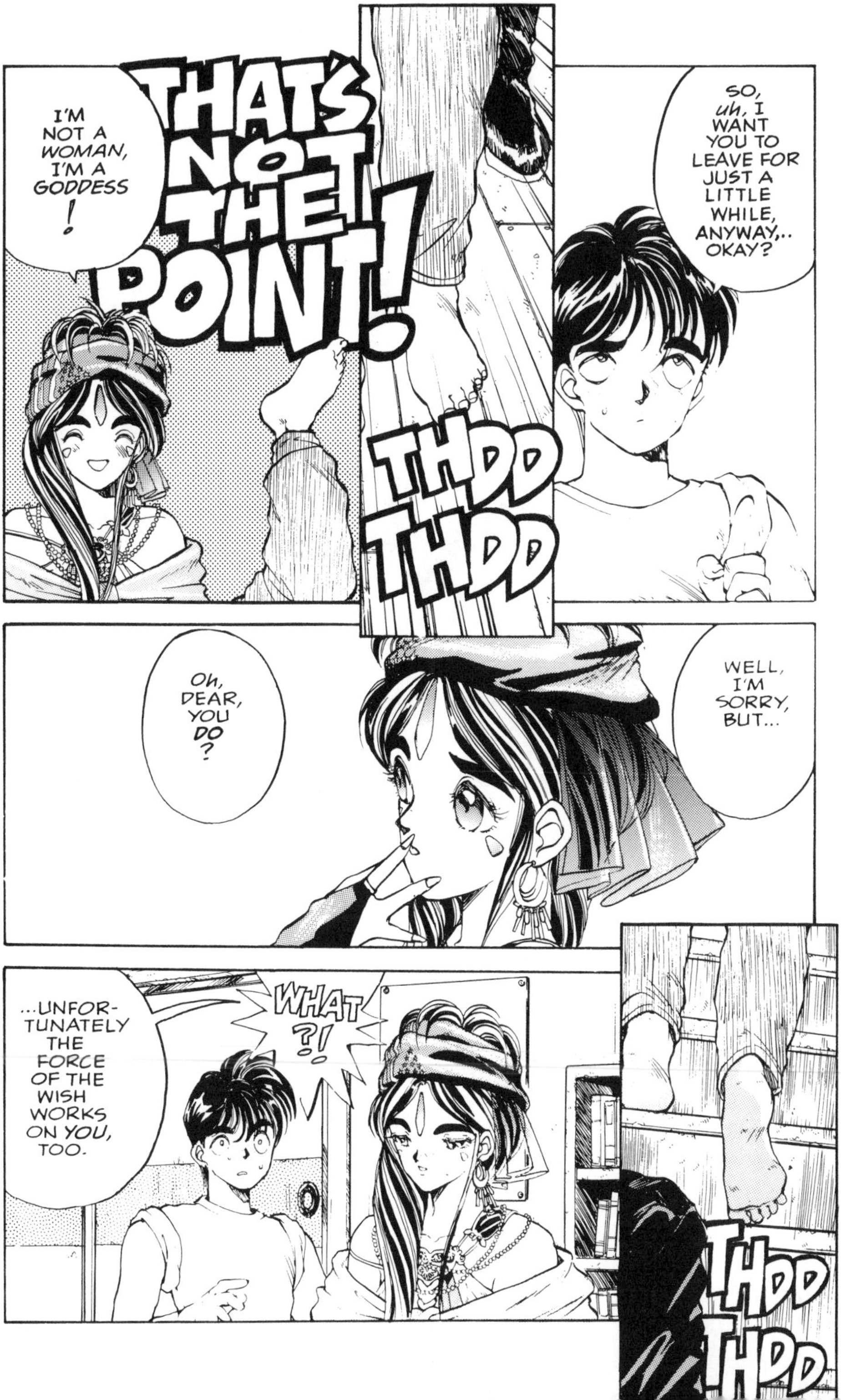
I'M NOT A WOMAN, I'M A GODDESS!
THAT'S NOT THE POINT!
THDD THDD
SO, uh, I WANT YOU TO LEAVE FOR JUST A LITTLE WHILE, ANYWAY... OKAY?
Oh, DEAR, YOU DO?
WELL, I'M SORRY, BUT...
...UNFORTUNATELY THE FORCE OF THE WISH WORKS ON YOU, TOO.
WHAT?!
THDD THDD

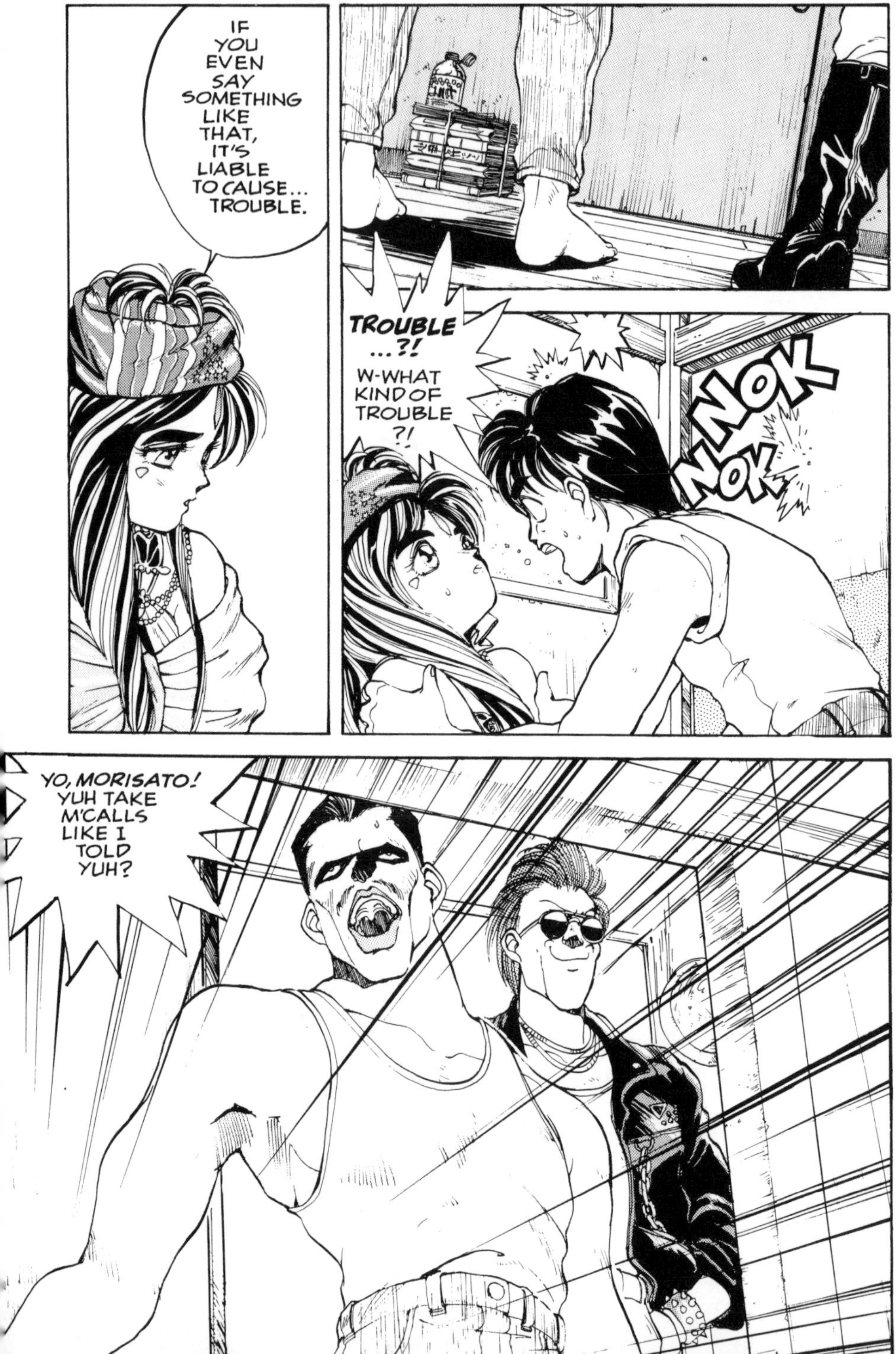
IF YOU EVEN SAY SOMETHING LIKE THAT, IT'S LIABLE TO CAUSE... TROUBLE.
TROUBLE ...?!
W-WHAT KIND OF TROUBLE ?!
NOK NOK
YO, MORISATO! YUH TAKE M'CALLS LIKE I TOLD YUH?

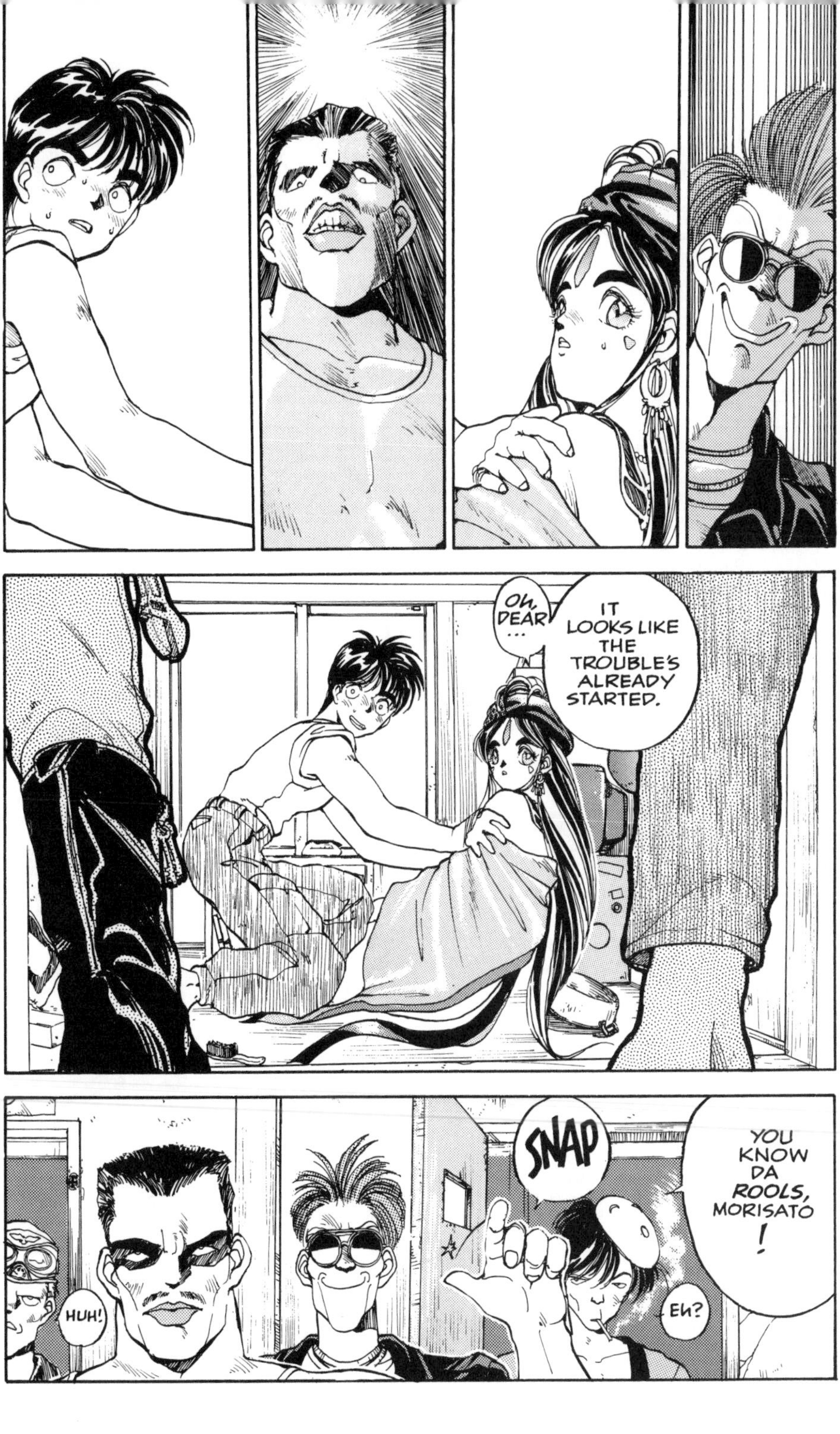

Oh, DEAR...
IT LOOKS LIKE THE TROUBLE'S ALREADY STARTED.
HUH!
SNAP
Eh?
YOU KNOW DA ROOLS, MORISATO!

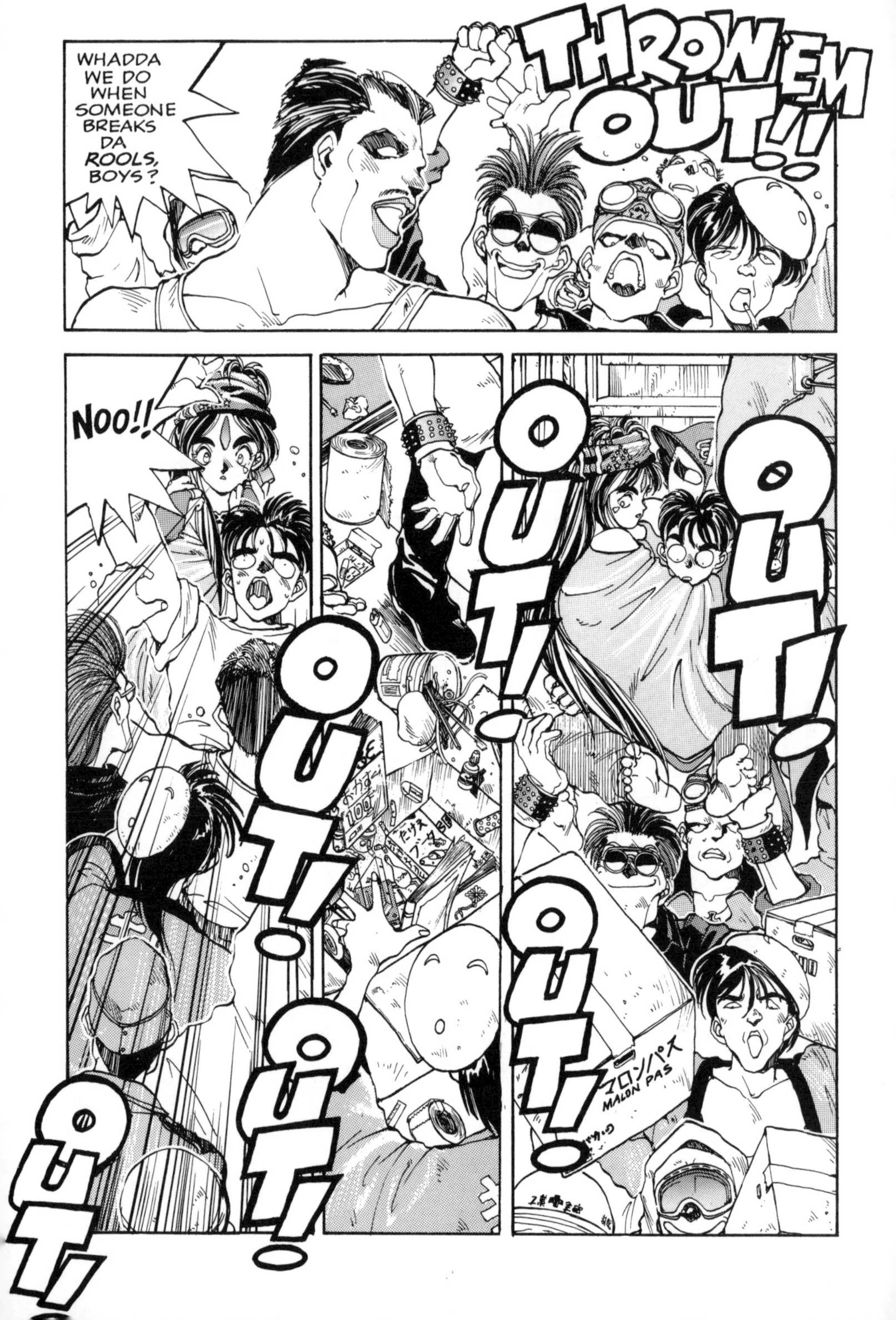
WHADDA WE DO WHEN SOMEONE BREAKS DA ROOLS, BOYS?
THROW 'EM OUT!!
NOO!!
OUT!
OUT!
OUT!
OUT!
OUT!
OUT!
マロンパス
MALON PAS

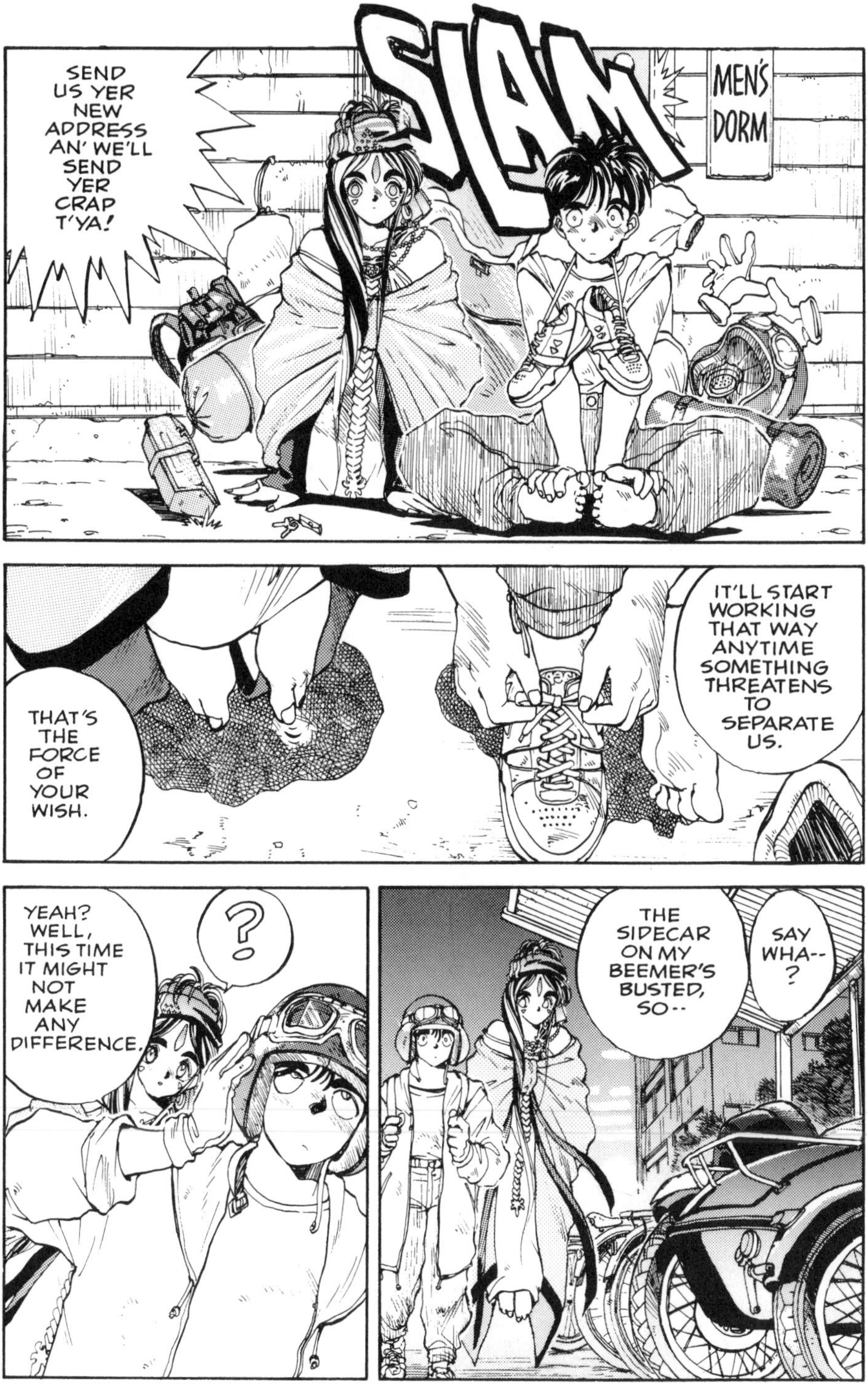
SLAM
SEND US YER NEW ADDRESS AN' WE'LL SEND YER CRAP T'YA!
MEN'S DORM
THAT'S THE FORCE OF YOUR WISH.
IT'LL START WORKING THAT WAY ANYTIME SOMETHING THREATENS TO SEPARATE US.
YEAH? WELL, THIS TIME IT MIGHT NOT MAKE ANY DIFFERENCE.
?
THE SIDECAR ON MY BEEMER'S BUSTED, SO--
SAY WHA--?

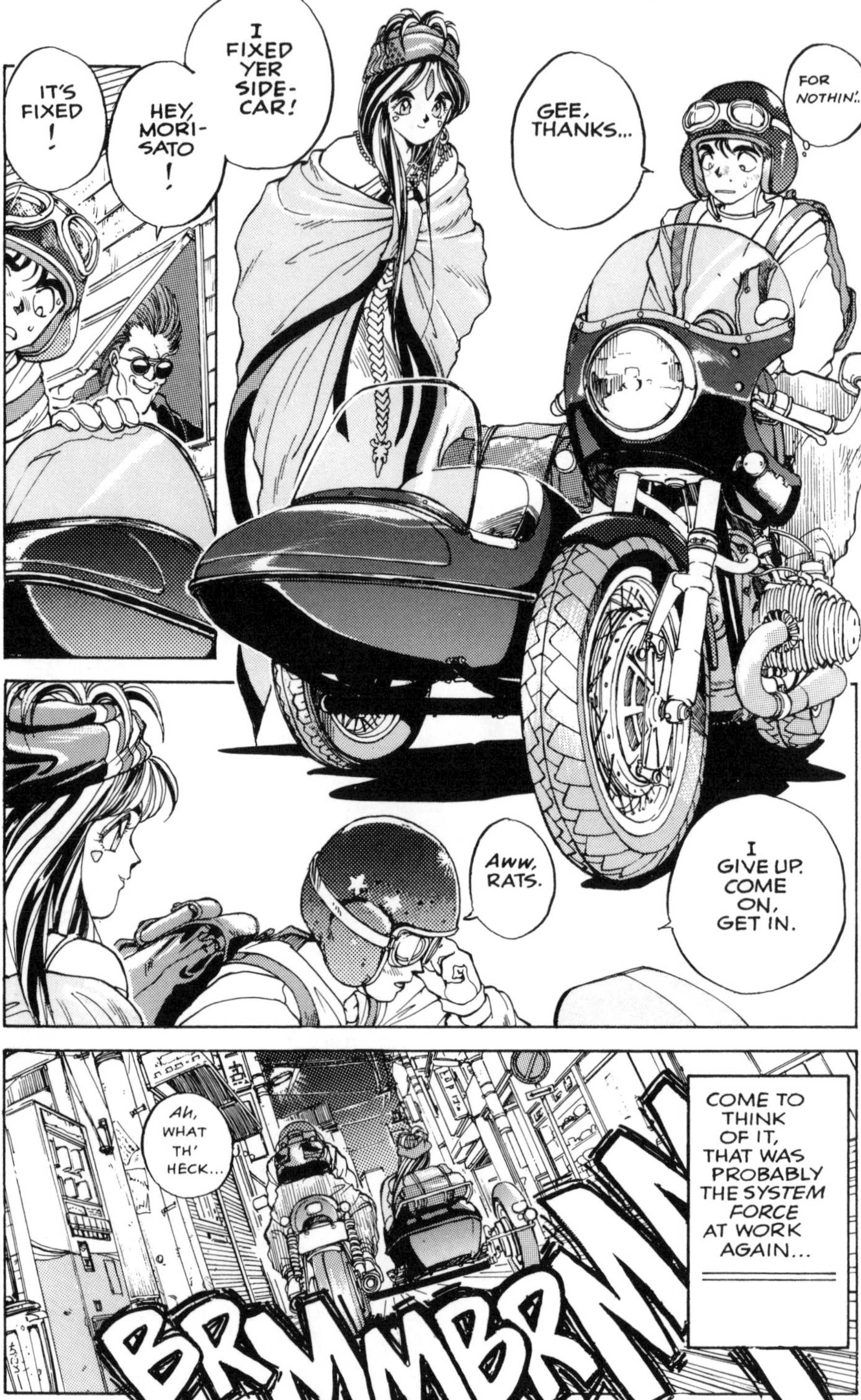
IT'S FIXED!
HEY, MORISATO!
I FIXED YER SIDE-CAR!
GEE, THANKS...
FOR NOTHIN'...
AWW, RATS.
I GIVE UP. COME ON, GET IN.
AH, WHAT TH' HECK...
COME TO THINK OF IT, THAT WAS PROBABLY THE *SYSTEM FORCE* AT WORK AGAIN...
BRMMBRMM

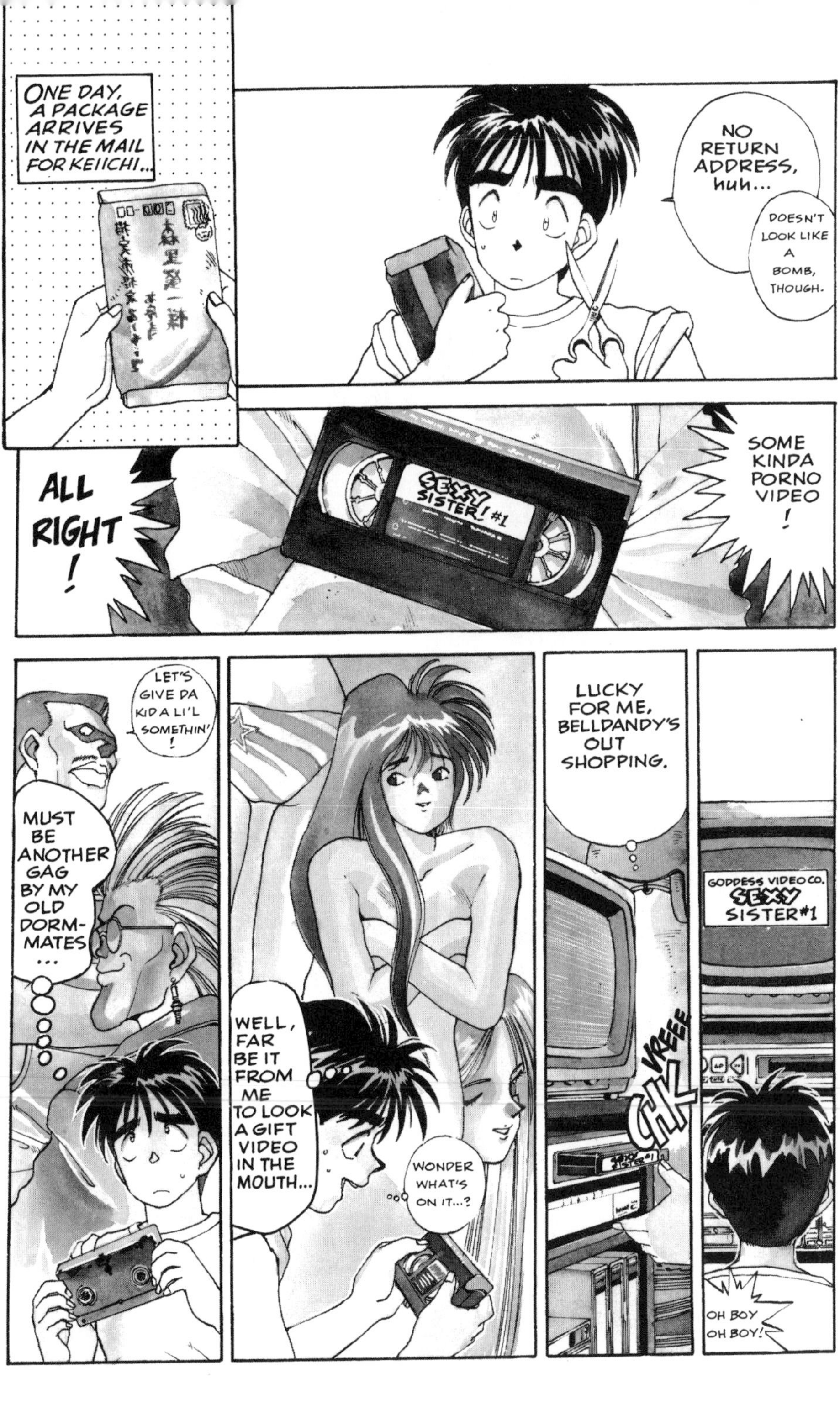
ONE DAY, A PACKAGE ARRIVES IN THE MAIL FOR KEIICHI...
NO RETURN ADDRESS, huh...
DOESN'T LOOK LIKE A BOMB, THOUGH.
ALL RIGHT!
SEXY SISTER! #1
SOME KINDA PORNO VIDEO!
LET'S GIVE DA KID A LI'L SOMETHIN'!
MUST BE ANOTHER GAG BY MY OLD DORM-MATES...
WELL, FAR BE IT FROM ME TO LOOK A GIFT VIDEO IN THE MOUTH...
WONDER WHAT'S ON IT...?
LUCKY FOR ME, BELLDANDY'S OUT SHOPPING.
VREEE
CHK
GODDESS VIDEO CO. SEXY SISTER #1
OH BOY OH BOY!

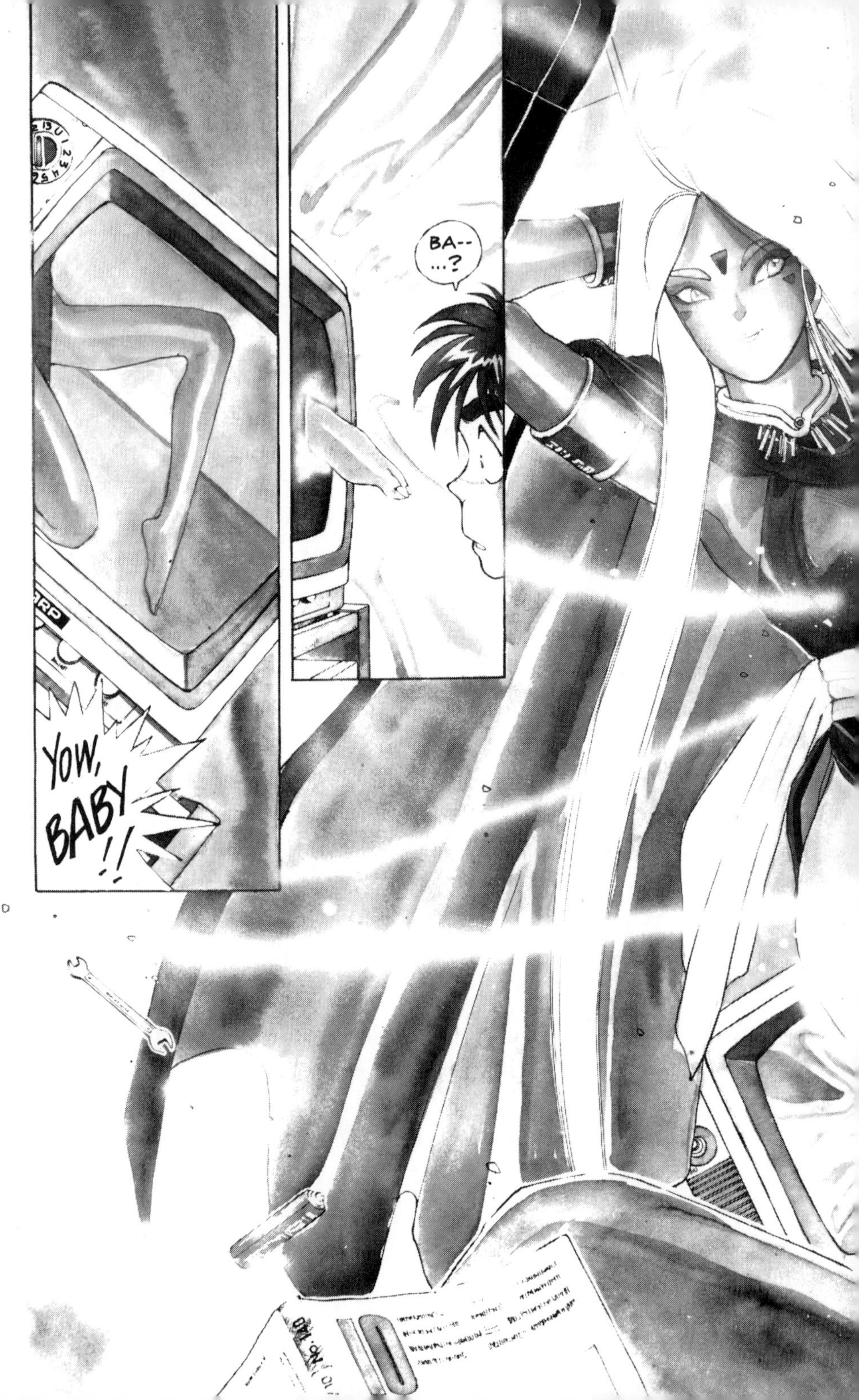
YOW, BABY!!
BA-- ...?

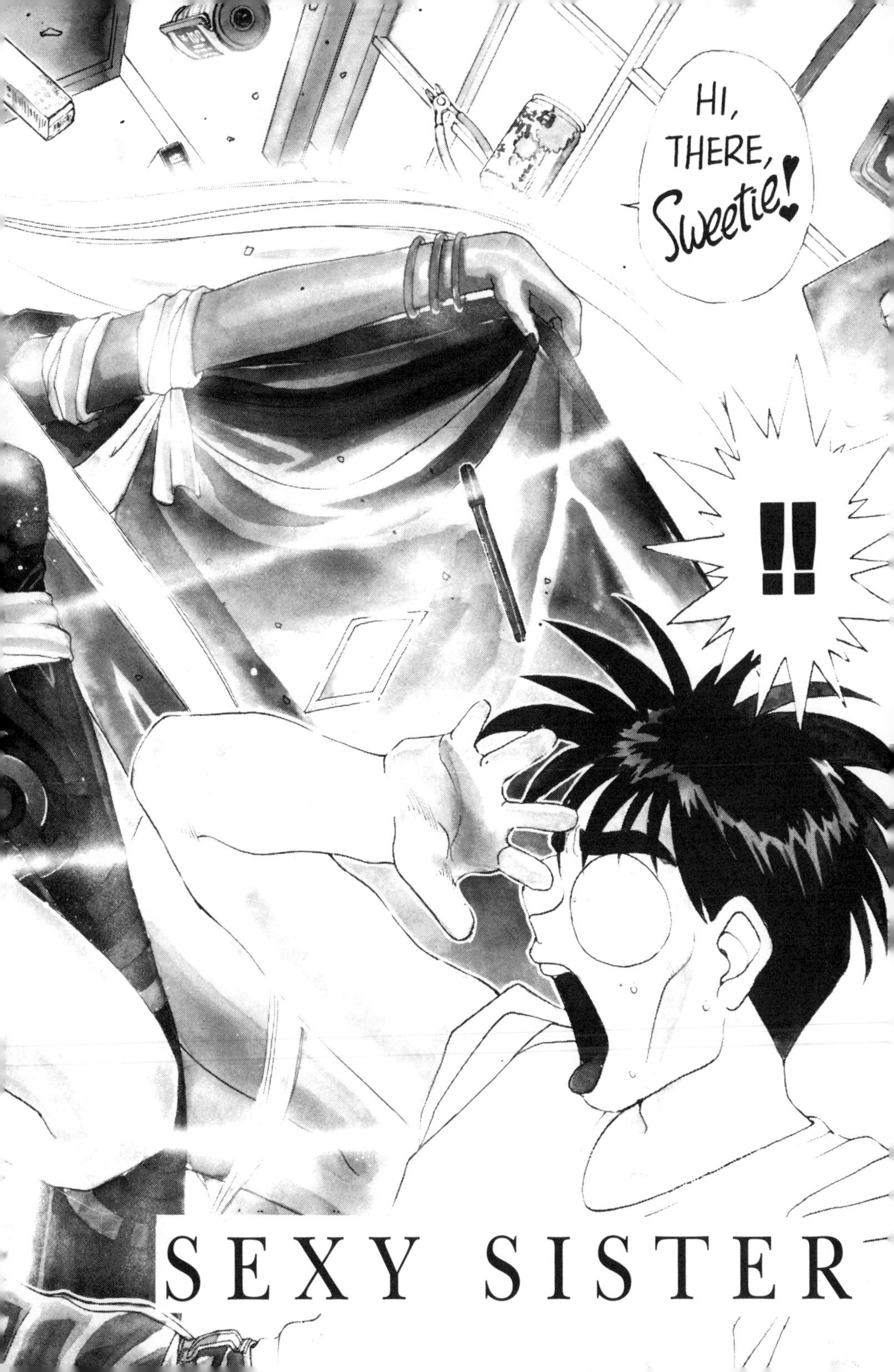
HI, THERE, Sweetie!♥
!!
SEXY SISTER

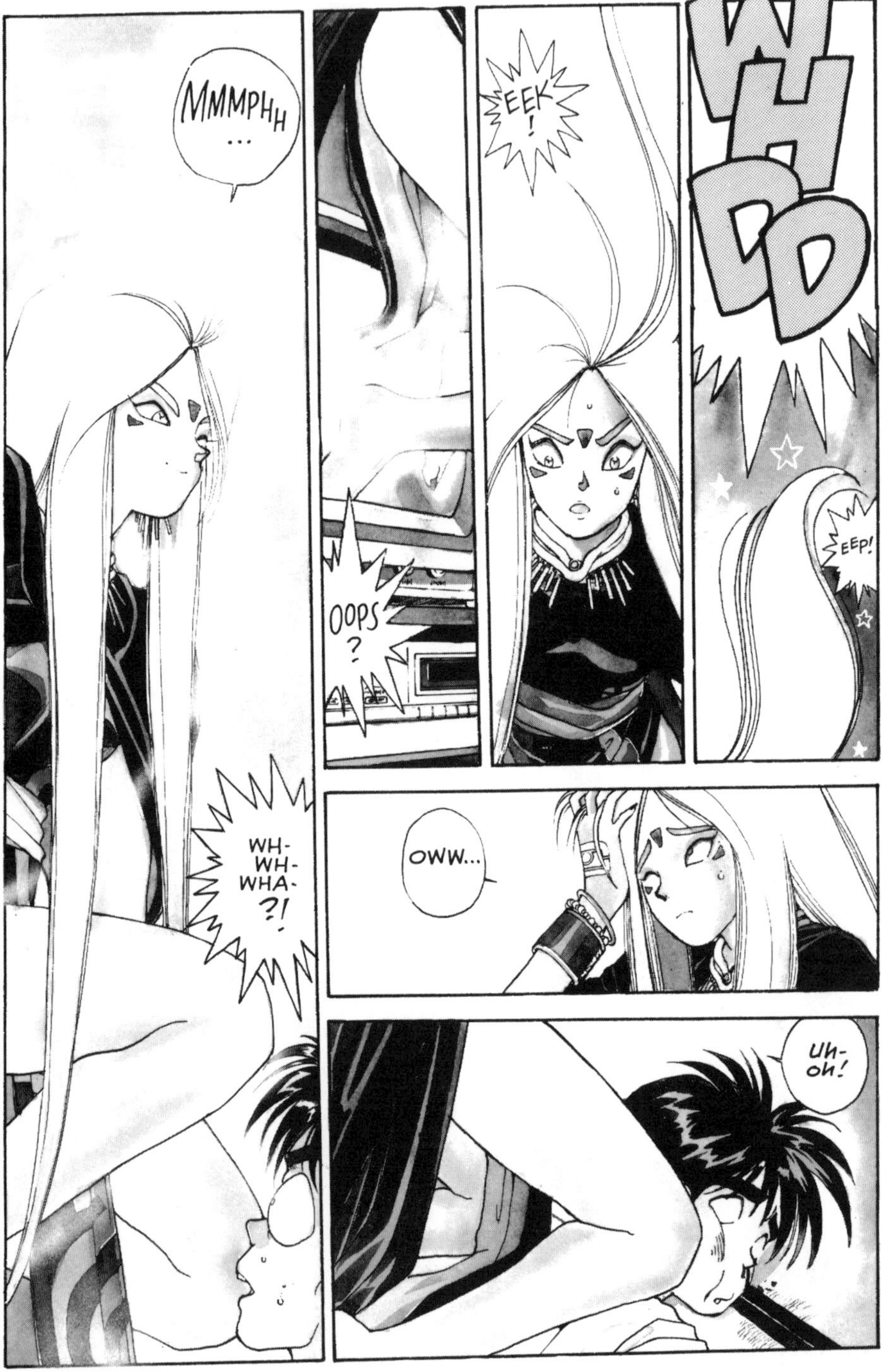
MMMPHH ...
WH- WH- WHA- ?!
OOPS ?
EEK !
WHDD
EEP!
OWW...
Uh-oh!

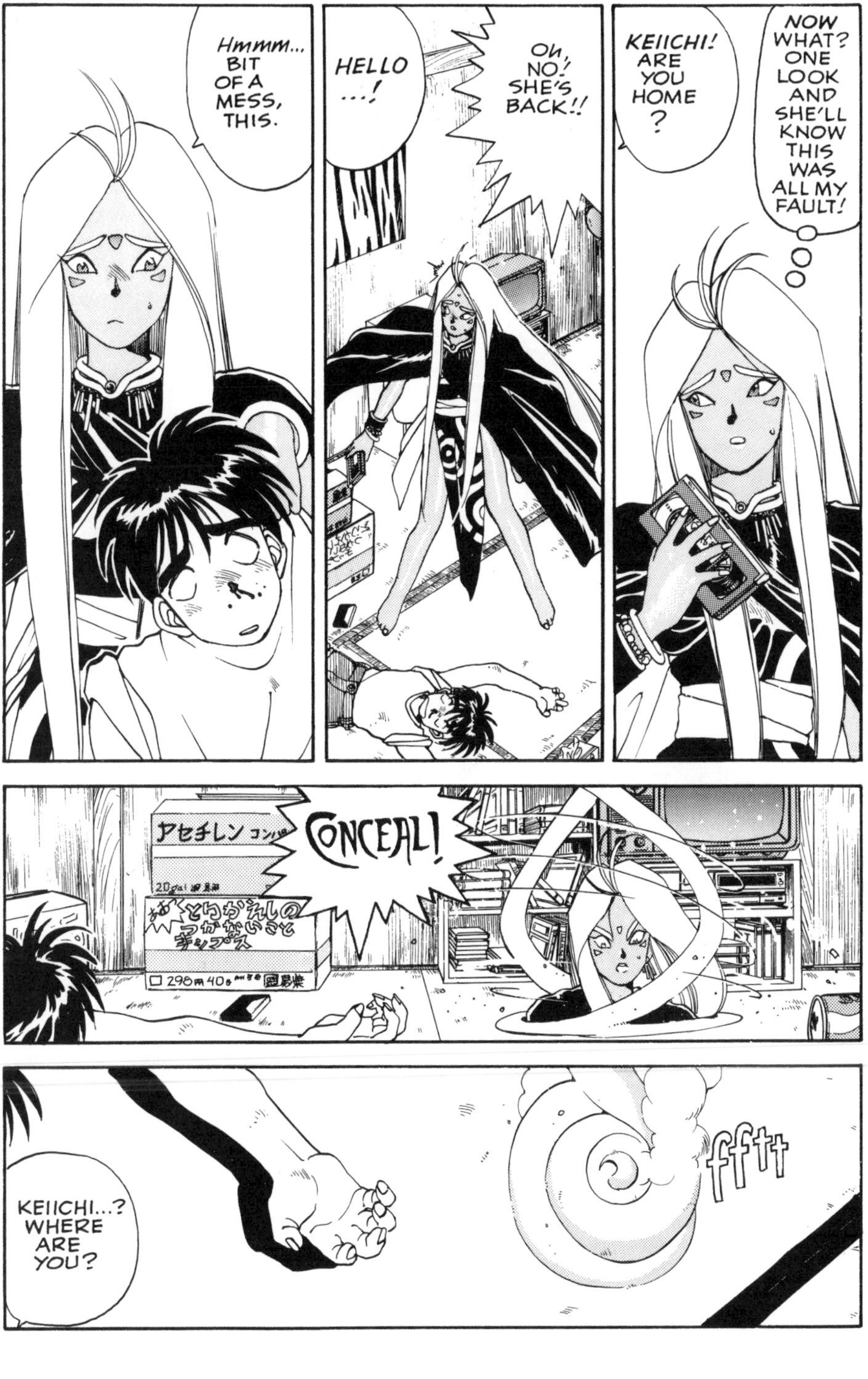

Hmmm... BIT OF A MESS, THIS.
HELLO ...!
Oh, NO! SHE'S BACK!!
KEIICHI! ARE YOU HOME ?
NOW WHAT? ONE LOOK AND SHE'LL KNOW THIS WAS ALL MY FAULT!
アセチレン
CONCEAL!
KEIICHI...? WHERE ARE YOU?
ffft

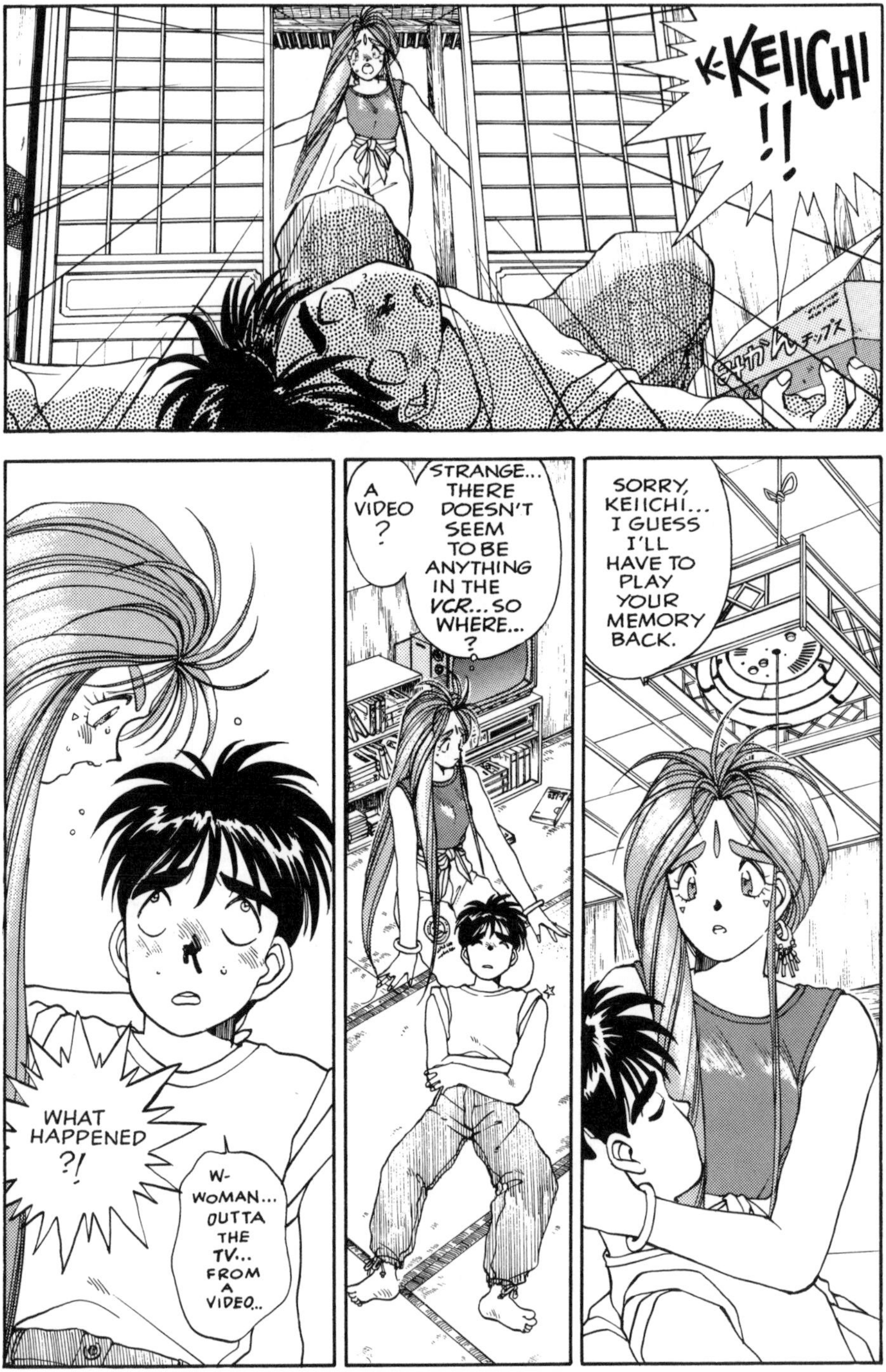
K-KEIICHI !!
WHAT HAPPENED ?!
W-WOMAN... OUTTA THE TV... FROM A VIDEO...
A VIDEO ?
STRANGE... THERE DOESN'T SEEM TO BE ANYTHING IN THE VCR... SO WHERE... ?
SORRY, KEIICHI... I GUESS I'LL HAVE TO PLAY YOUR MEMORY BACK.

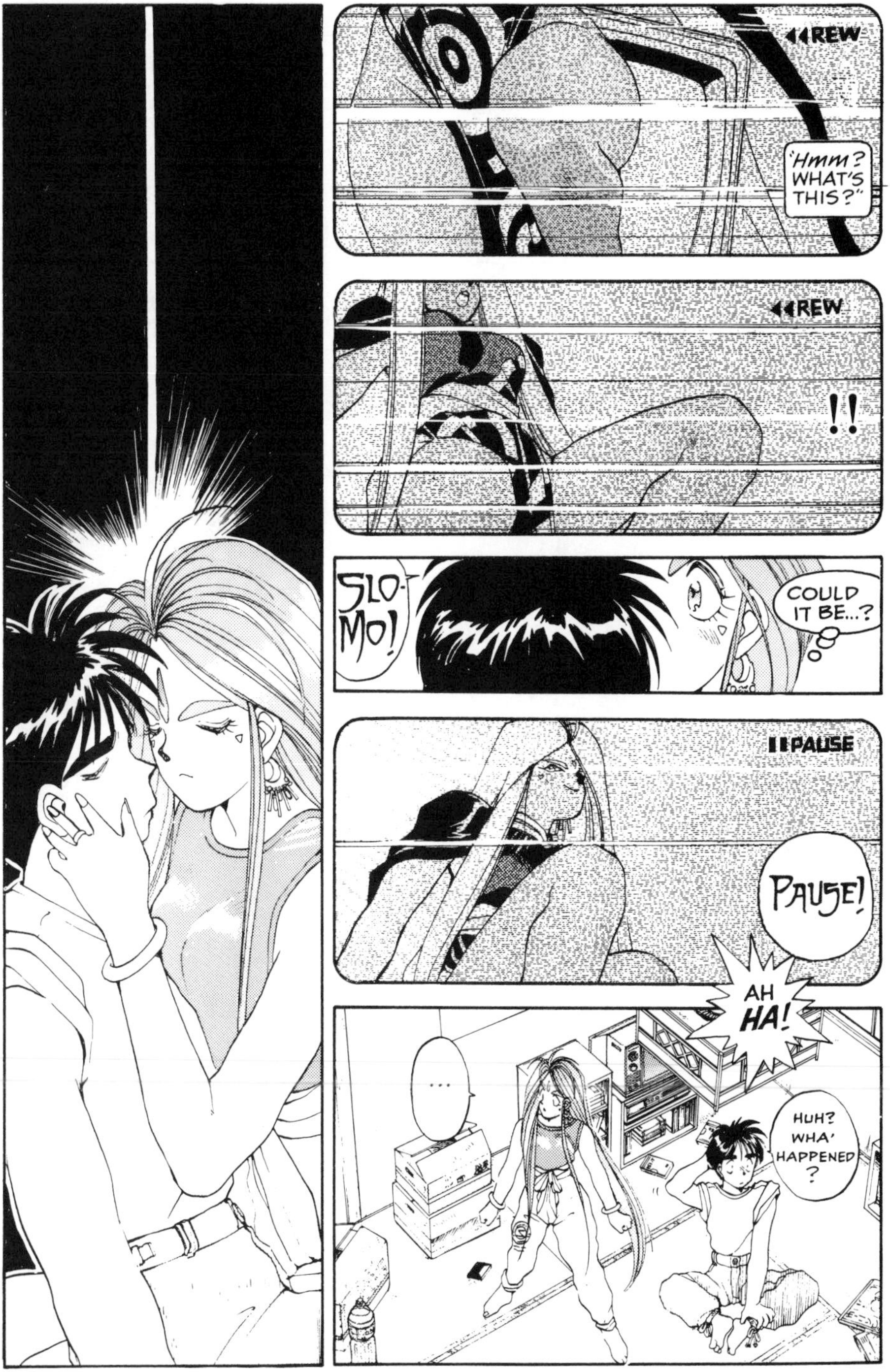

◀◀REW
"Hmm? WHAT'S THIS?"
◀◀REW
!!
SLO-MO!
COULD IT BE...?
❚❚PAUSE
PAUSE!
AH HA!
...
HUH? WHA' HAPPENED?

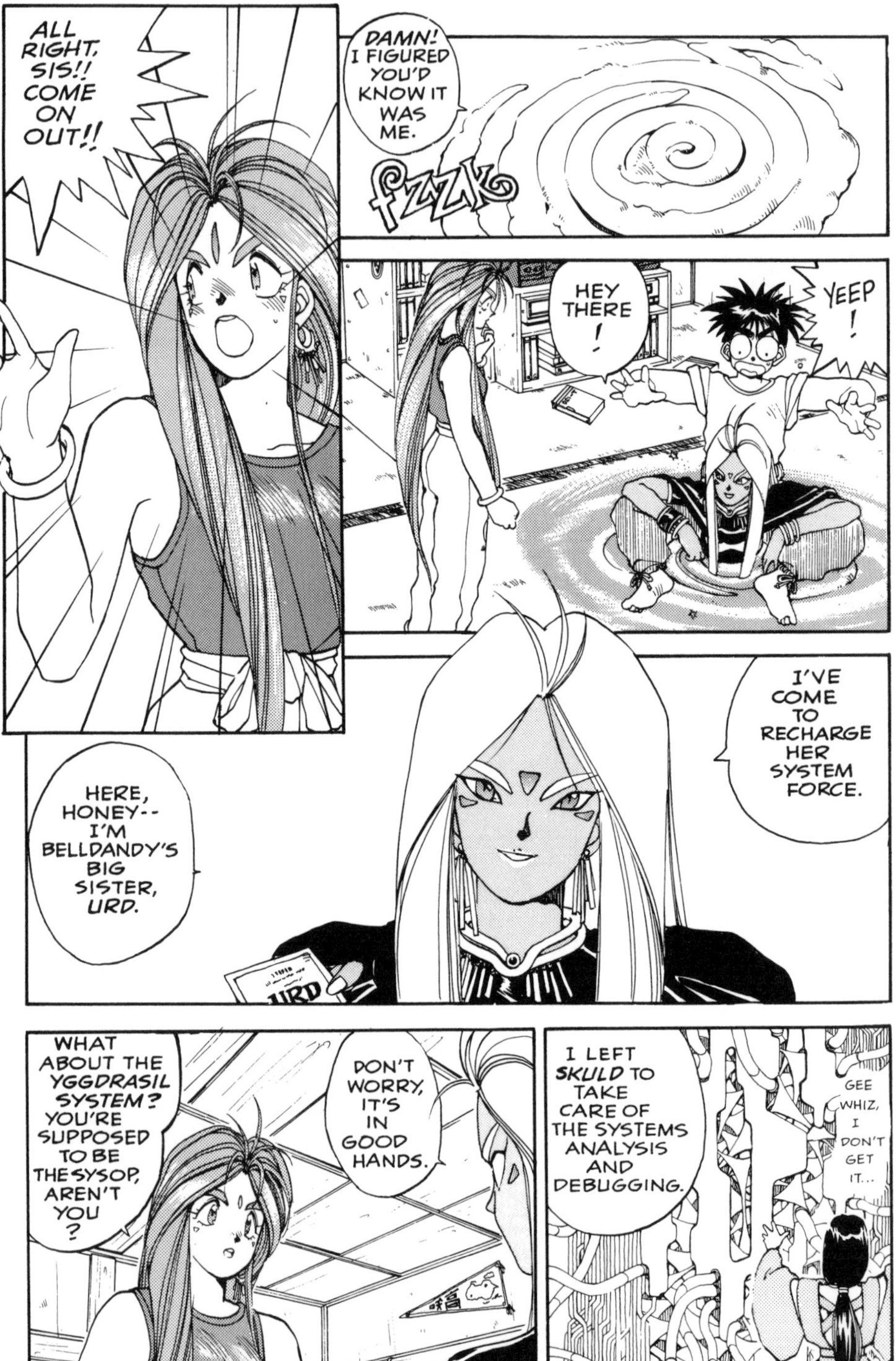
ALL RIGHT, SIS!! COME ON OUT!!
DAMN! I FIGURED YOU'D KNOW IT WAS ME.
fzzk
HEY THERE!
YEEP!
HERE, HONEY-- I'M BELLDANDY'S BIG SISTER, URD.
I'VE COME TO RECHARGE HER SYSTEM FORCE.
WHAT ABOUT THE YGGDRASIL SYSTEM? YOU'RE SUPPOSED TO BE THE SYSOP, AREN'T YOU?
DON'T WORRY, IT'S IN GOOD HANDS.
I LEFT SKULD TO TAKE CARE OF THE SYSTEMS ANALYSIS AND DEBUGGING.
GEE WHIZ, I DON'T GET IT...

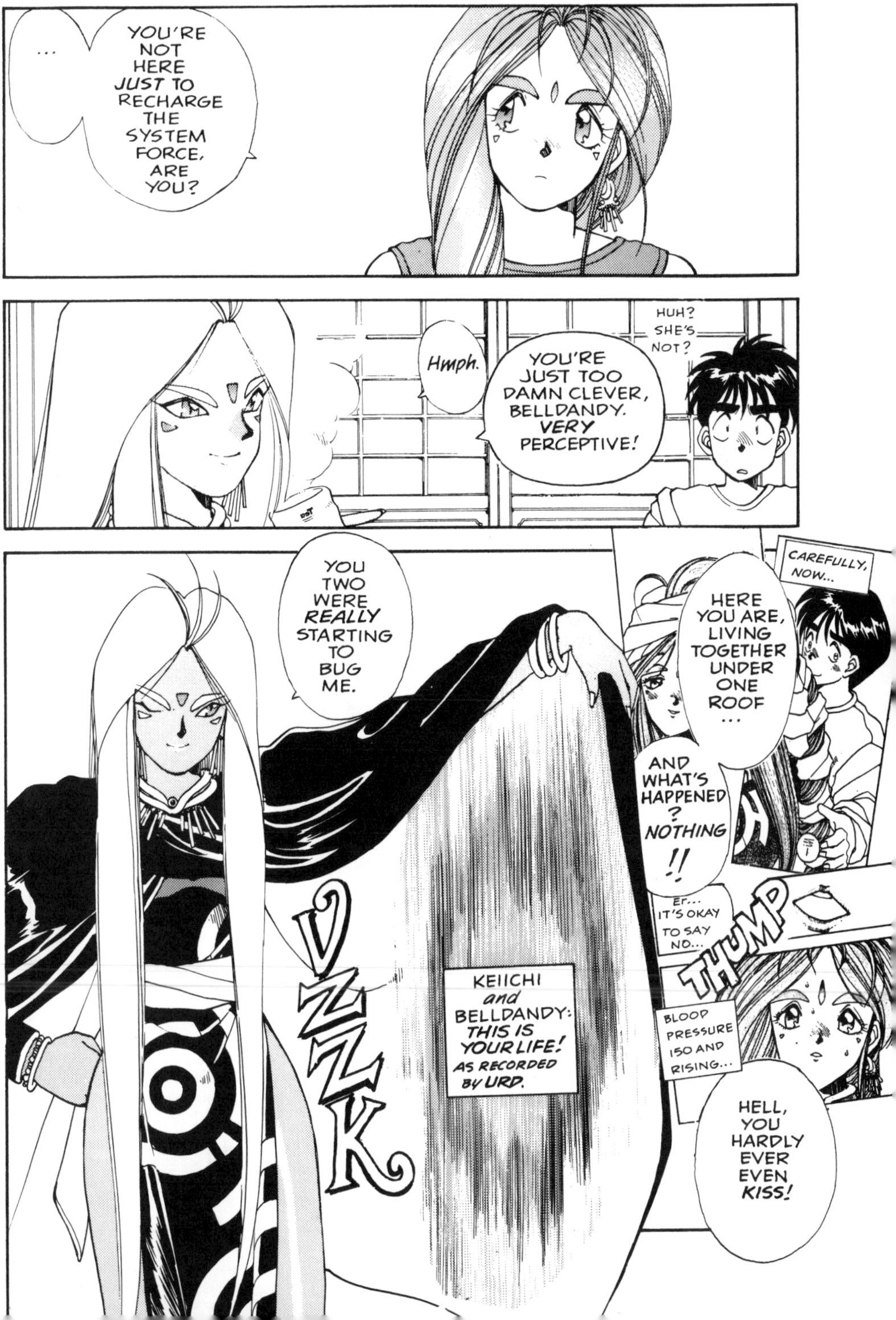
...
YOU'RE NOT HERE *JUST* TO RECHARGE THE SYSTEM FORCE, ARE YOU?
Hmph.
YOU'RE JUST TOO DAMN CLEVER, BELLDANDY. *VERY* PERCEPTIVE!
HUH? SHE'S NOT?
YOU TWO WERE *REALLY* STARTING TO BUG ME.
VZZK
KEIICHI *and* BELLDANDY: *THIS IS YOUR LIFE!* AS RECORDED BY *URD*.
CAREFULLY, NOW...
HERE YOU ARE, LIVING TOGETHER UNDER ONE ROOF ...
AND WHAT'S HAPPENED? *NOTHING* !!
ER... IT'S OKAY TO SAY NO...
THUMP
BLOOD PRESSURE 150 AND RISING...
HELL, YOU HARDLY EVER EVEN *KISS!*

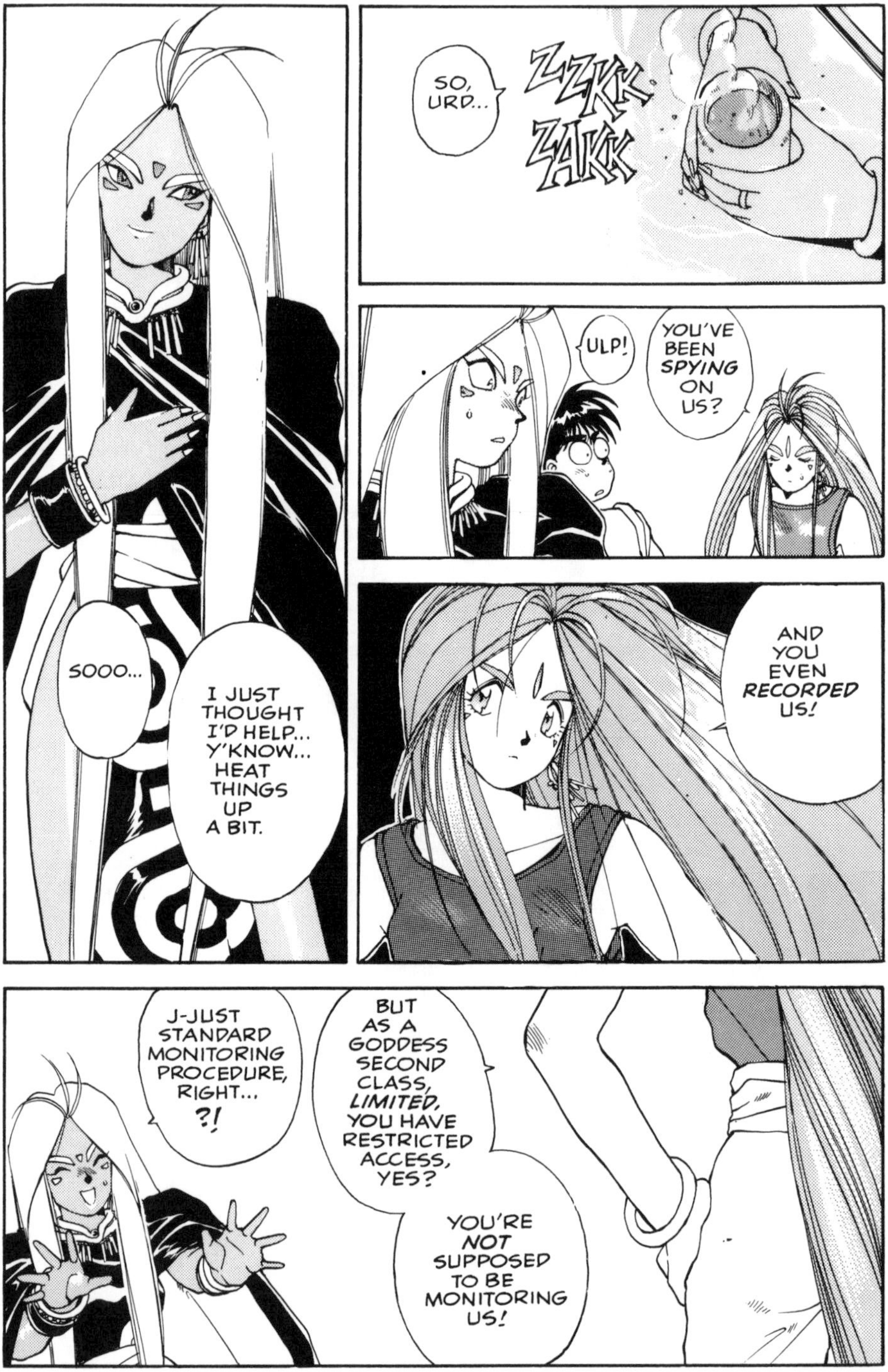
SOOO...
I JUST THOUGHT I'D HELP... Y'KNOW... HEAT THINGS UP A BIT.
SO, URD...
ZZKK ZAKK
ULP!
YOU'VE BEEN SPYING ON US?
AND YOU EVEN RECORDED US!
J-JUST STANDARD MONITORING PROCEDURE, RIGHT... ?!
BUT AS A GODDESS SECOND CLASS, LIMITED, YOU HAVE RESTRICTED ACCESS, YES?
YOU'RE NOT SUPPOSED TO BE MONITORING US!

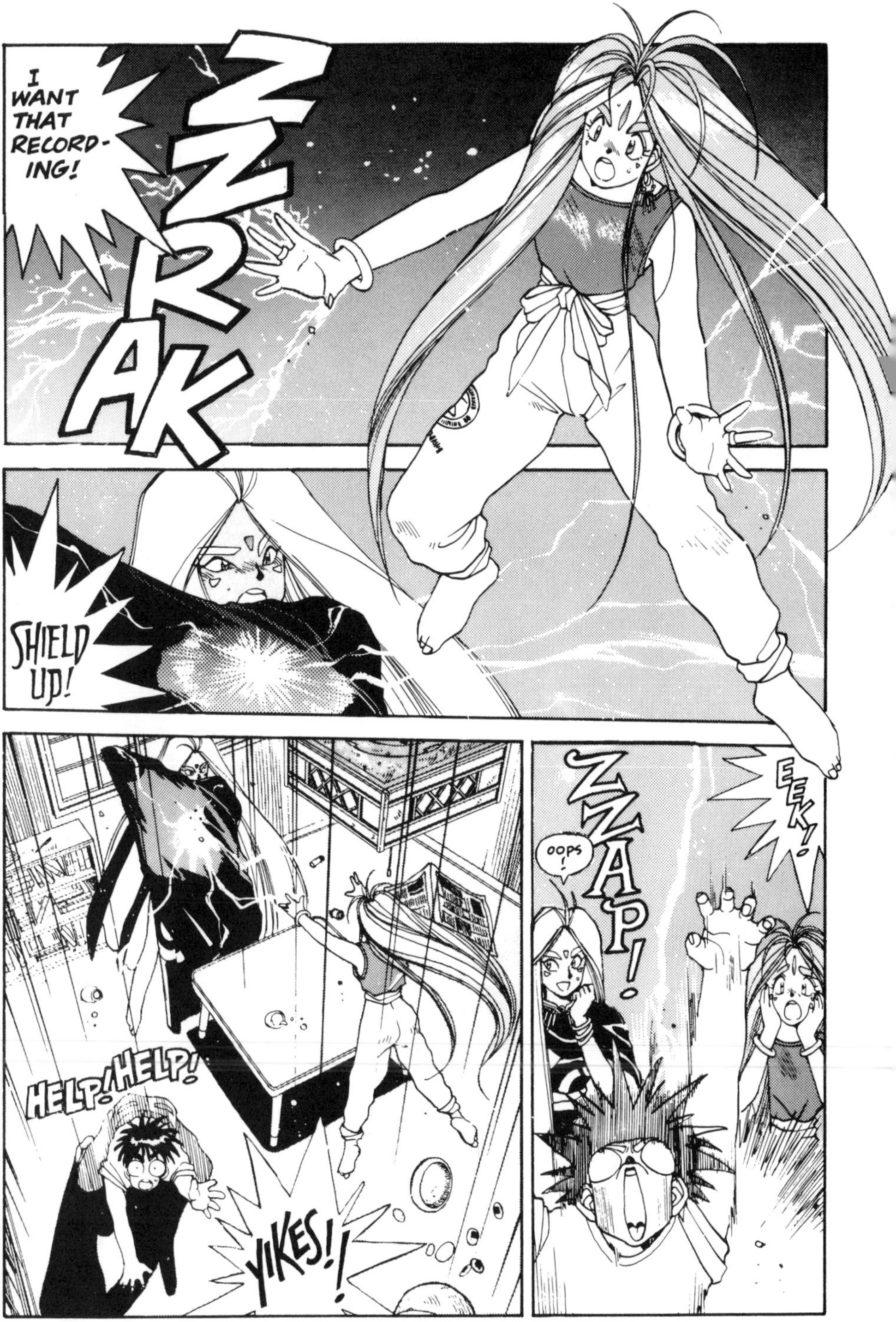

I WANT THAT RECORD-ING!
ZZRAK
SHIELD UP!
HELP! HELP!
YIKES!!
ZZAP!
OOPS!
EEK!

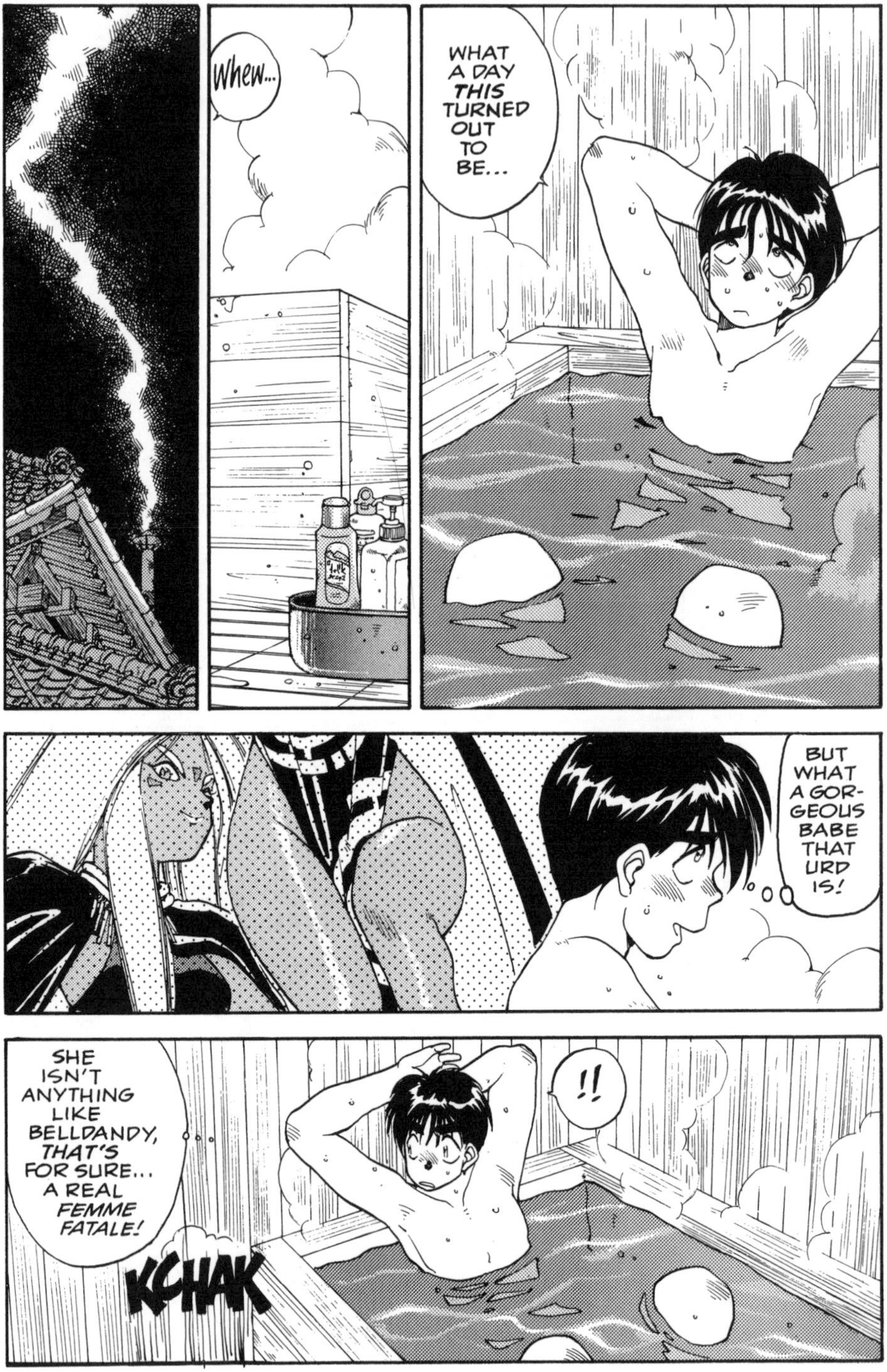
Whew...
WHAT A DAY THIS TURNED OUT TO BE...
BUT WHAT A GORGEOUS BABE THAT URD IS!
SHE ISN'T ANYTHING LIKE BELLDANDY, THAT'S FOR SURE... A REAL FEMME FATALE!
!!
KCHAK

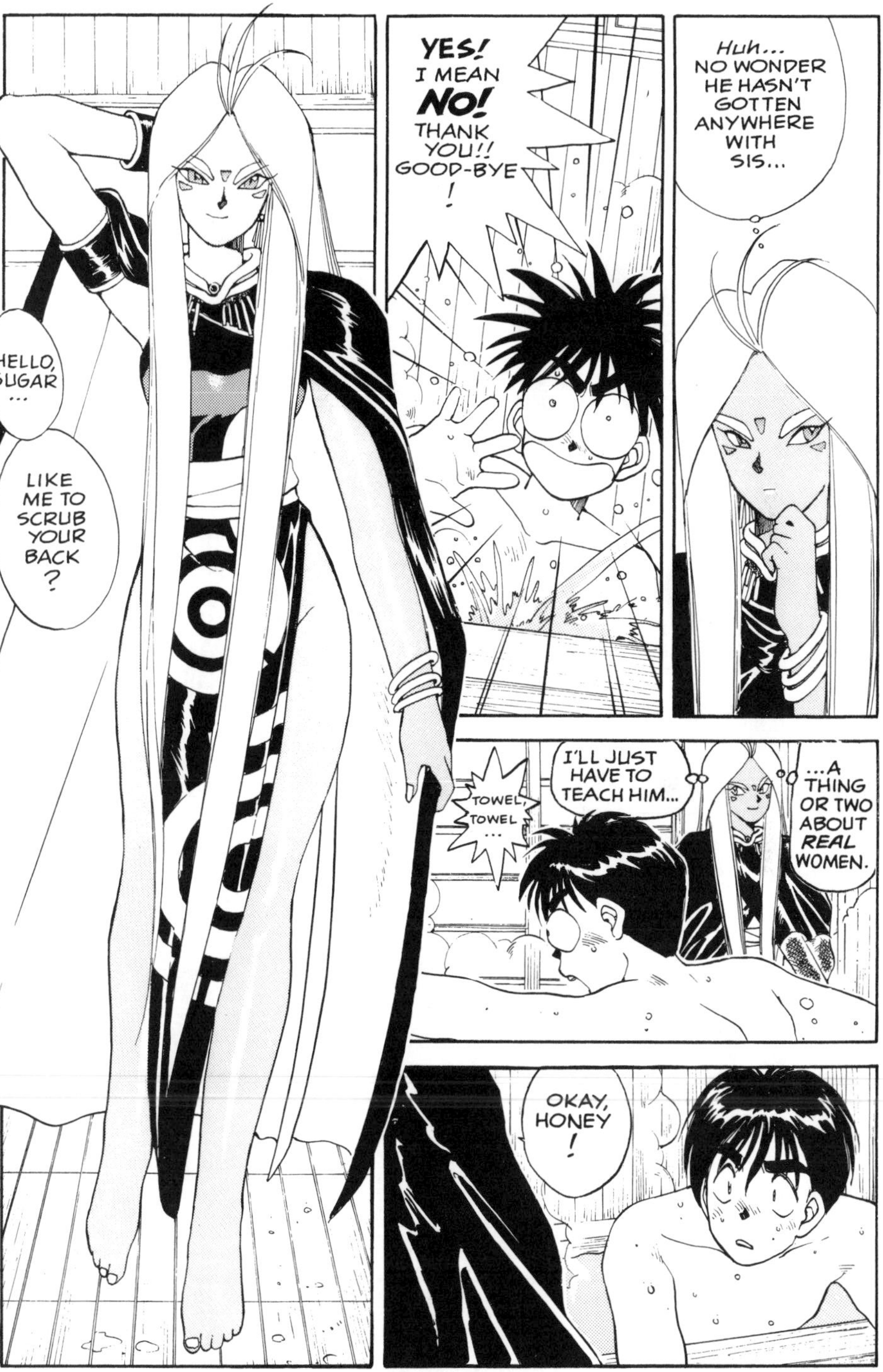

HELLO, SUGAR ...
LIKE ME TO SCRUB YOUR BACK ?
YES! I MEAN NO! THANK YOU!! GOOD-BYE !
Huh... NO WONDER HE HASN'T GOTTEN ANYWHERE WITH SIS...
TOWEL, TOWEL ...
I'LL JUST HAVE TO TEACH HIM...
...A THING OR TWO ABOUT REAL WOMEN.
OKAY, HONEY !

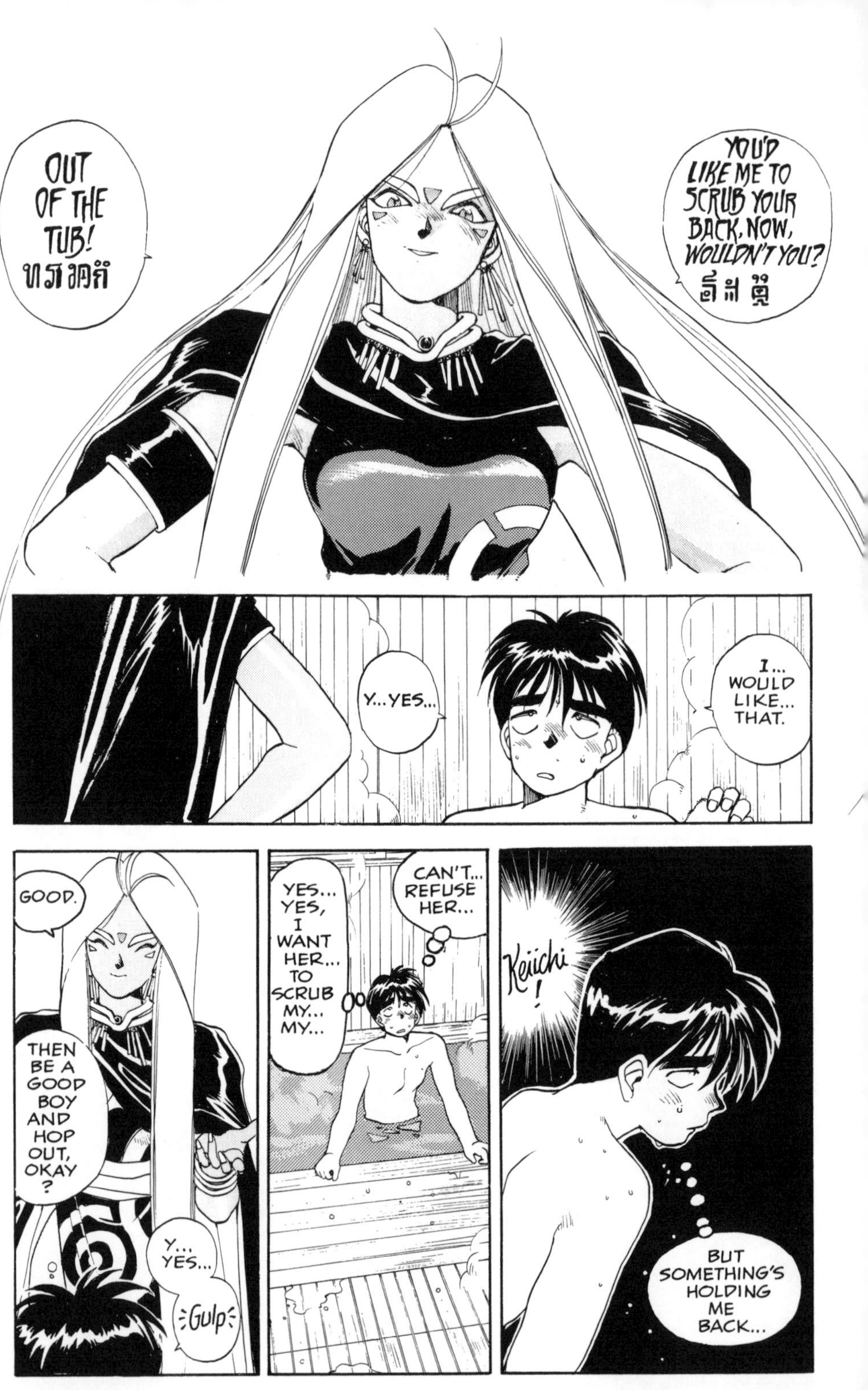
OUT OF THE TUB!
YOU'D LIKE ME TO SCRUB YOUR BACK, NOW, WOULDN'T YOU?
Y... YES...
I... WOULD LIKE... THAT.
GOOD.
THEN BE A GOOD BOY AND HOP OUT, OKAY?
Y..., YES...
Gulp
YES... YES, I WANT HER... TO SCRUB MY... MY...
CAN'T... REFUSE HER...
Keiichi!
BUT SOMETHING'S HOLDING ME BACK...

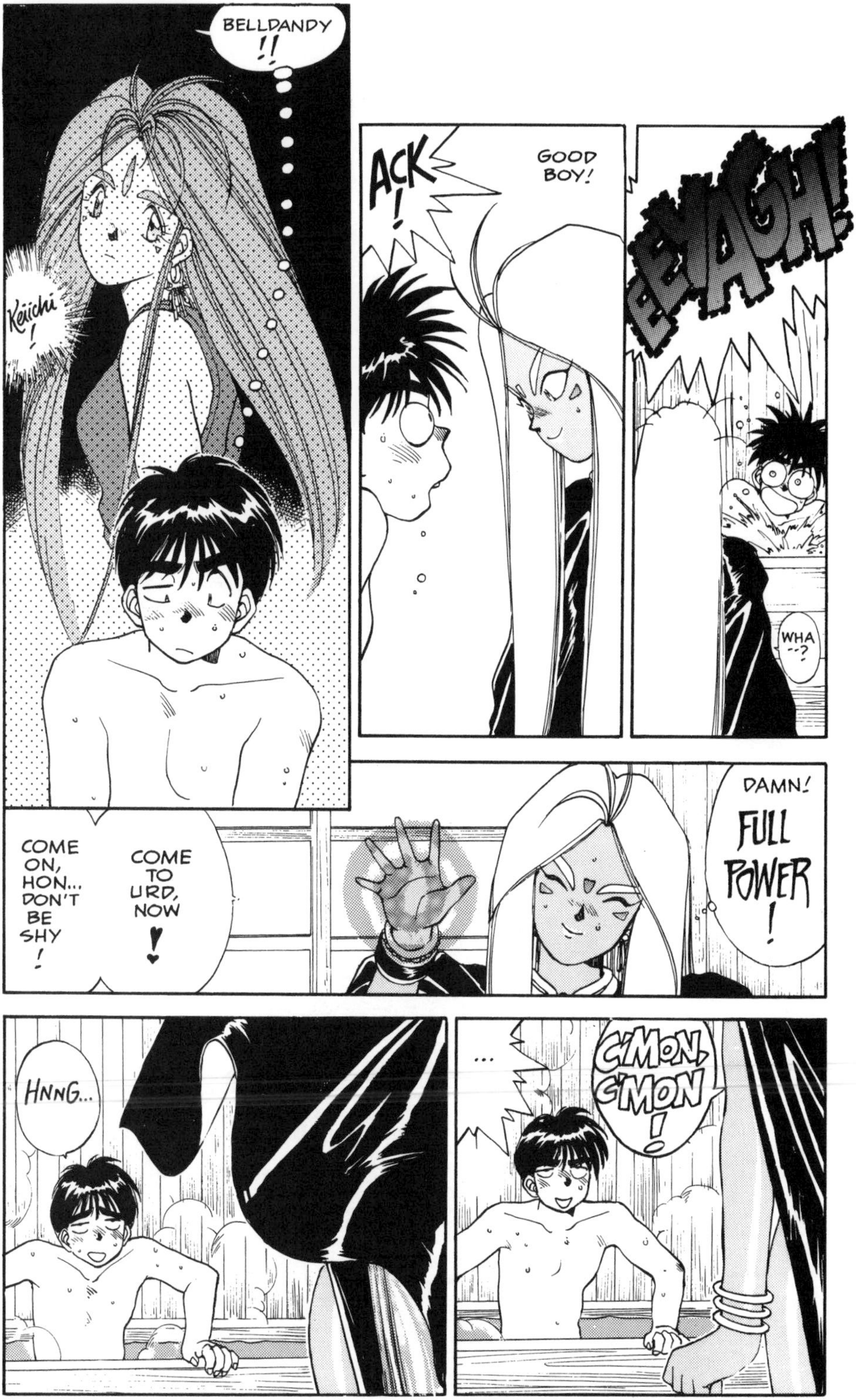

BELLDANDY !!
Keiichi !
ACK !
GOOD BOY!
EEYAGH!
WHA --?
COME ON, HON... DON'T BE SHY !
COME TO URD, NOW ♥!
DAMN! FULL POWER !
HNNG...
...
C'MON, C'MON !

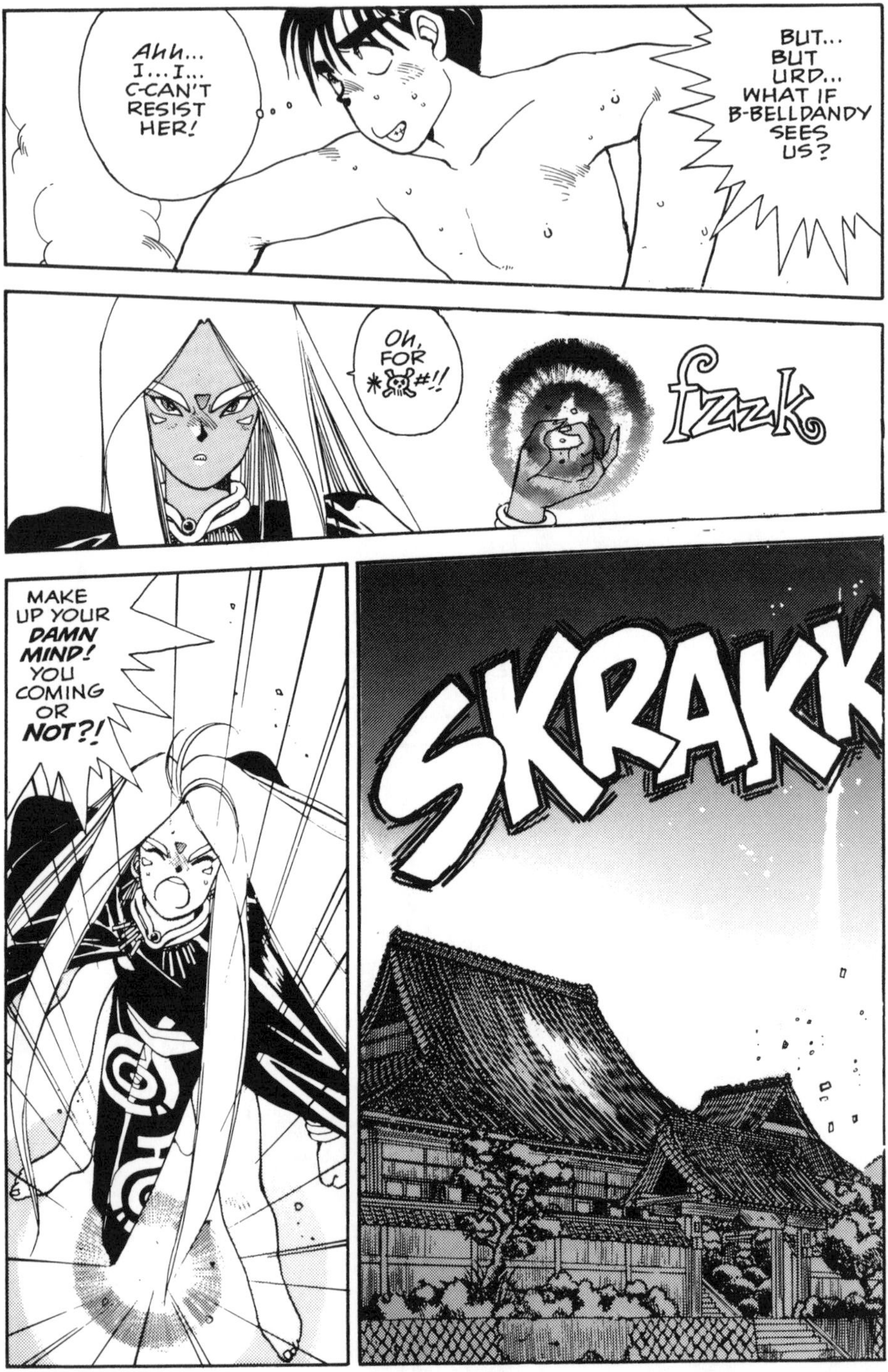
Ahh... I... I... C-CAN'T RESIST HER!
BUT... BUT URD... WHAT IF B-BELLDANDY SEES US?
Oh, FOR *☠#!!
fzzk
MAKE UP YOUR DAMN MIND! YOU COMING OR NOT?!
SKRAKK

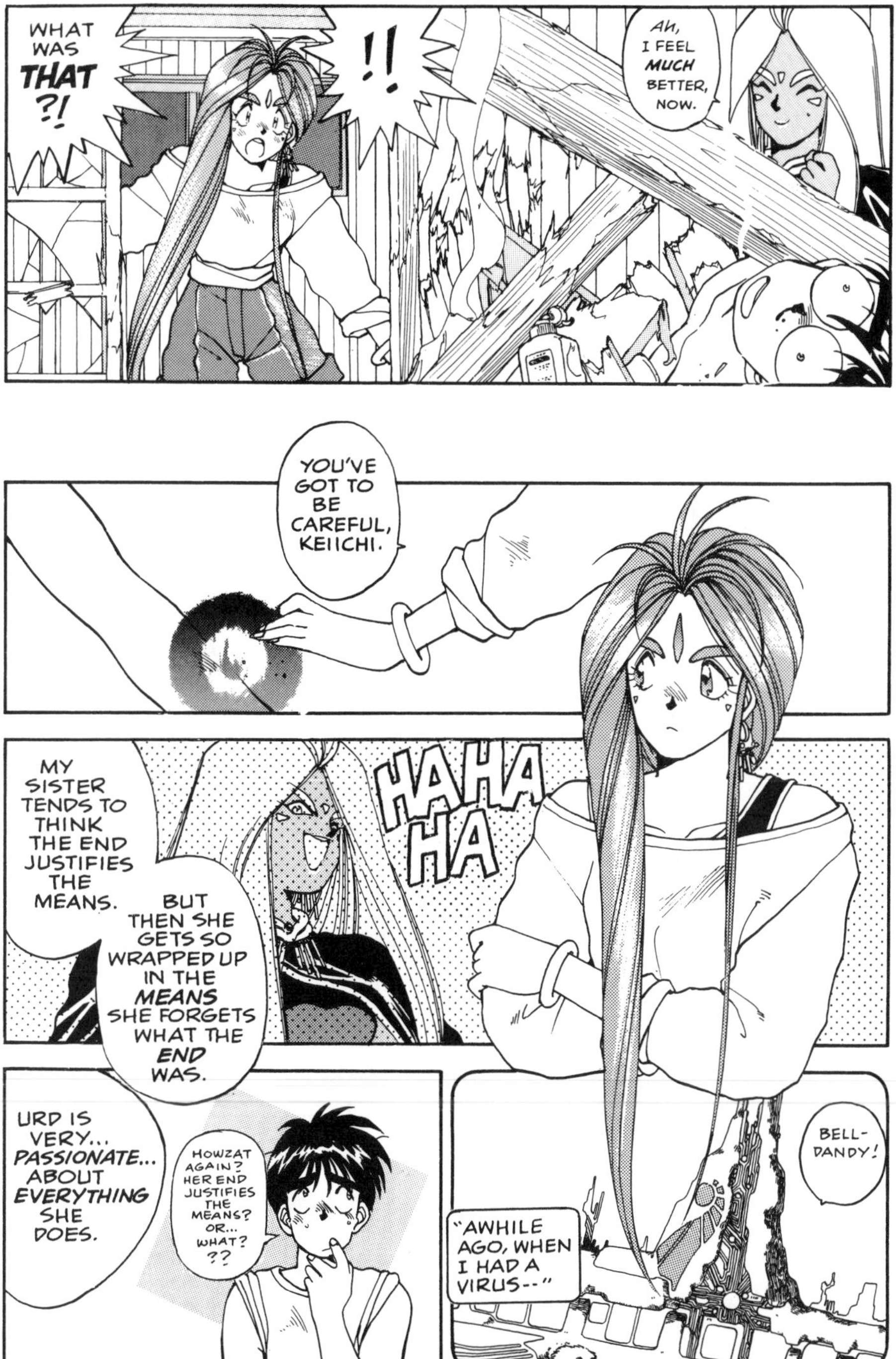
WHAT WAS **THAT** ?!
!!
Ah, I FEEL **MUCH** BETTER, NOW.
YOU'VE GOT TO BE CAREFUL, KEIICHI.
MY SISTER TENDS TO THINK THE END JUSTIFIES THE MEANS.
HAHA HA
BUT THEN SHE GETS SO WRAPPED UP IN THE ***MEANS*** SHE FORGETS WHAT THE ***END*** WAS.
URD IS VERY... ***PASSIONATE...*** ABOUT ***EVERYTHING*** SHE DOES.
HOWZAT AGAIN? HER END JUSTIFIES THE MEANS? OR... WHAT? ??
BELL-DANDY!
"AWHILE AGO, WHEN I HAD A VIRUS--"

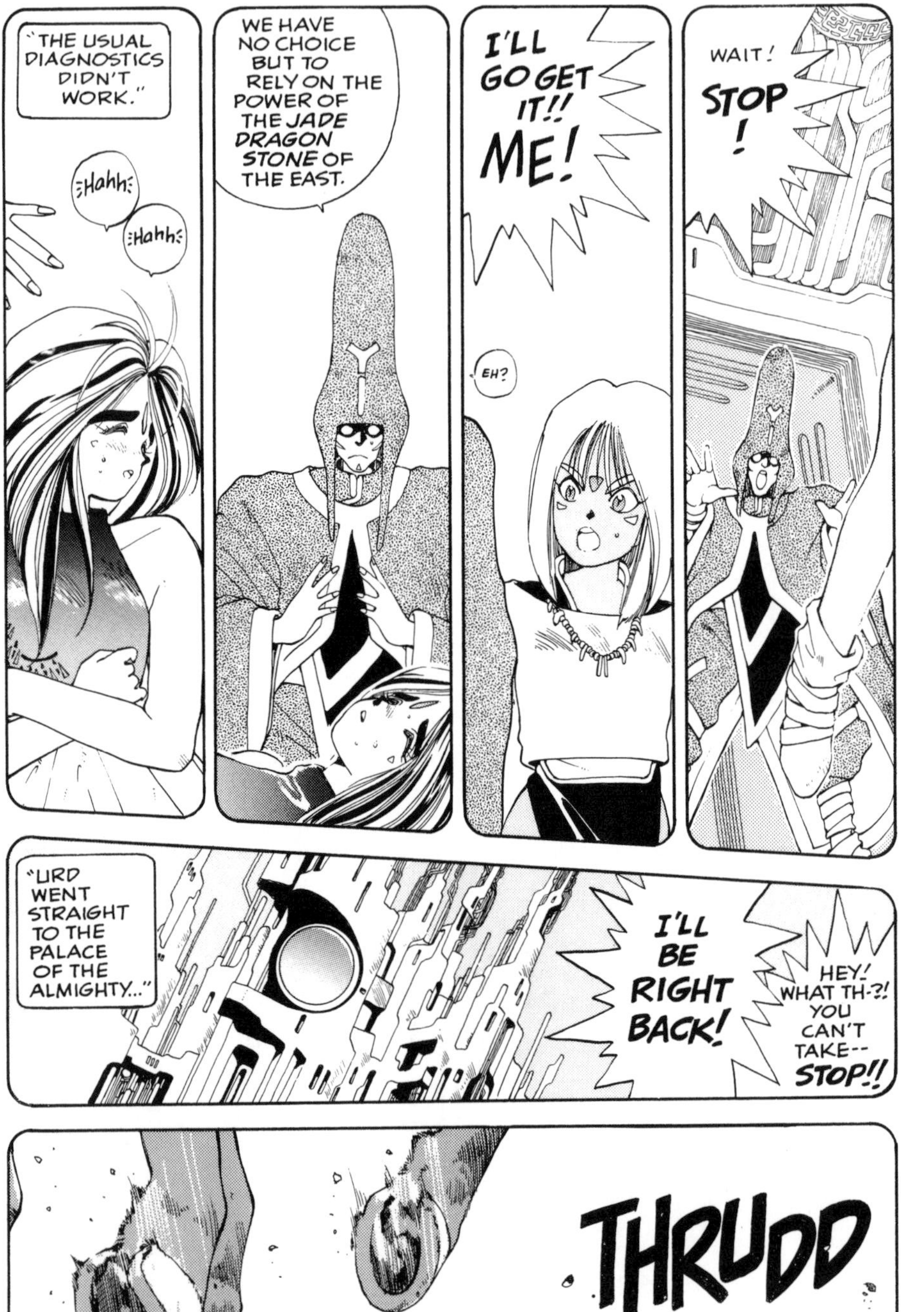
"THE USUAL DIAGNOSTICS DIDN'T WORK."
HAHH
HAHH
WE HAVE NO CHOICE BUT TO RELY ON THE POWER OF THE JADE DRAGON STONE OF THE EAST.
I'LL GO GET IT!! ME!
EH?
WAIT!
STOP!
"URD WENT STRAIGHT TO THE PALACE OF THE ALMIGHTY..."
I'LL BE RIGHT BACK!
HEY! WHAT TH-?! YOU CAN'T TAKE-- STOP!!
THRUDD

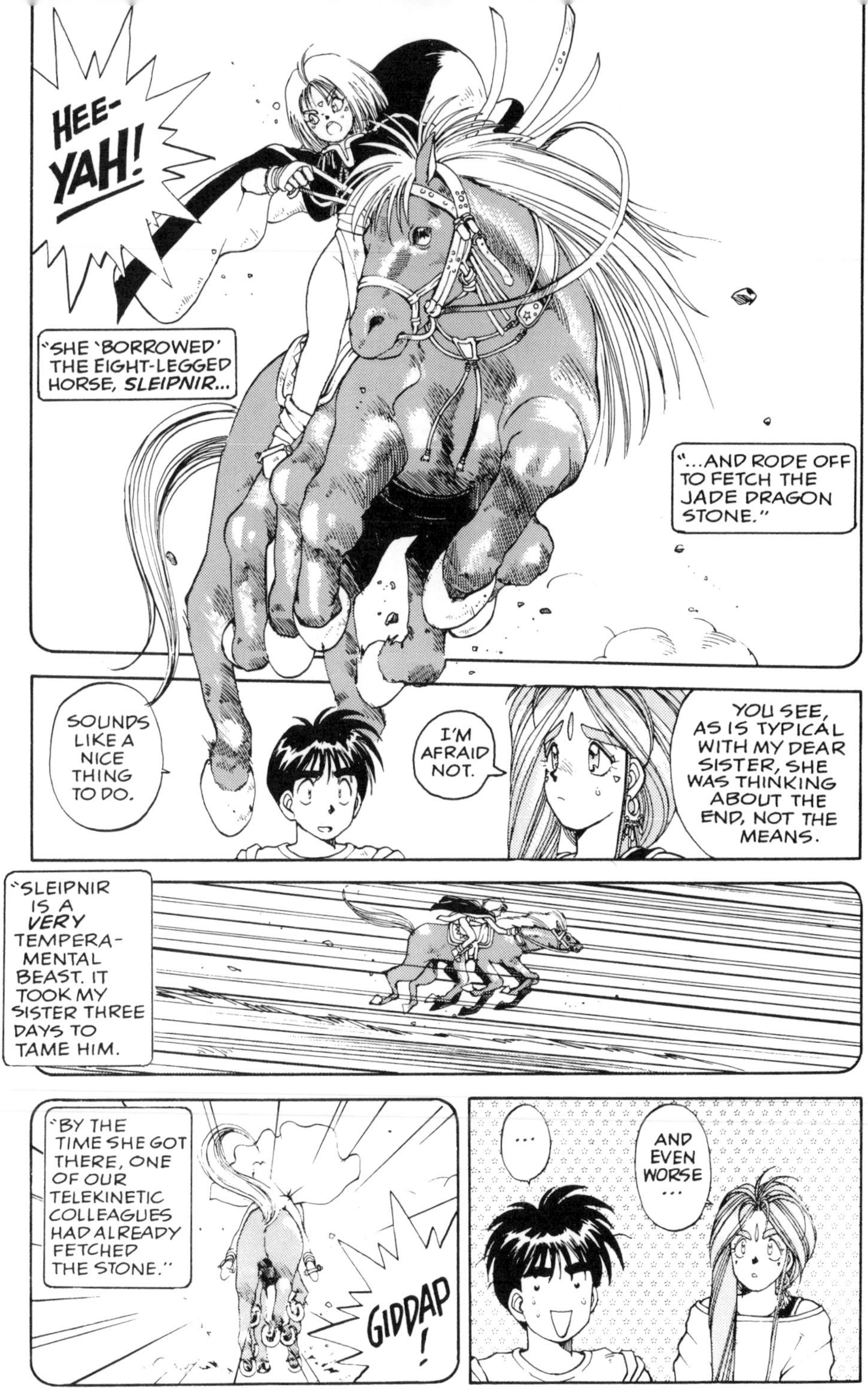
HEE-YAH!
"SHE 'BORROWED' THE EIGHT-LEGGED HORSE, *SLEIPNIR*...
"...AND RODE OFF TO FETCH THE JADE DRAGON STONE."
SOUNDS LIKE A NICE THING TO DO.
I'M AFRAID NOT.
YOU SEE, AS IS TYPICAL WITH MY DEAR SISTER, SHE WAS THINKING ABOUT THE END, NOT THE MEANS.
"SLEIPNIR IS A ***VERY*** TEMPERA-MENTAL BEAST. IT TOOK MY SISTER THREE DAYS TO TAME HIM.
"BY THE TIME SHE GOT THERE, ONE OF OUR TELEKINETIC COLLEAGUES HAD ALREADY FETCHED THE STONE."
GIDDAP!
...
AND EVEN WORSE...

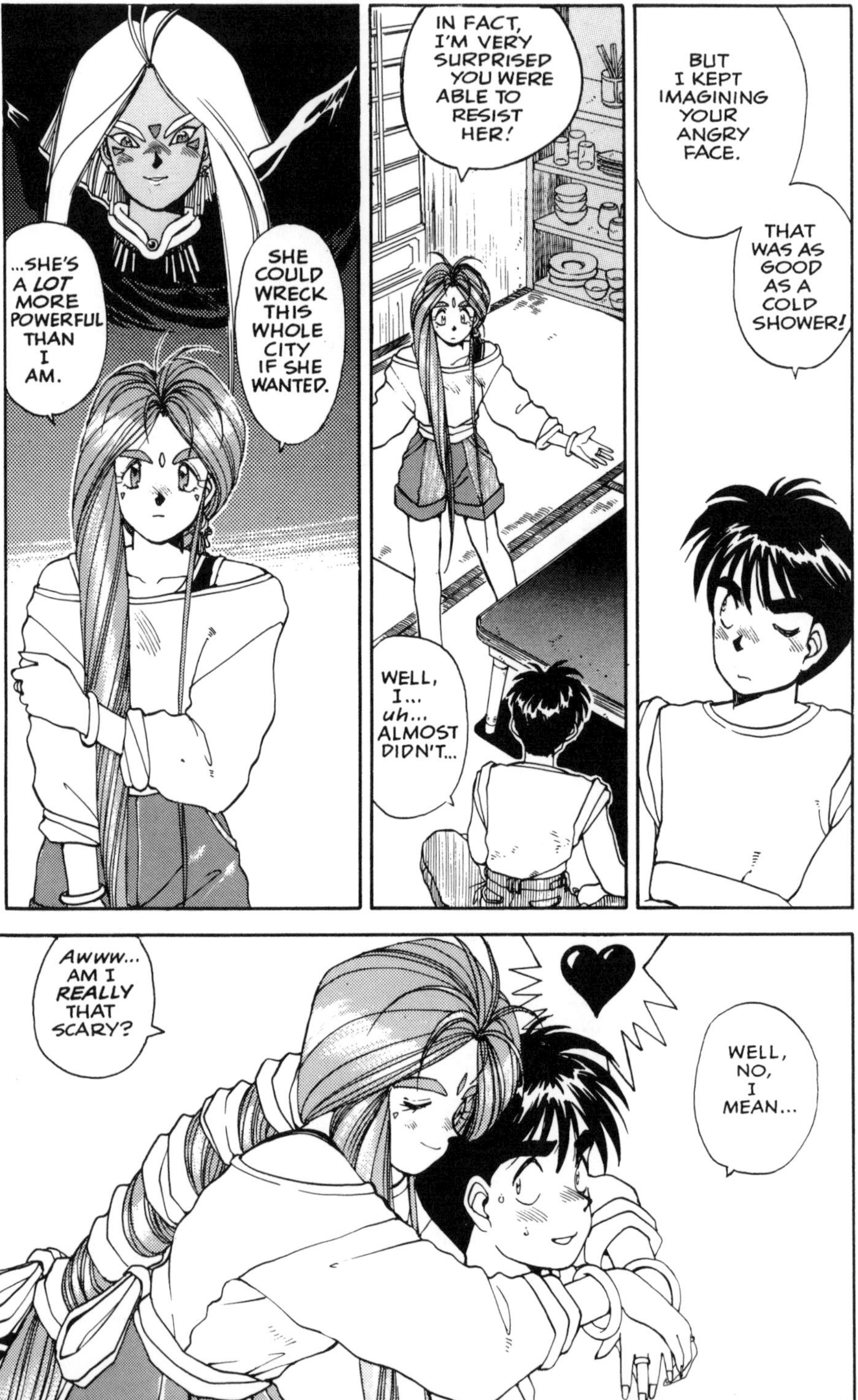
...SHE'S A *LOT* MORE POWERFUL THAN I AM.
SHE COULD WRECK THIS WHOLE CITY IF SHE WANTED.
IN FACT, I'M VERY SURPRISED YOU WERE ABLE TO RESIST HER!
WELL, I... *uh...* ALMOST DIDN'T...
BUT I KEPT IMAGINING YOUR ANGRY FACE.
THAT WAS AS GOOD AS A COLD SHOWER!
AWWW... AM I ***REALLY*** THAT SCARY?
WELL, NO, I MEAN...

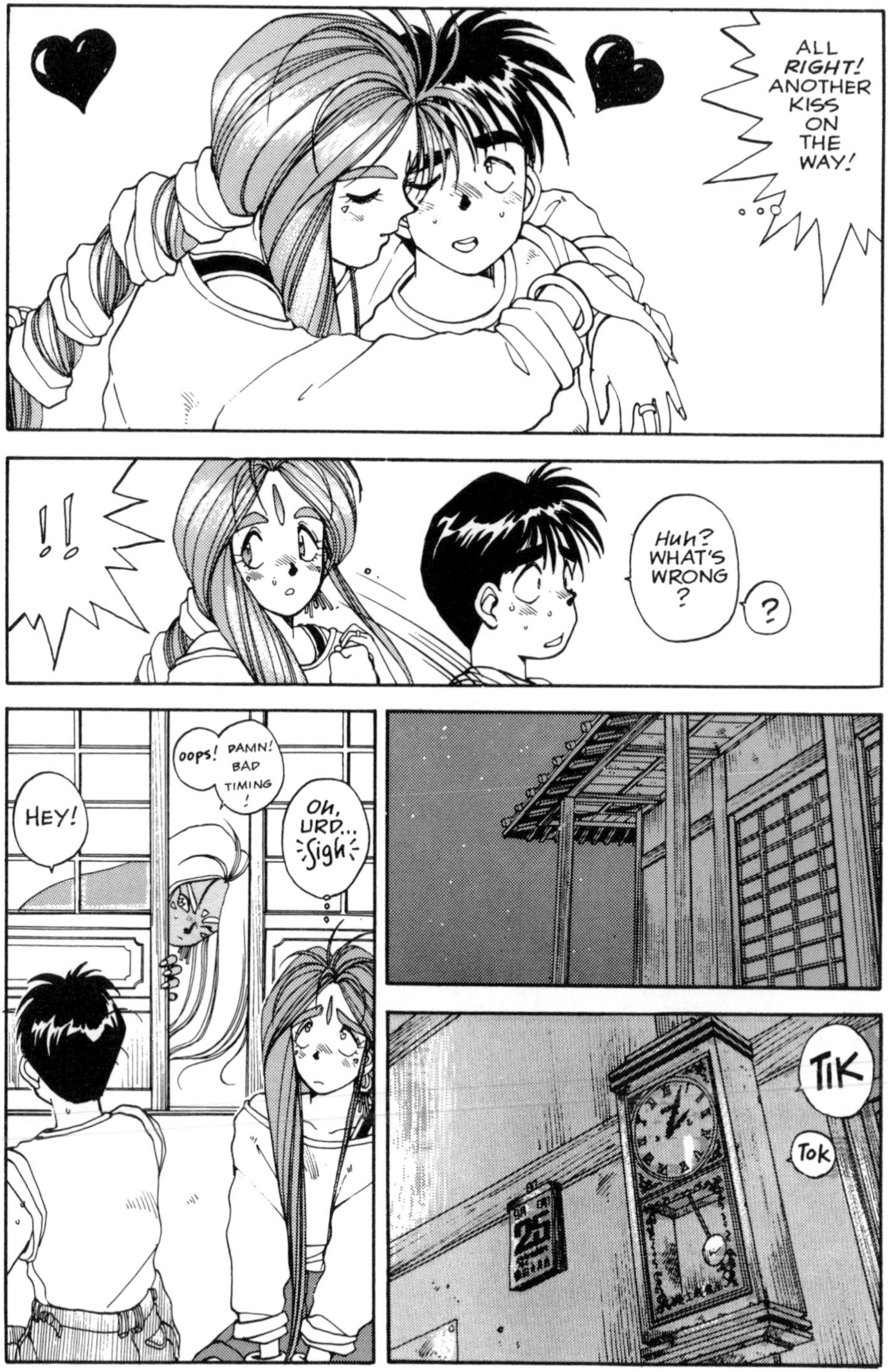

ALL RIGHT! ANOTHER KISS ON THE WAY!
!!
Huh? WHAT'S WRONG?
?
HEY!
oops! DAMN! BAD TIMING!
Oh, URD... Sigh
TIK
Tok

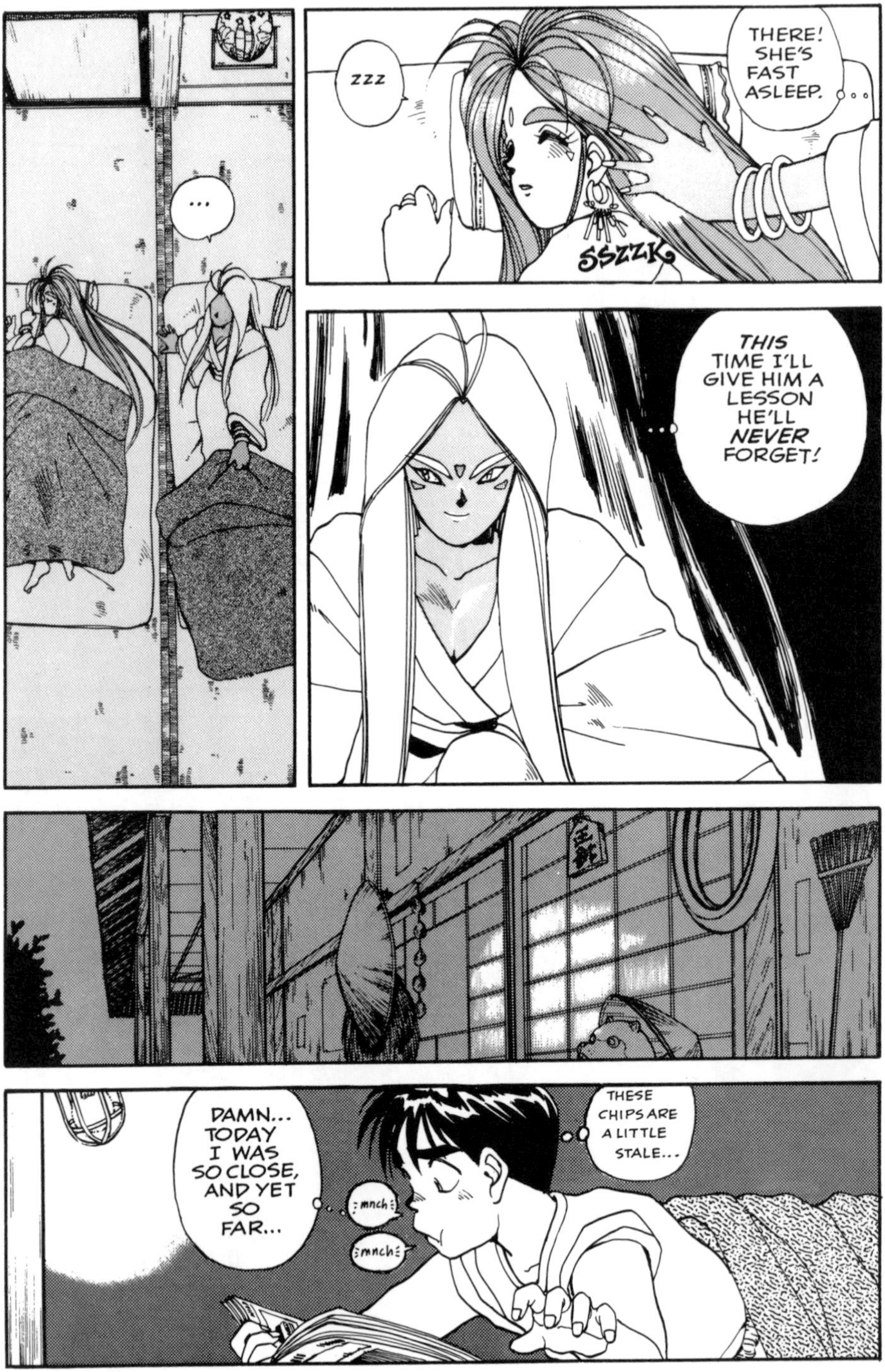
...
ZZZ
THERE! SHE'S FAST ASLEEP. . .
SSZZK
THIS TIME I'LL GIVE HIM A LESSON HE'LL NEVER FORGET!
DAMN... TODAY I WAS SO CLOSE, AND YET SO FAR...
mnch
mnch
THESE CHIPS ARE A LITTLE STALE...

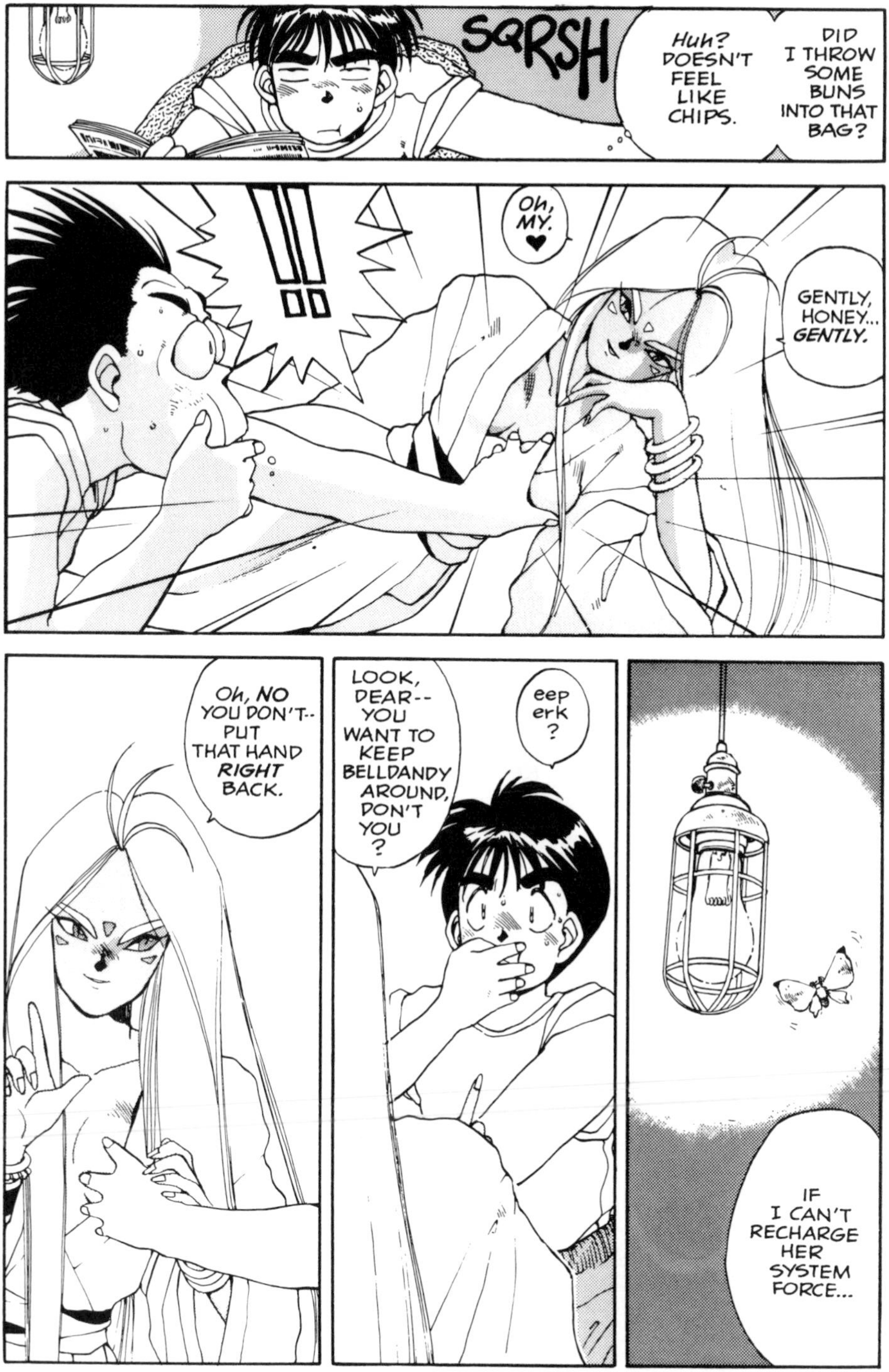
SQRSH
Huh? DOESN'T FEEL LIKE CHIPS.
DID I THROW SOME BUNS INTO THAT BAG?
!!!!
Oh, MY. ♥
GENTLY, HONEY... GENTLY.
Oh, NO YOU DON'T-- PUT THAT HAND RIGHT BACK.
LOOK, DEAR-- YOU WANT TO KEEP BELLDANDY AROUND, DON'T YOU?
eep erk ?
IF I CAN'T RECHARGE HER SYSTEM FORCE...

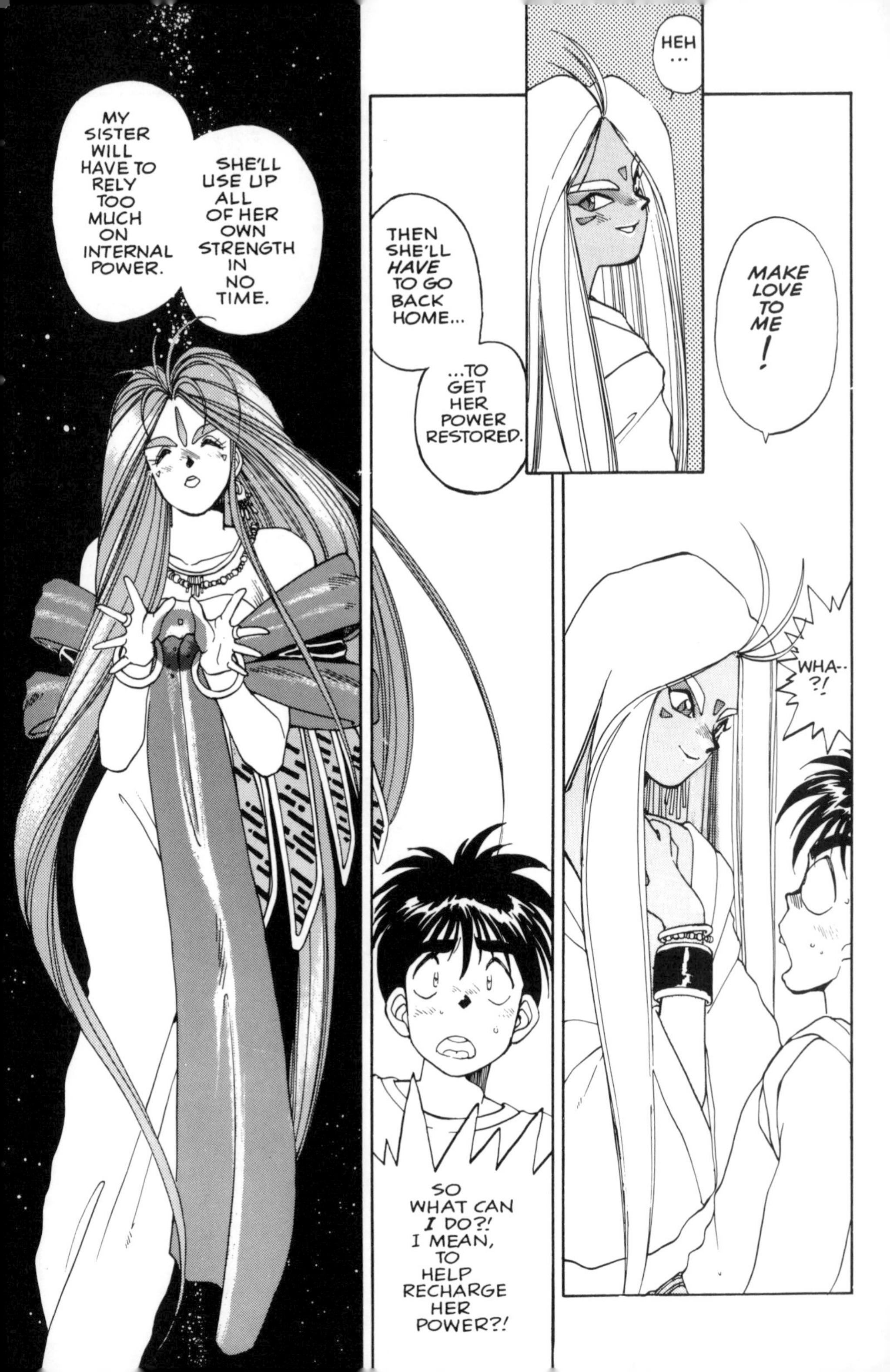
MY SISTER WILL HAVE TO RELY TOO MUCH ON INTERNAL POWER.
SHE'LL USE UP ALL OF HER OWN STRENGTH IN NO TIME.
THEN SHE'LL *HAVE* TO GO BACK HOME...
...TO GET HER POWER RESTORED.
SO WHAT CAN *I* DO?! I MEAN, TO HELP RECHARGE HER POWER?!
HEH ...
MAKE LOVE TO ME!
WHA-- ?!

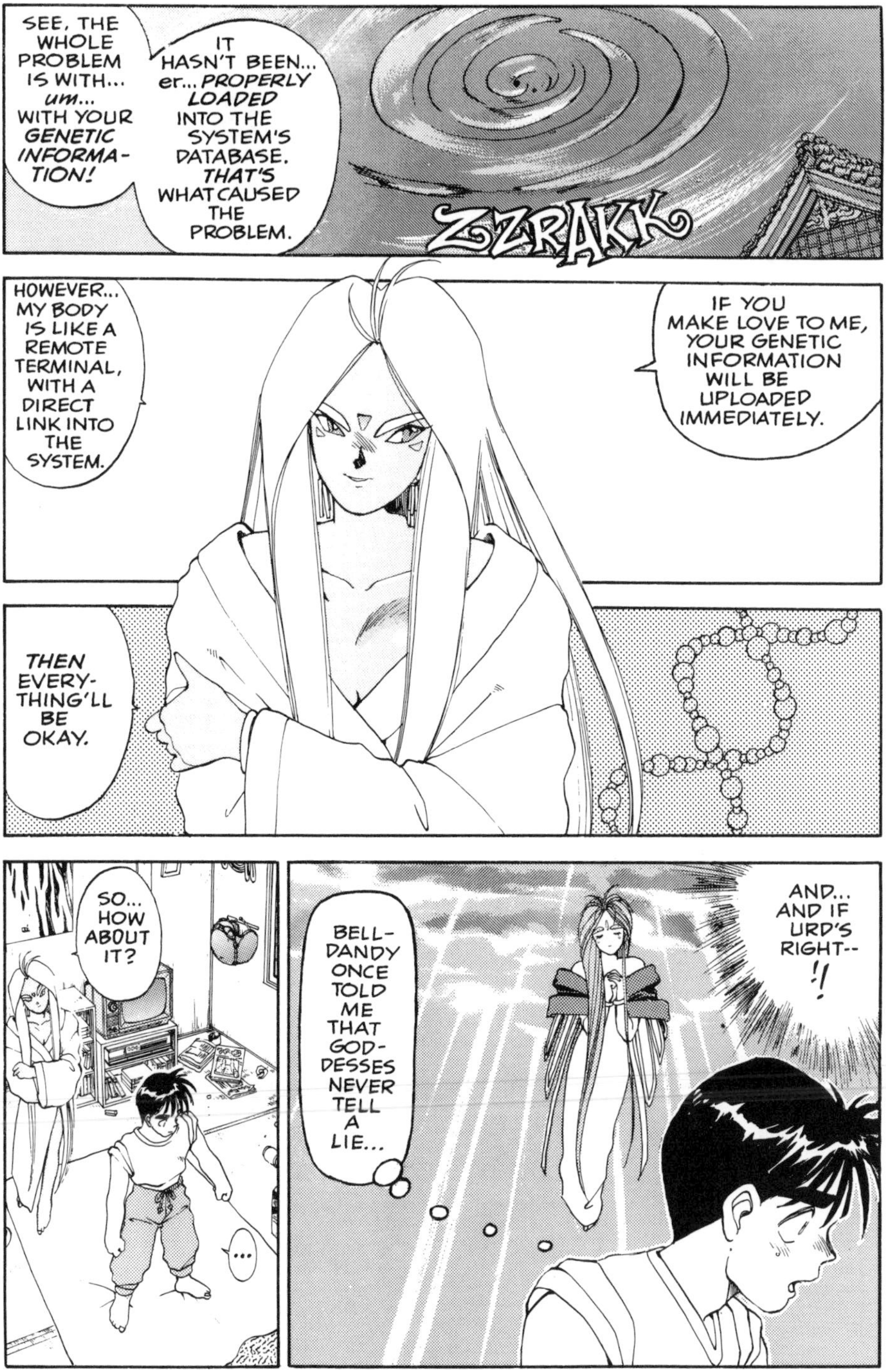
SEE, THE WHOLE PROBLEM IS WITH... *um*... WITH YOUR *GENETIC INFORMATION!*
IT HASN'T BEEN... er... *PROPERLY LOADED* INTO THE SYSTEM'S DATABASE. *THAT'S* WHAT CAUSED THE PROBLEM.
ZZRAKK
HOWEVER... MY BODY IS LIKE A REMOTE TERMINAL, WITH A DIRECT LINK INTO THE SYSTEM.
IF YOU MAKE LOVE TO ME, YOUR GENETIC INFORMATION WILL BE UPLOADED IMMEDIATELY.
THEN EVERY-THING'LL BE OKAY.
SO... HOW ABOUT IT?
...
BELL-DANDY ONCE TOLD ME THAT GOD-DESSES NEVER TELL A LIE...
AND... AND IF URD'S RIGHT--
!!

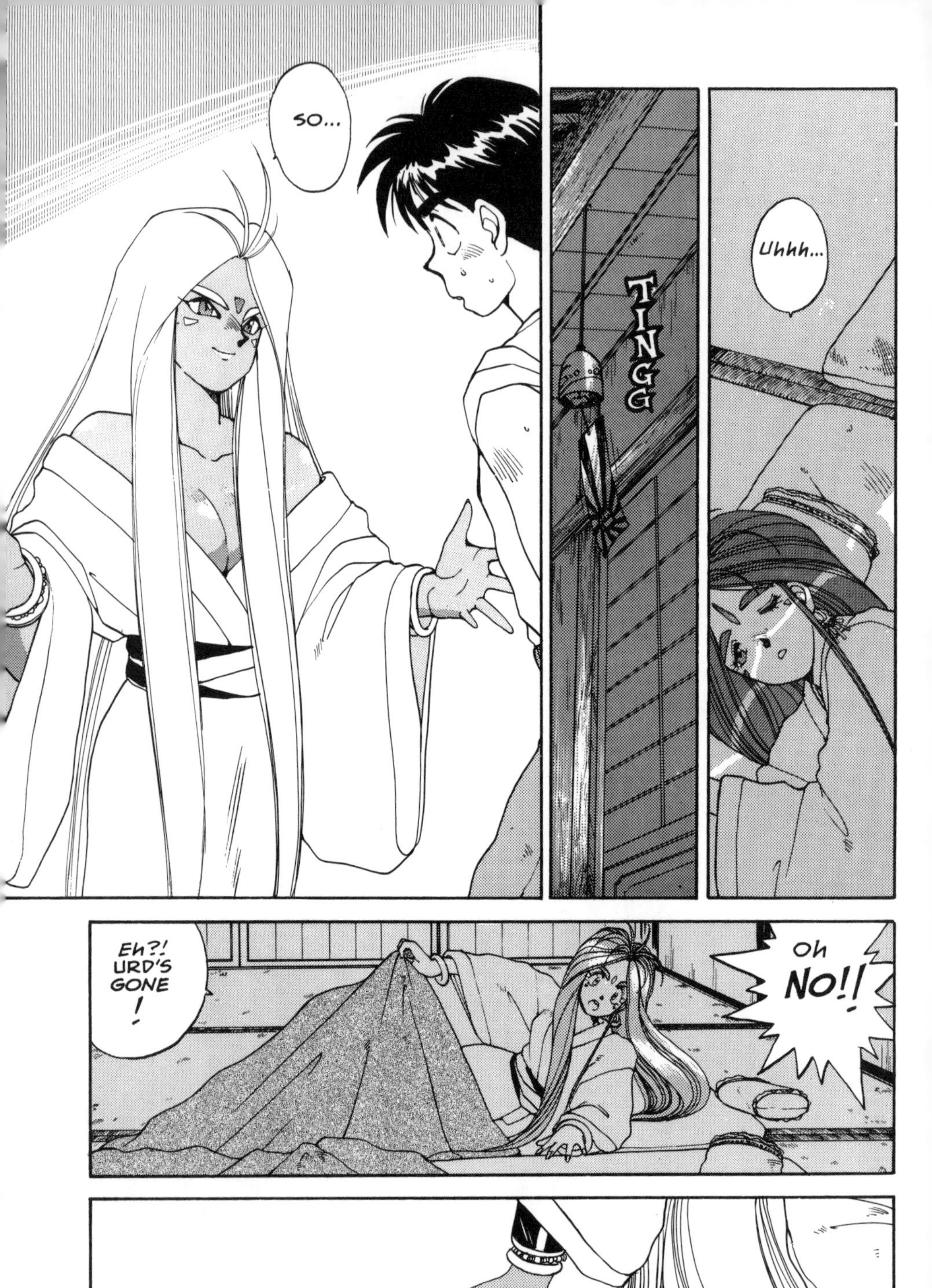
SO...
TINGG
Uhhh...
Eh?! URD'S GONE !
Oh NO!!

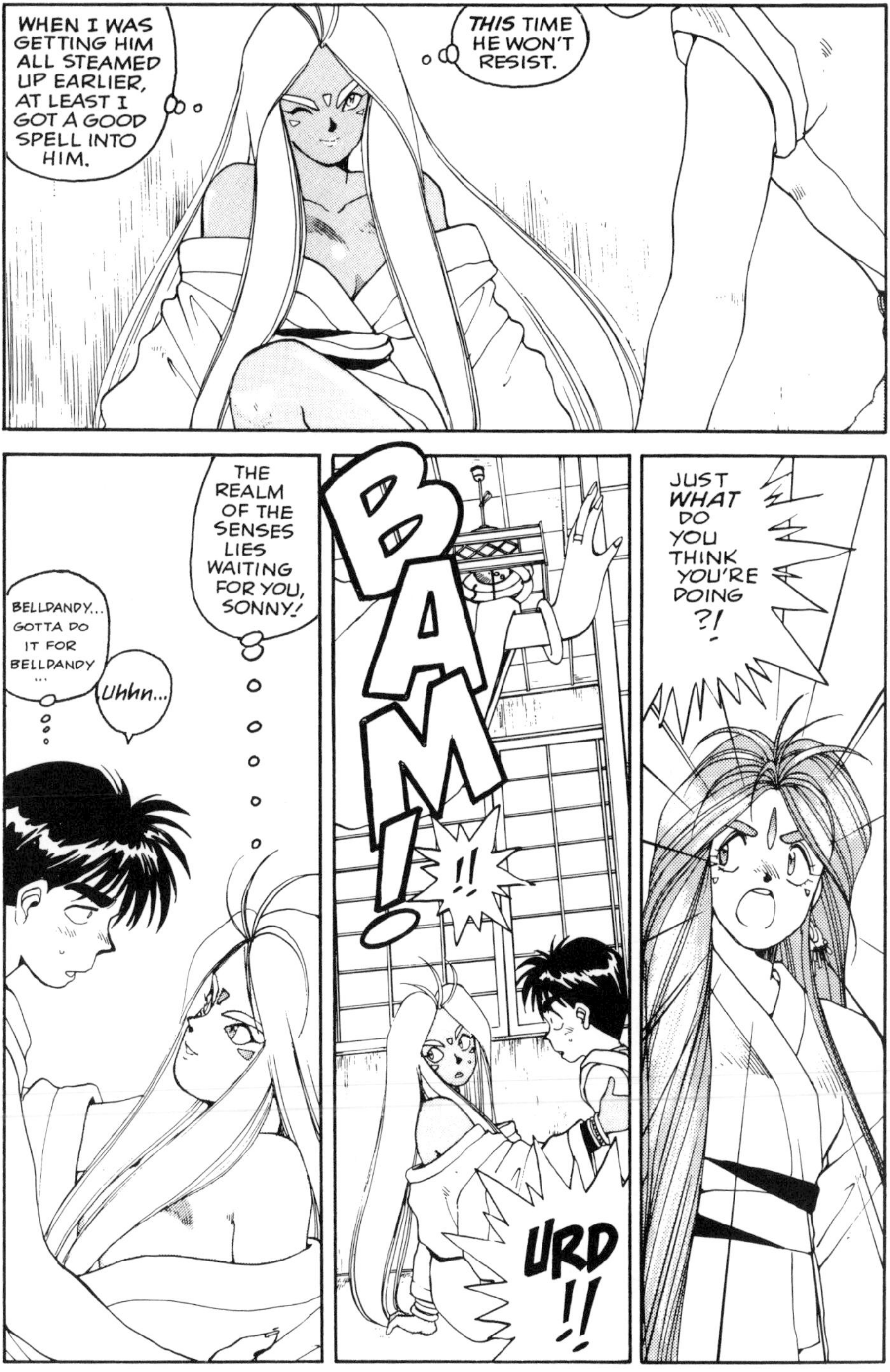
WHEN I WAS GETTING HIM ALL STEAMED UP EARLIER, AT LEAST I GOT A GOOD SPELL INTO HIM.
THIS TIME HE WON'T RESIST.
THE REALM OF THE SENSES LIES WAITING FOR YOU, SONNY!
BELLDANDY... GOTTA DO IT FOR BELLDANDY...
Uhhn...
BAM!
!!
URD!!
JUST WHAT DO YOU THINK YOU'RE DOING?!

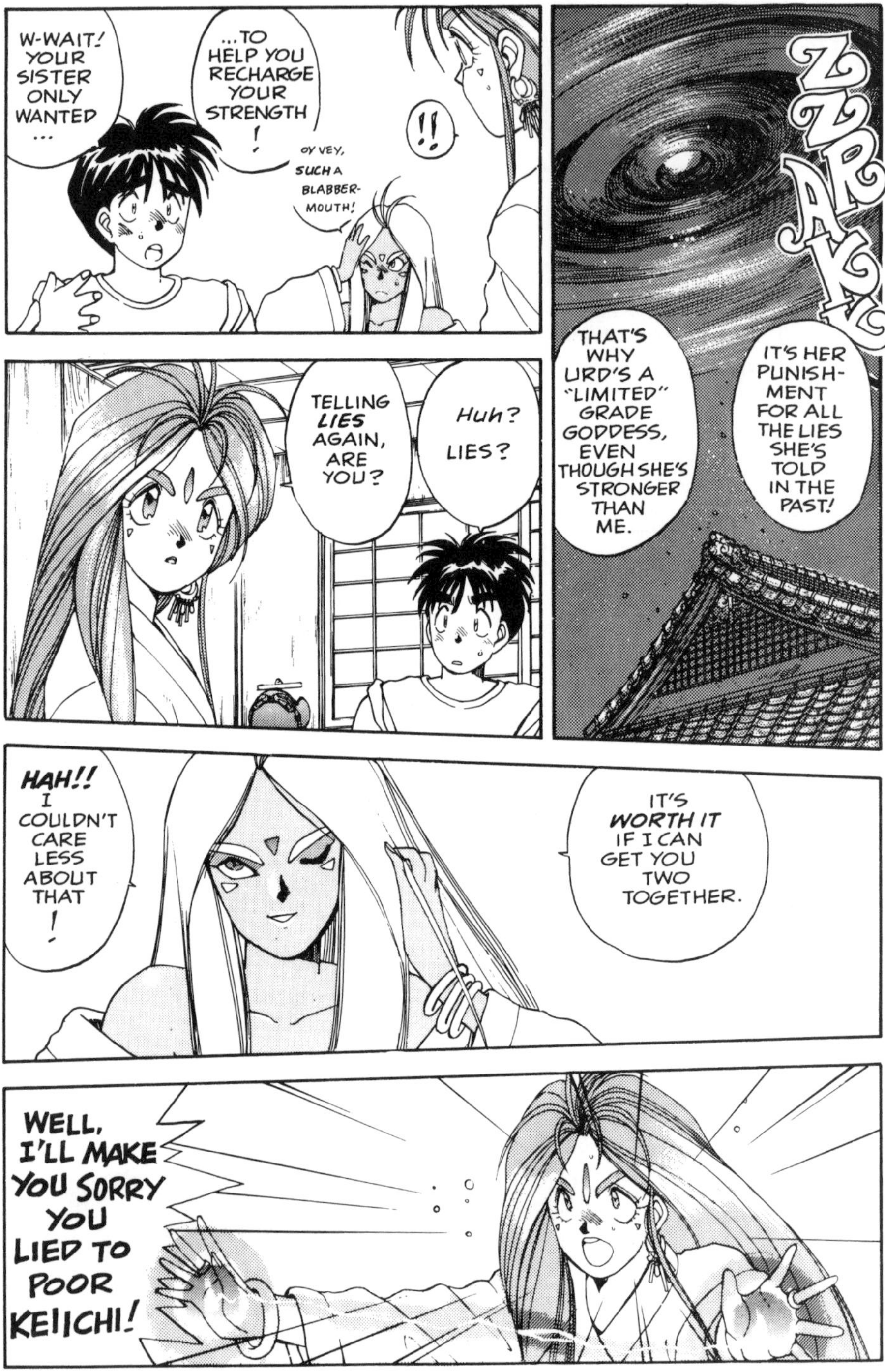
W-WAIT! YOUR SISTER ONLY WANTED ...
...TO HELP YOU RECHARGE YOUR STRENGTH!
!!
OY VEY, SUCH A BLABBER-MOUTH!
ZZRAAKK
IT'S HER PUNISH-MENT FOR ALL THE LIES SHE'S TOLD IN THE PAST!
THAT'S WHY URD'S A "LIMITED" GRADE GODDESS, EVEN THOUGH SHE'S STRONGER THAN ME.
Huh? LIES?
TELLING LIES AGAIN, ARE YOU?
IT'S WORTH IT IF I CAN GET YOU TWO TOGETHER.
HAH!! I COULDN'T CARE LESS ABOUT THAT!
WELL, I'LL MAKE YOU SORRY YOU LIED TO POOR KEIICHI!

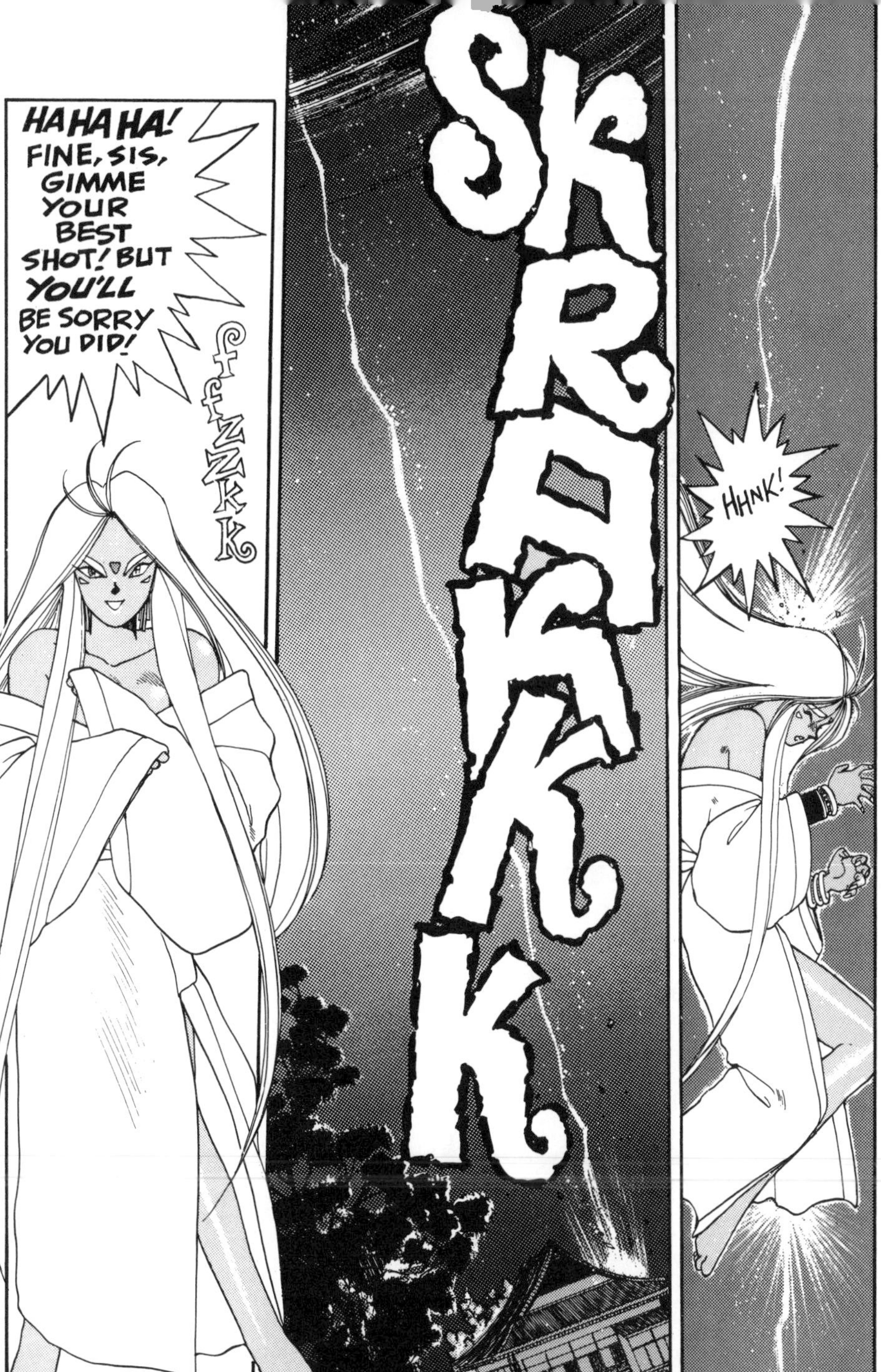
HA HA HA! FINE, SIS, GIMME YOUR BEST SHOT! BUT YOU'LL BE SORRY YOU DID!
ffZZKK
SKRAKAKAK
HHNK!

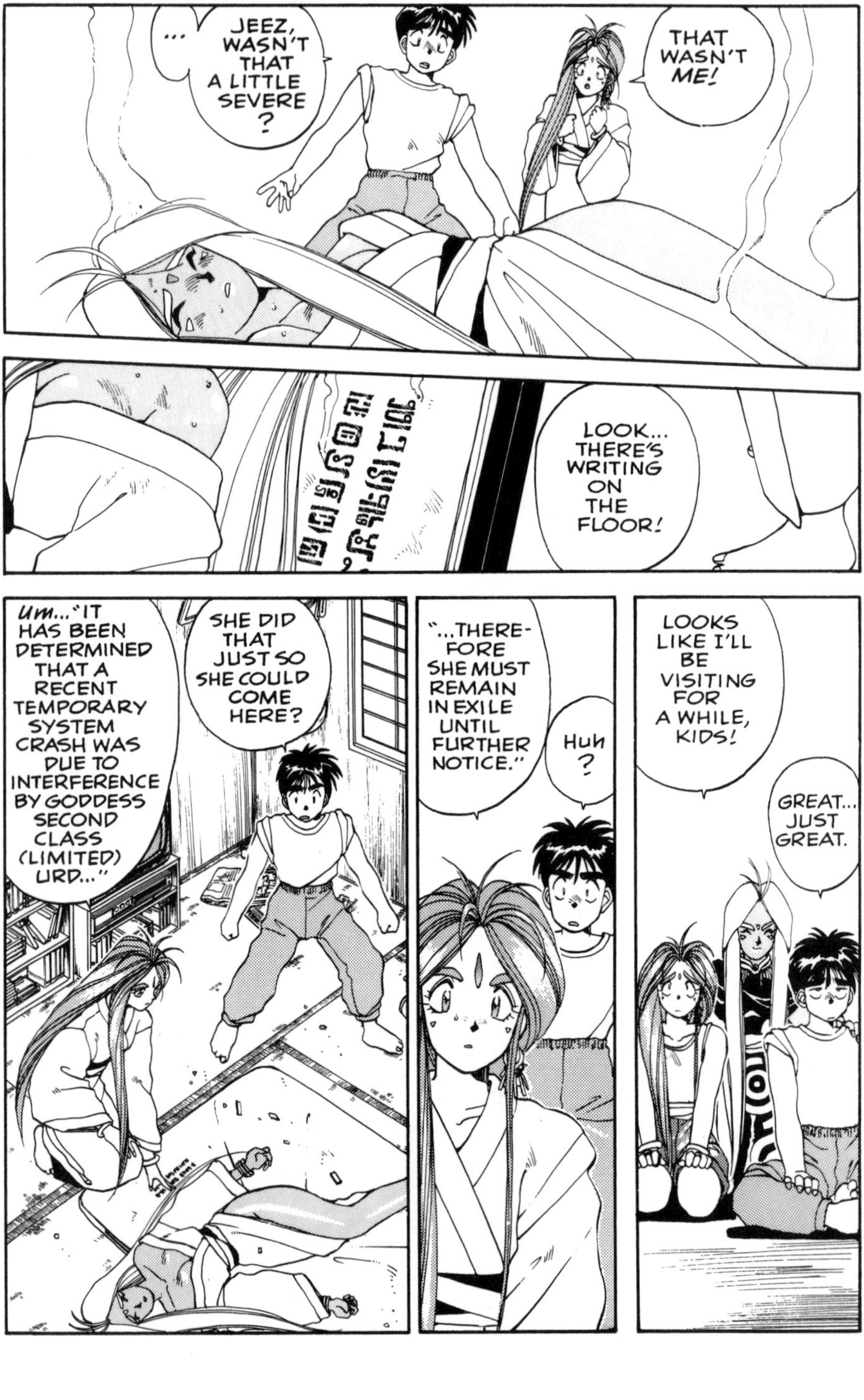
...
JEEZ, WASN'T THAT A LITTLE SEVERE?
THAT WASN'T ME!
LOOK... THERE'S WRITING ON THE FLOOR!
Um... "IT HAS BEEN DETERMINED THAT A RECENT TEMPORARY SYSTEM CRASH WAS DUE TO INTERFERENCE BY GODDESS SECOND CLASS (LIMITED) URD..."
SHE DID THAT JUST SO SHE COULD COME HERE?
"...THEREFORE SHE MUST REMAIN IN EXILE UNTIL FURTHER NOTICE."
Huh?
LOOKS LIKE I'LL BE VISITING FOR A WHILE, KIDS!
GREAT... JUST GREAT.

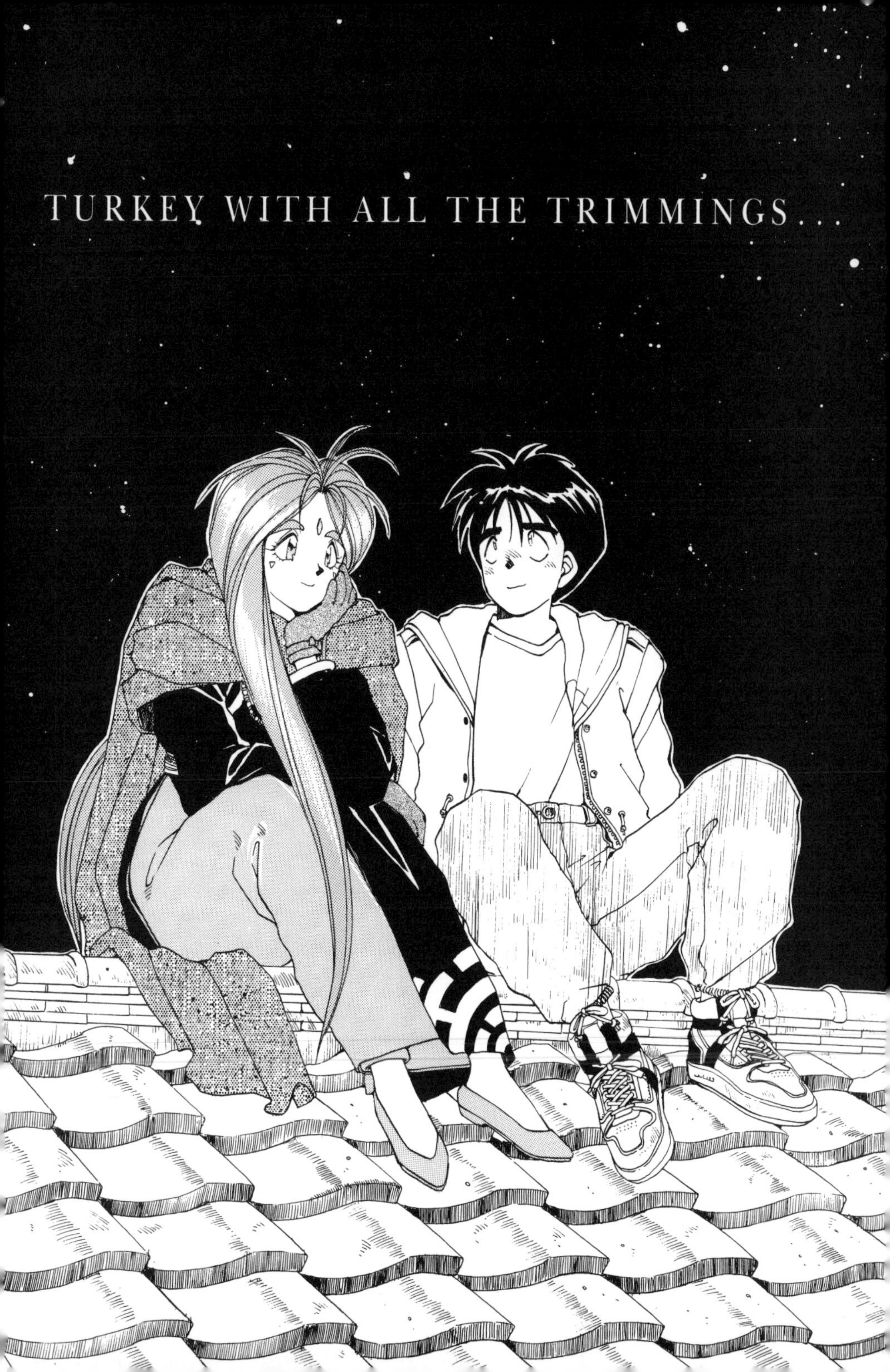
TURKEY WITH ALL THE TRIMMINGS...

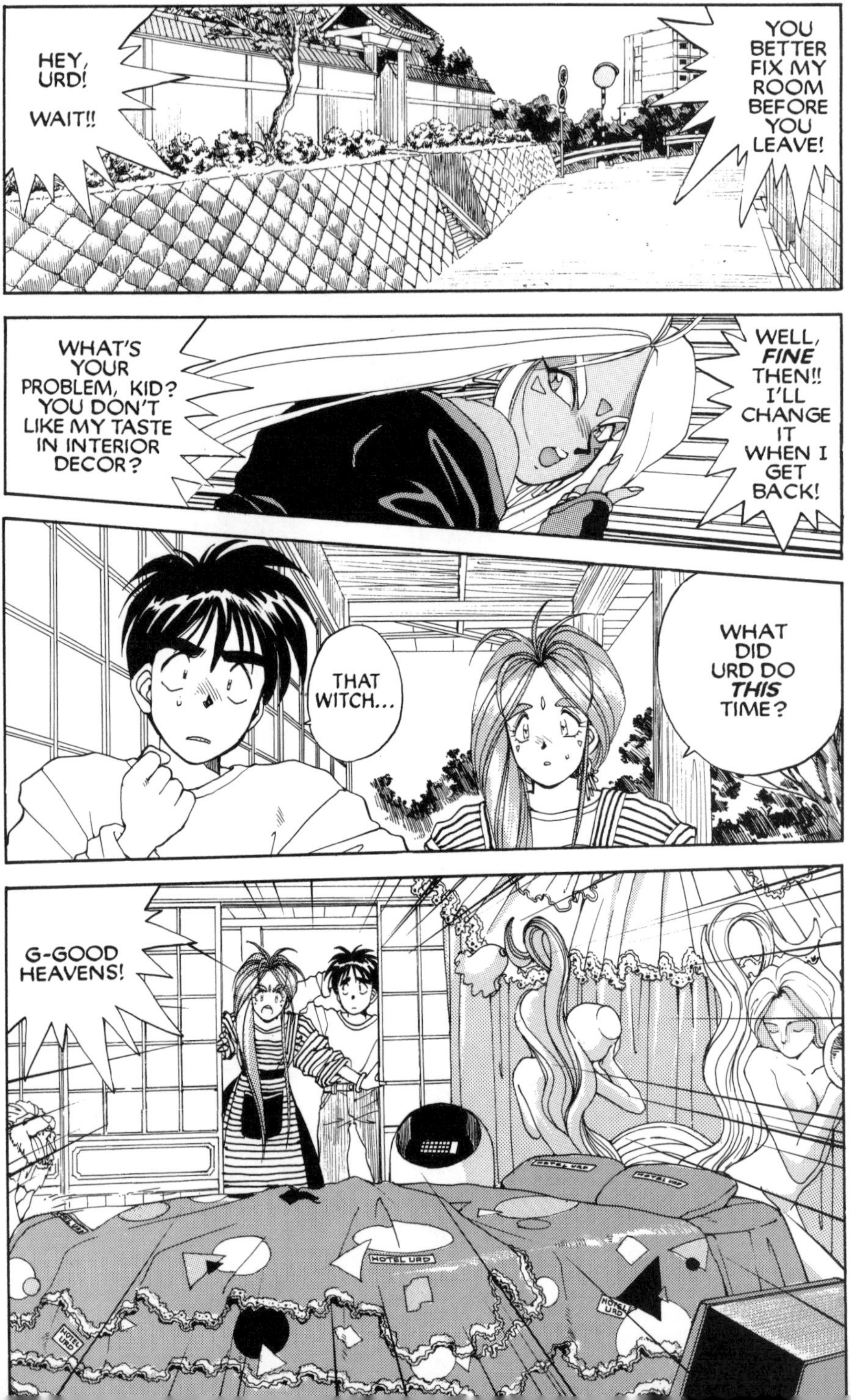
HEY, URD!
WAIT!!
YOU BETTER FIX MY ROOM BEFORE YOU LEAVE!
WHAT'S YOUR PROBLEM, KID? YOU DON'T LIKE MY TASTE IN INTERIOR DECOR?
WELL, *FINE* THEN!! I'LL CHANGE IT WHEN I GET BACK!
THAT WITCH...
WHAT DID URD DO *THIS* TIME?
G-GOOD HEAVENS!
HOTEL URD

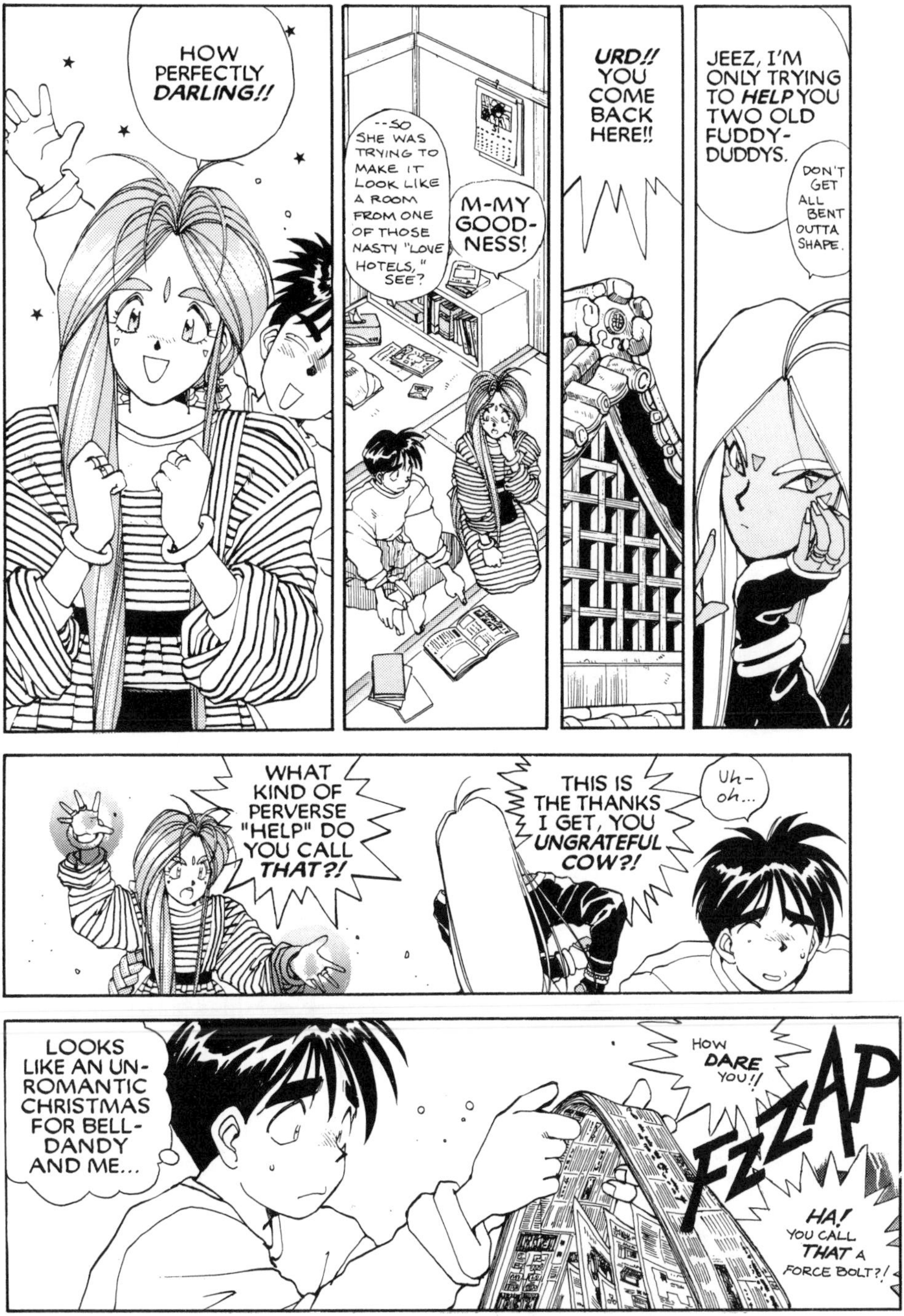
HOW PERFECTLY DARLING!!
--SO SHE WAS TRYING TO MAKE IT LOOK LIKE A ROOM FROM ONE OF THOSE NASTY "LOVE HOTELS," SEE?
M-MY GOODNESS!
URD!! YOU COME BACK HERE!!
JEEZ, I'M ONLY TRYING TO HELP YOU TWO OLD FUDDY-DUDDYS.
DON'T GET ALL BENT OUTTA SHAPE.
WHAT KIND OF PERVERSE "HELP" DO YOU CALL THAT?!
THIS IS THE THANKS I GET, YOU UNGRATEFUL COW?!
Uh-oh...
LOOKS LIKE AN UN-ROMANTIC CHRISTMAS FOR BELL-DANDY AND ME...
HOW DARE YOU!!
FZZZAP
HA! YOU CALL THAT A FORCE BOLT?!

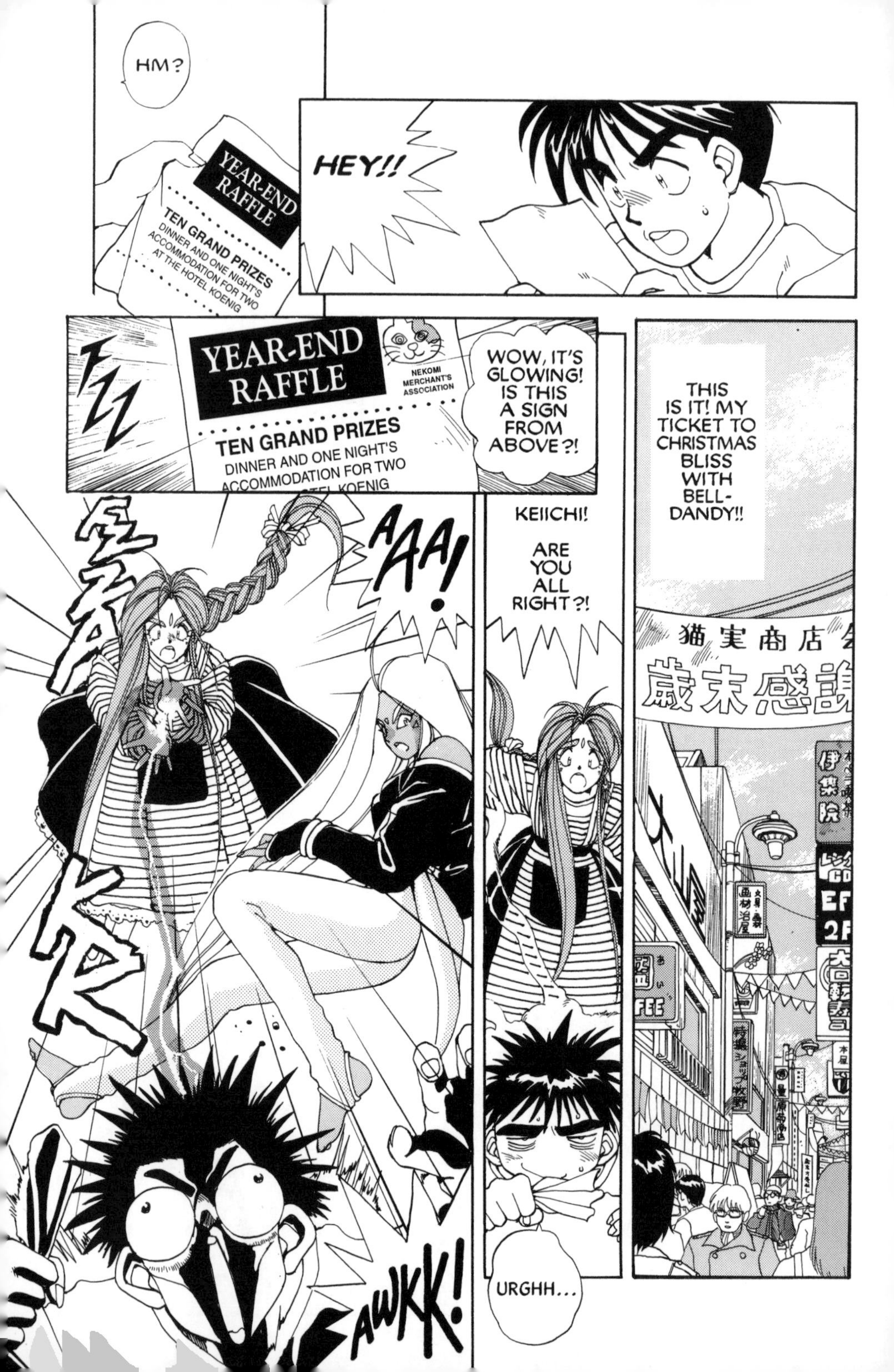
HM?
YEAR-END RAFFLE
TEN GRAND PRIZES
DINNER AND ONE NIGHT'S ACCOMMODATION FOR TWO AT THE HOTEL KOENIG
HEY!!
YEAR-END RAFFLE
NEKOMI MERCHANT'S ASSOCIATION
TEN GRAND PRIZES
DINNER AND ONE NIGHT'S ACCOMMODATION FOR TWO
WOW, IT'S GLOWING! IS THIS A SIGN FROM ABOVE?!
AAA!
AWKK!
KEIICHI!
ARE YOU ALL RIGHT?!
URGHH...
THIS IS IT! MY TICKET TO CHRISTMAS BLISS WITH BELL-DANDY!!
猫実商店会

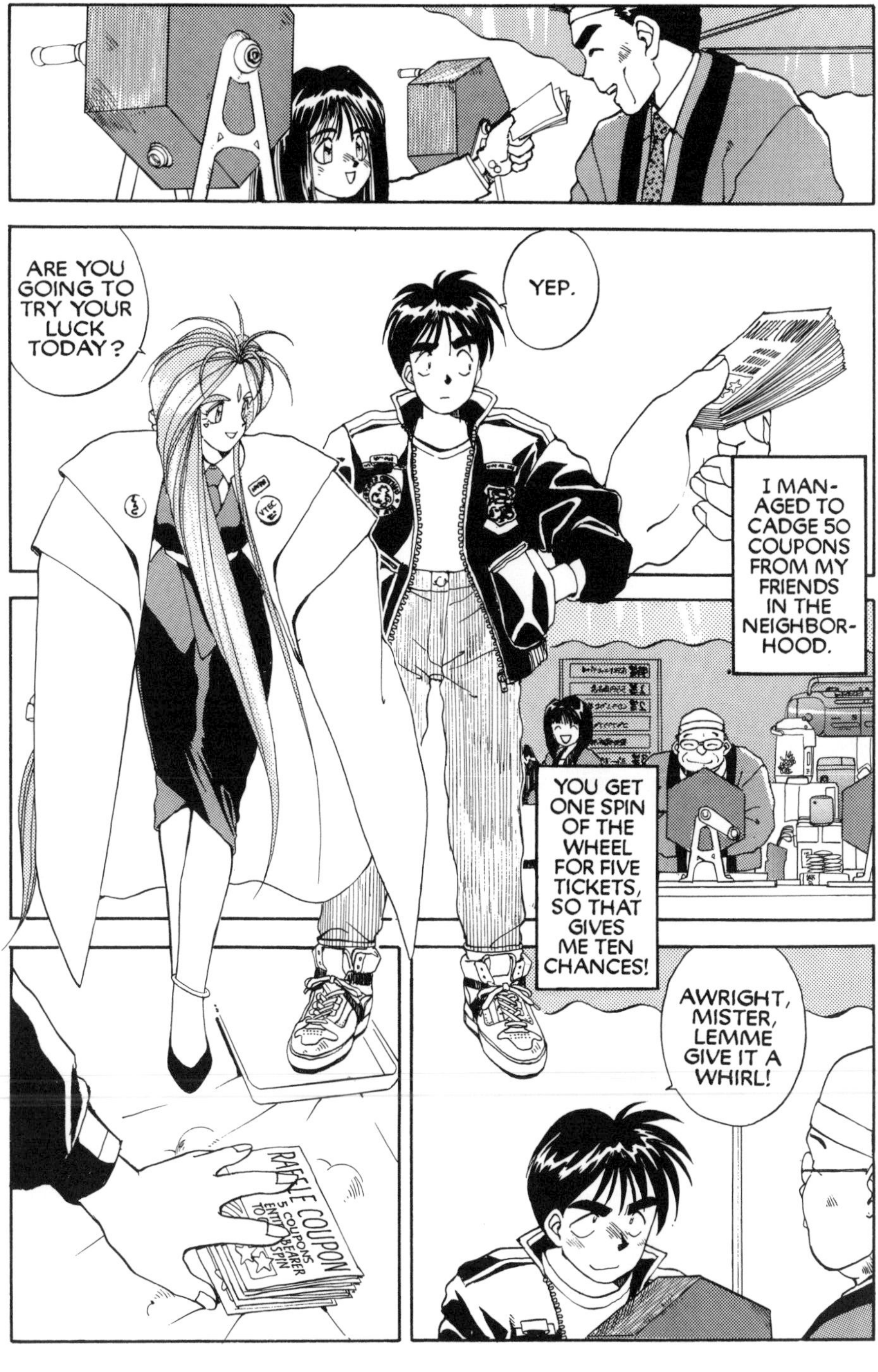
ARE YOU GOING TO TRY YOUR LUCK TODAY?
YEP.
I MANAGED TO CADGE 50 COUPONS FROM MY FRIENDS IN THE NEIGHBORHOOD.
YOU GET ONE SPIN OF THE WHEEL FOR FIVE TICKETS, SO THAT GIVES ME TEN CHANCES!
RAFFLE COUPON
5 COUPONS
AWRIGHT, MISTER, LEMME GIVE IT A WHIRL!

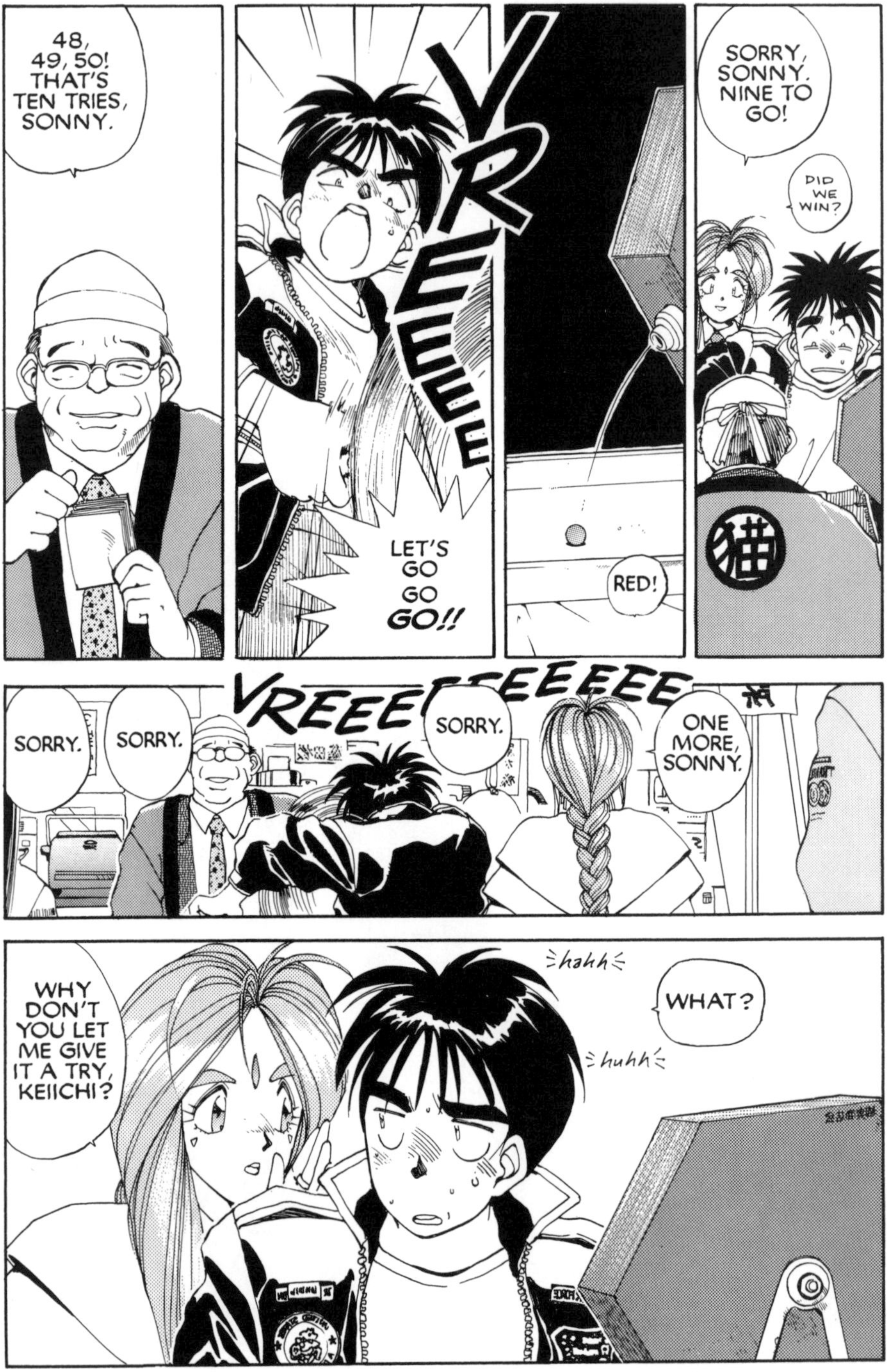
48, 49, 50! THAT'S TEN TRIES, SONNY.
VREEEEE
LET'S GO GO GO!!
RED!
SORRY, SONNY. NINE TO GO!
DID WE WIN?
VREEEEEEEEEEE
SORRY.
SORRY.
SORRY.
ONE MORE, SONNY.
WHY DON'T YOU LET ME GIVE IT A TRY, KEIICHI?
hahh
WHAT?
huhh

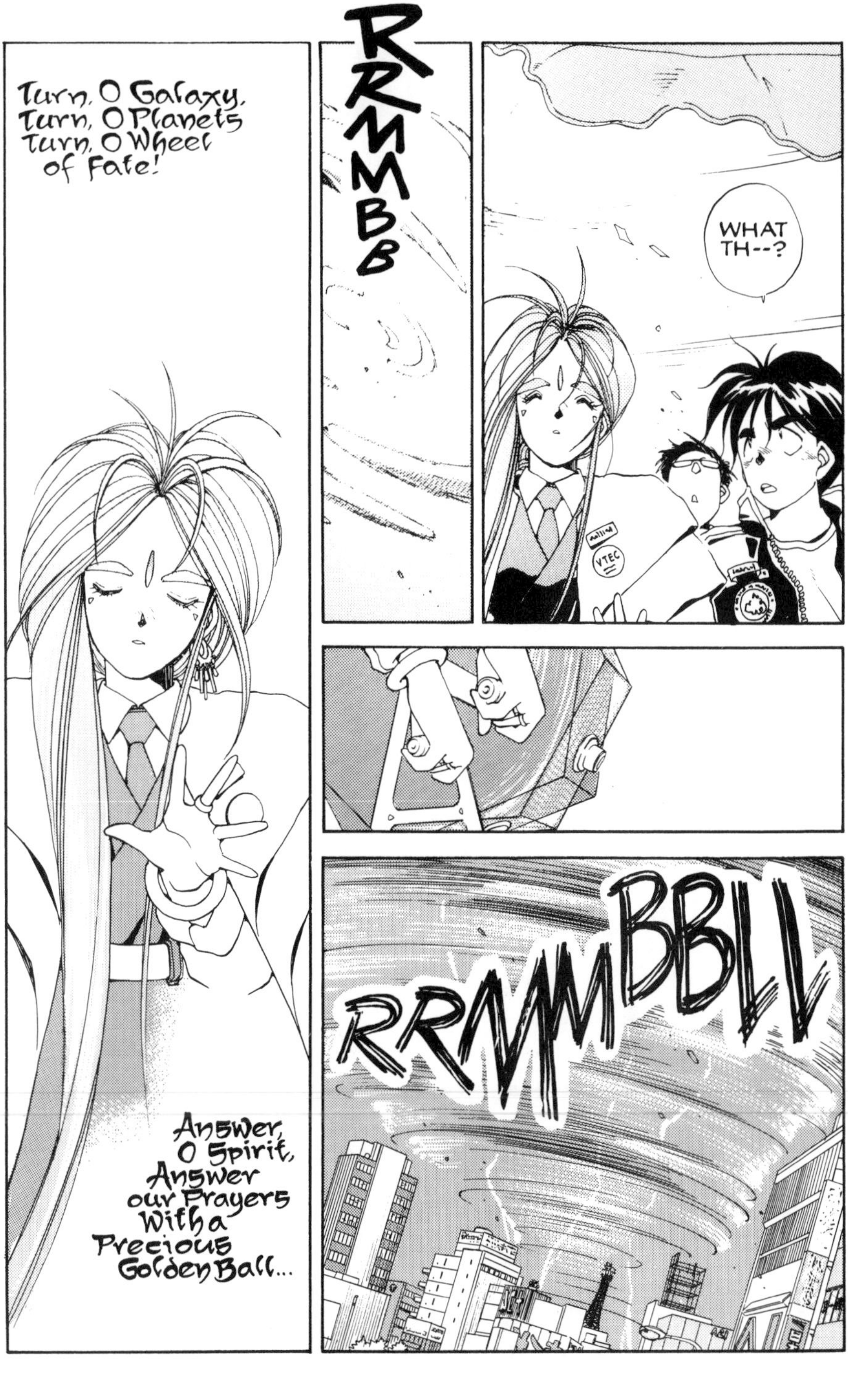
Turn, O Galaxy, Turn, O Planets Turn, O Wheel of Fate!
Answer, O Spirit, Answer our Prayers With a Precious Golden Ball...
RRMMBB
WHAT TH--?
RRMMBBLL

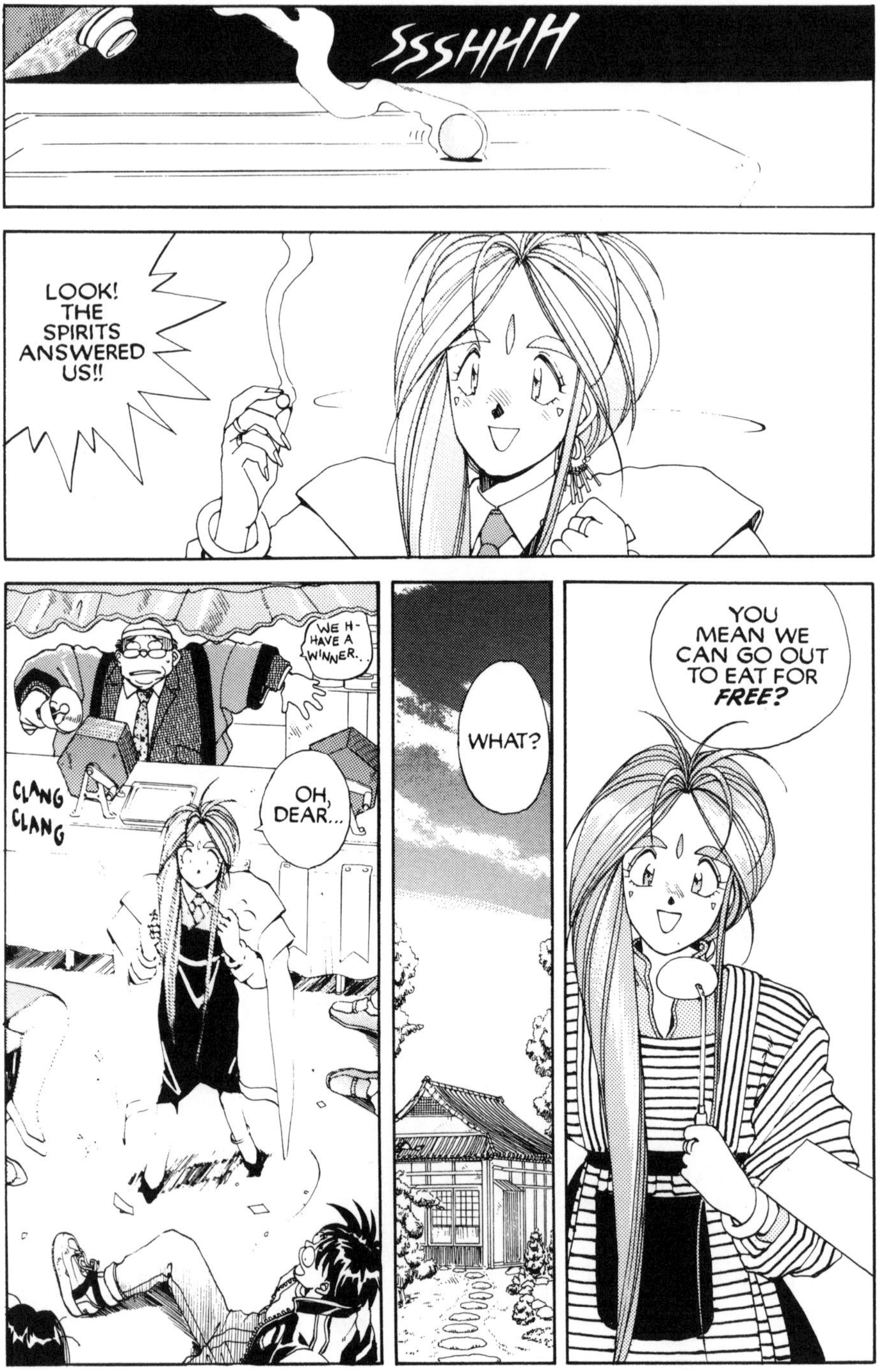
SSSHHH
LOOK! THE SPIRITS ANSWERED US!!
WE H-HAVE A WINNER...
CLANG CLANG
OH, DEAR...
WHAT?
YOU MEAN WE CAN GO OUT TO EAT FOR *FREE?*

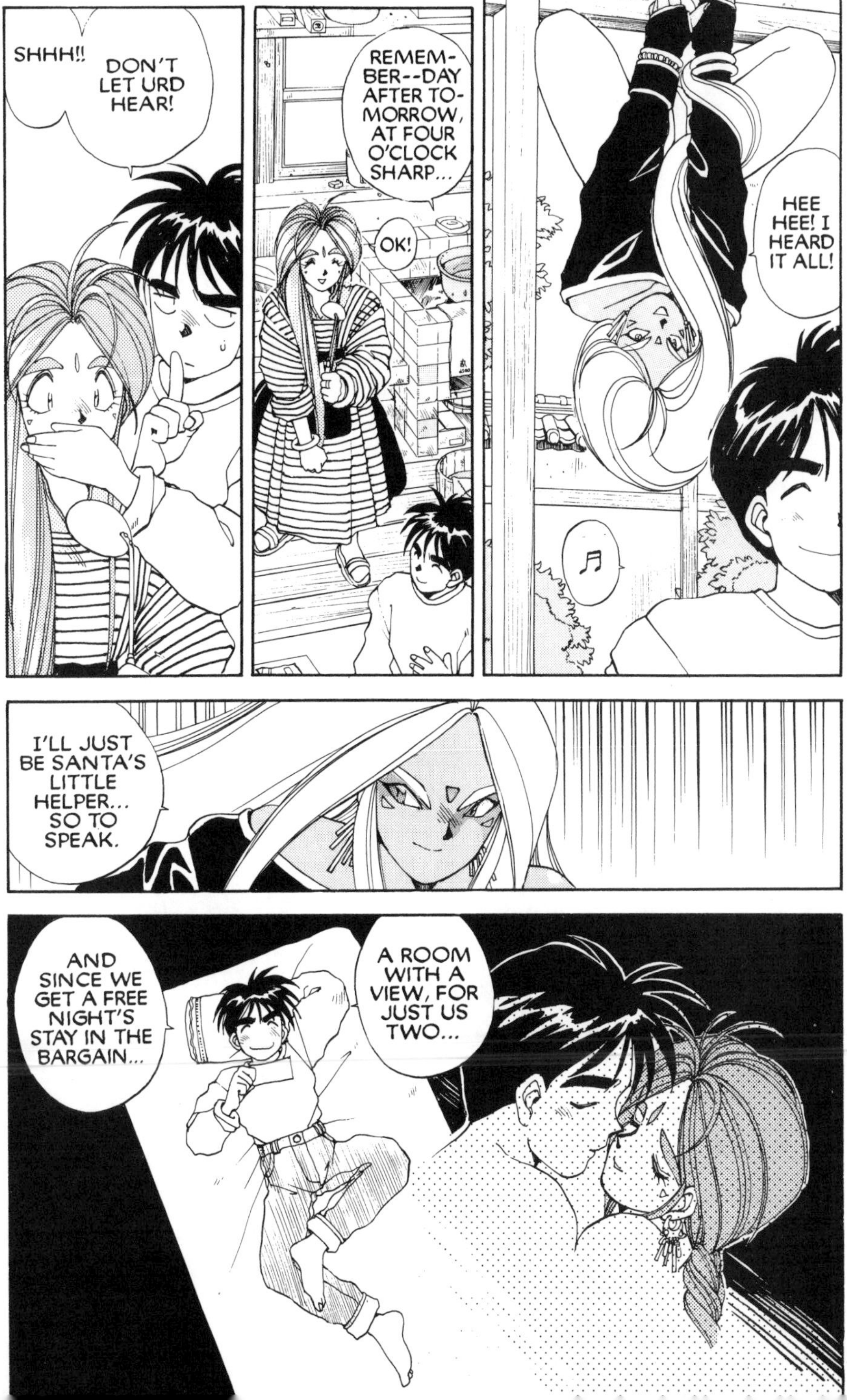
SHHH!! DON'T LET URD HEAR!
REMEMBER--DAY AFTER TOMORROW, AT FOUR O'CLOCK SHARP...
OK!
HEE HEE! I HEARD IT ALL!
♫
I'LL JUST BE SANTA'S LITTLE HELPER... SO TO SPEAK.
AND SINCE WE GET A FREE NIGHT'S STAY IN THE BARGAIN...
A ROOM WITH A VIEW, FOR JUST US TWO...

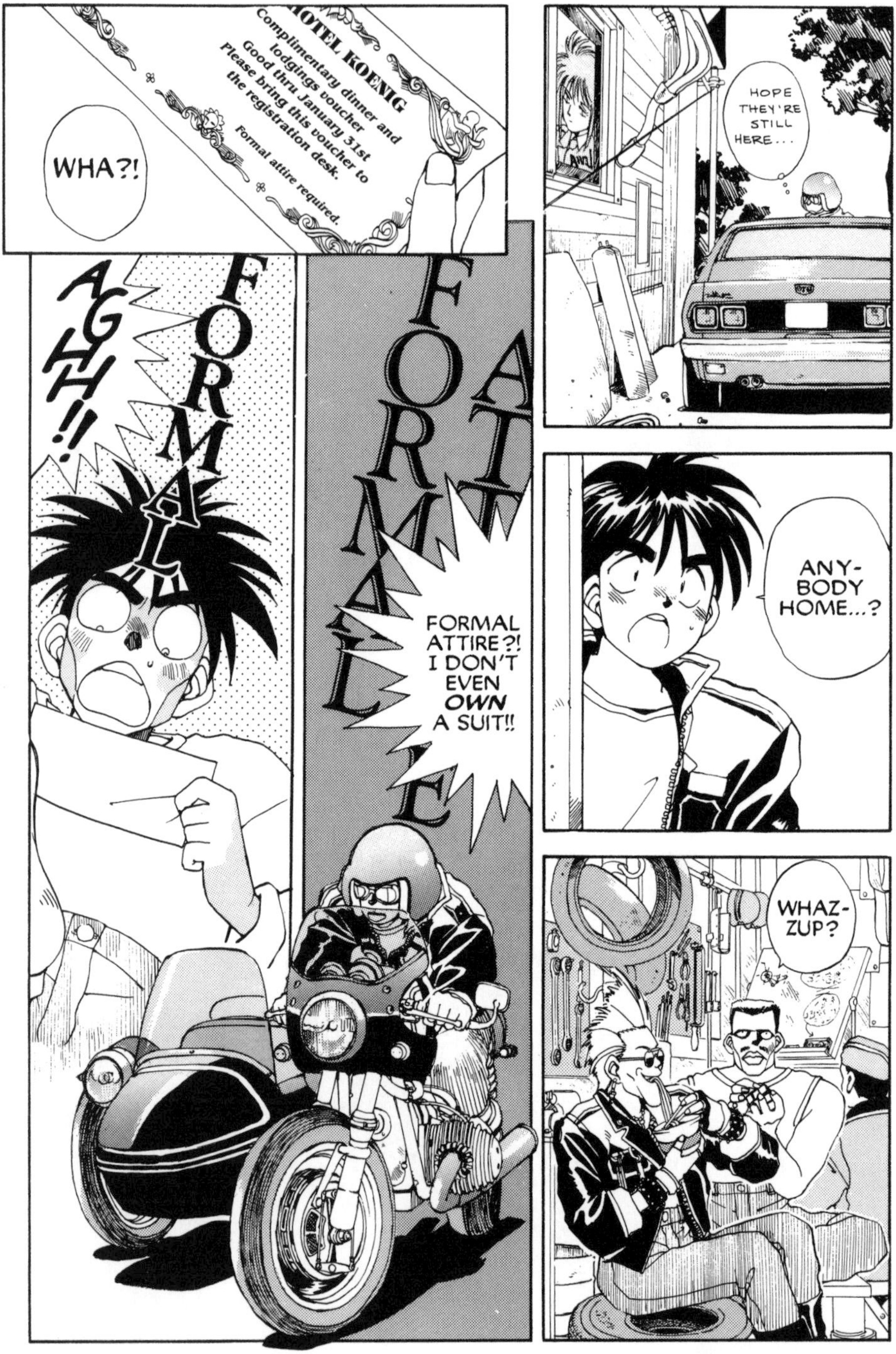
HOTEL KOENIG
Complimentary dinner and lodgings voucher
Good thru January 31st
Please bring this voucher to the registration desk.
Formal attire required.
WHA?!
HOPE THEY'RE STILL HERE...
FORMAL
AGHH!!
FORMAL ATTIRE
FORMAL ATTIRE?! I DON'T EVEN *OWN* A SUIT!!
ANY-BODY HOME...?
WHAZ-ZUP?

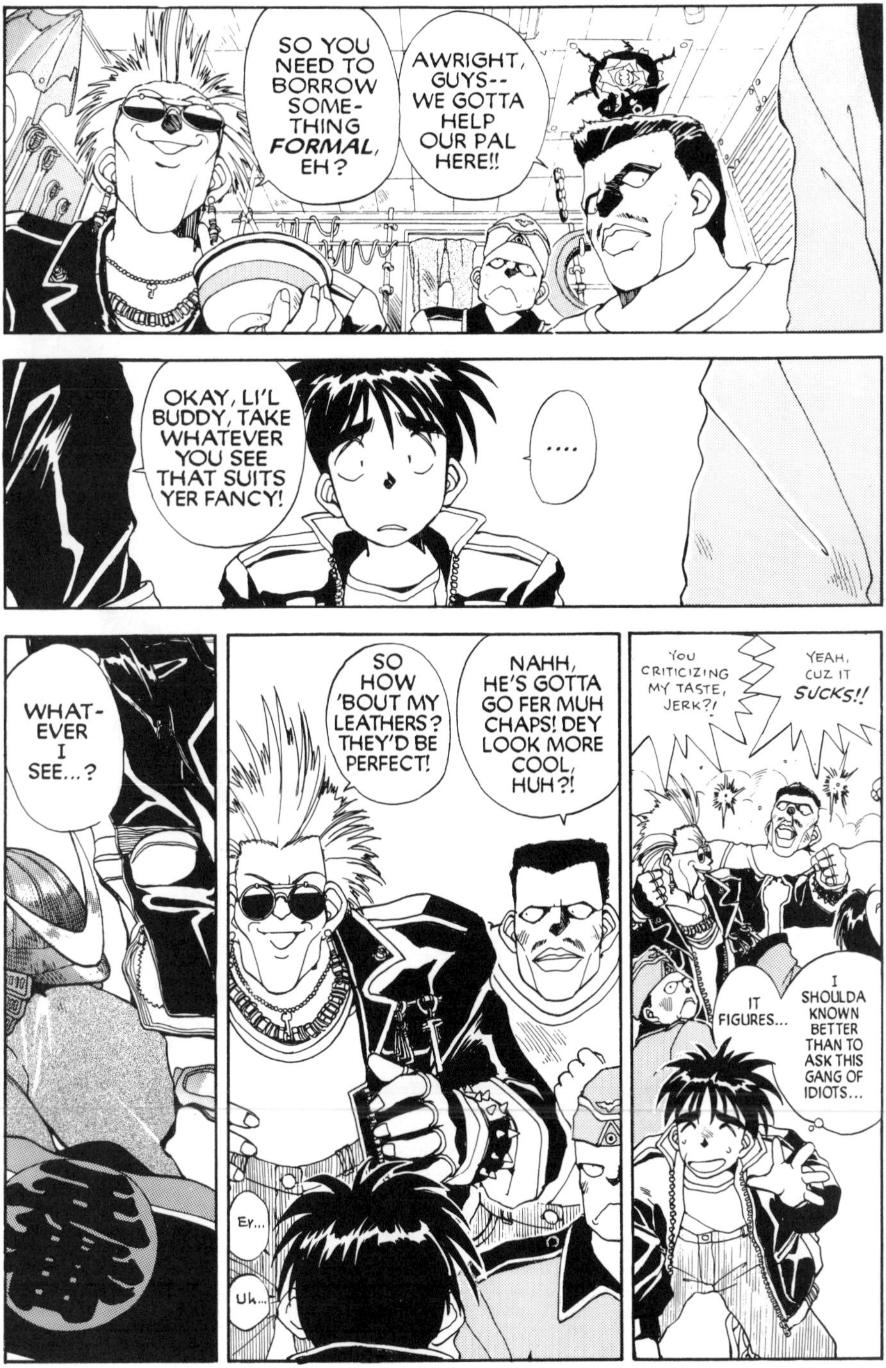
SO YOU NEED TO BORROW SOME-THING *FORMAL*, EH?
AWRIGHT, GUYS-- WE GOTTA HELP OUR PAL HERE!!
OKAY, LI'L BUDDY, TAKE WHATEVER YOU SEE THAT SUITS YER FANCY!
....
WHAT-EVER I SEE...?
SO HOW 'BOUT MY LEATHERS? THEY'D BE PERFECT!
NAHH, HE'S GOTTA GO FER MUH CHAPS! DEY LOOK MORE COOL, HUH?!
Er...
Uh...
YOU CRITICIZING MY TASTE, JERK?!
YEAH, CUZ IT *SUCKS!!*
IT FIGURES...
I SHOULDA KNOWN BETTER THAN TO ASK THIS GANG OF IDIOTS...

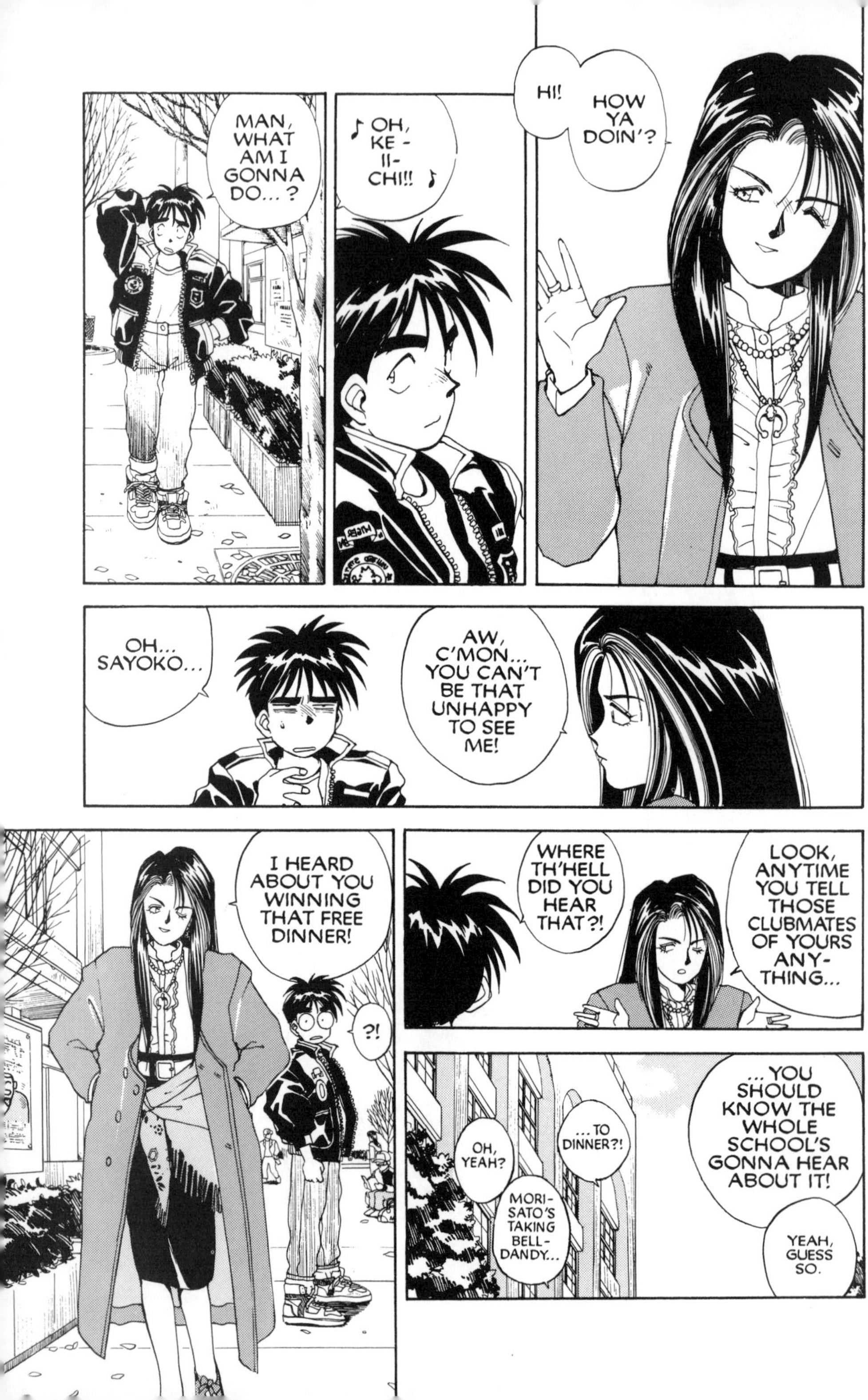
MAN, WHAT AM I GONNA DO...?
♪ OH, KE-II-CHI!! ♪
HI!
HOW YA DOIN'?
OH... SAYOKO...
AW, C'MON... YOU CAN'T BE THAT UNHAPPY TO SEE ME!
I HEARD ABOUT YOU WINNING THAT FREE DINNER!
?!
WHERE TH'HELL DID YOU HEAR THAT?!
LOOK, ANYTIME YOU TELL THOSE CLUBMATES OF YOURS ANY-THING...
...YOU SHOULD KNOW THE WHOLE SCHOOL'S GONNA HEAR ABOUT IT!
OH, YEAH?
...TO DINNER?!
MORI-SATO'S TAKING BELL-DANDY...
YEAH, GUESS SO.

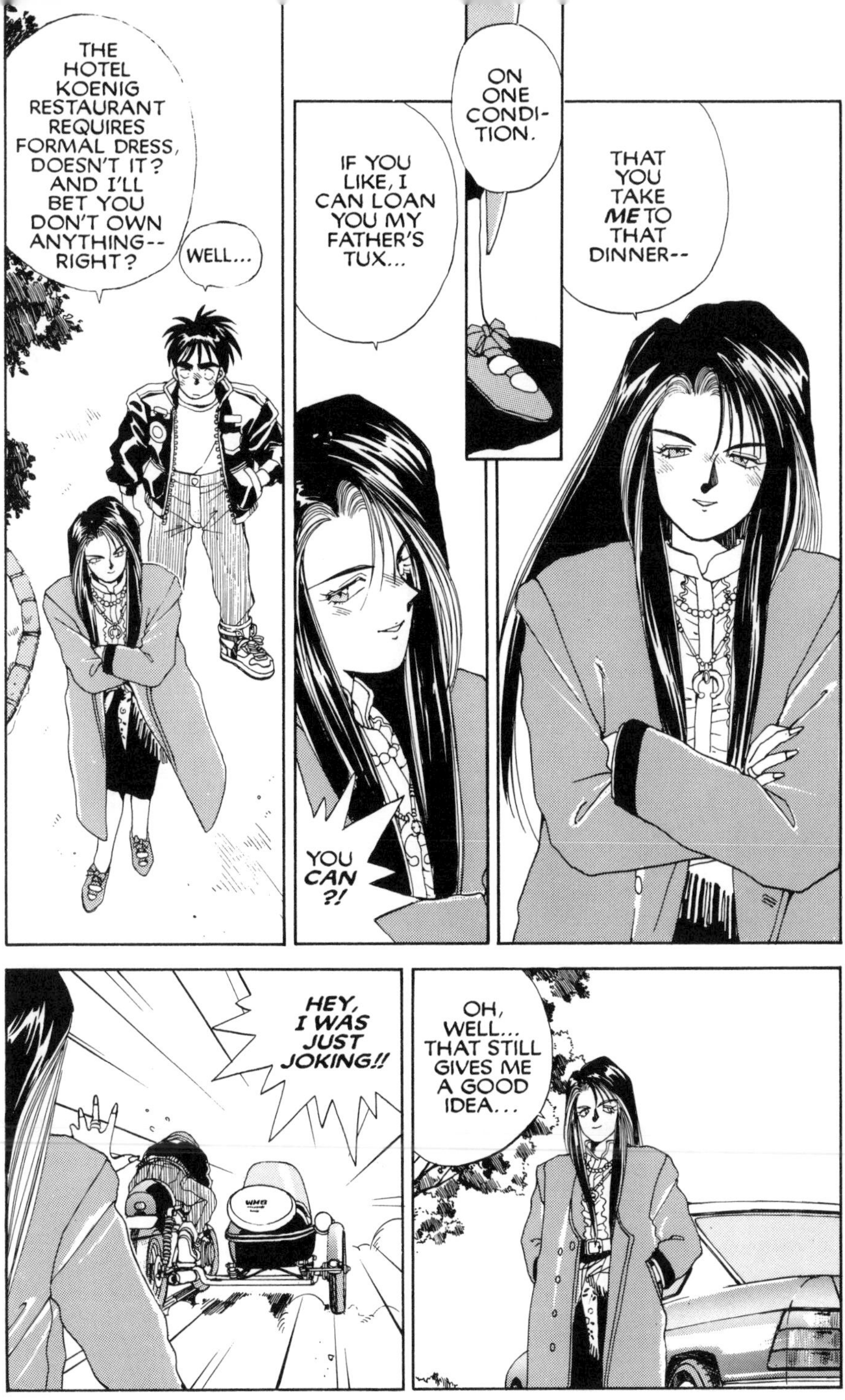
THE HOTEL KOENIG RESTAURANT REQUIRES FORMAL DRESS, DOESN'T IT? AND I'LL BET YOU DON'T OWN ANYTHING-- RIGHT?
WELL...
IF YOU LIKE, I CAN LOAN YOU MY FATHER'S TUX...
YOU *CAN* ?!
ON ONE CONDITION.
THAT YOU TAKE *ME* TO THAT DINNER--
HEY, I WAS JUST JOKING!!
OH, WELL... THAT STILL GIVES ME A GOOD IDEA...

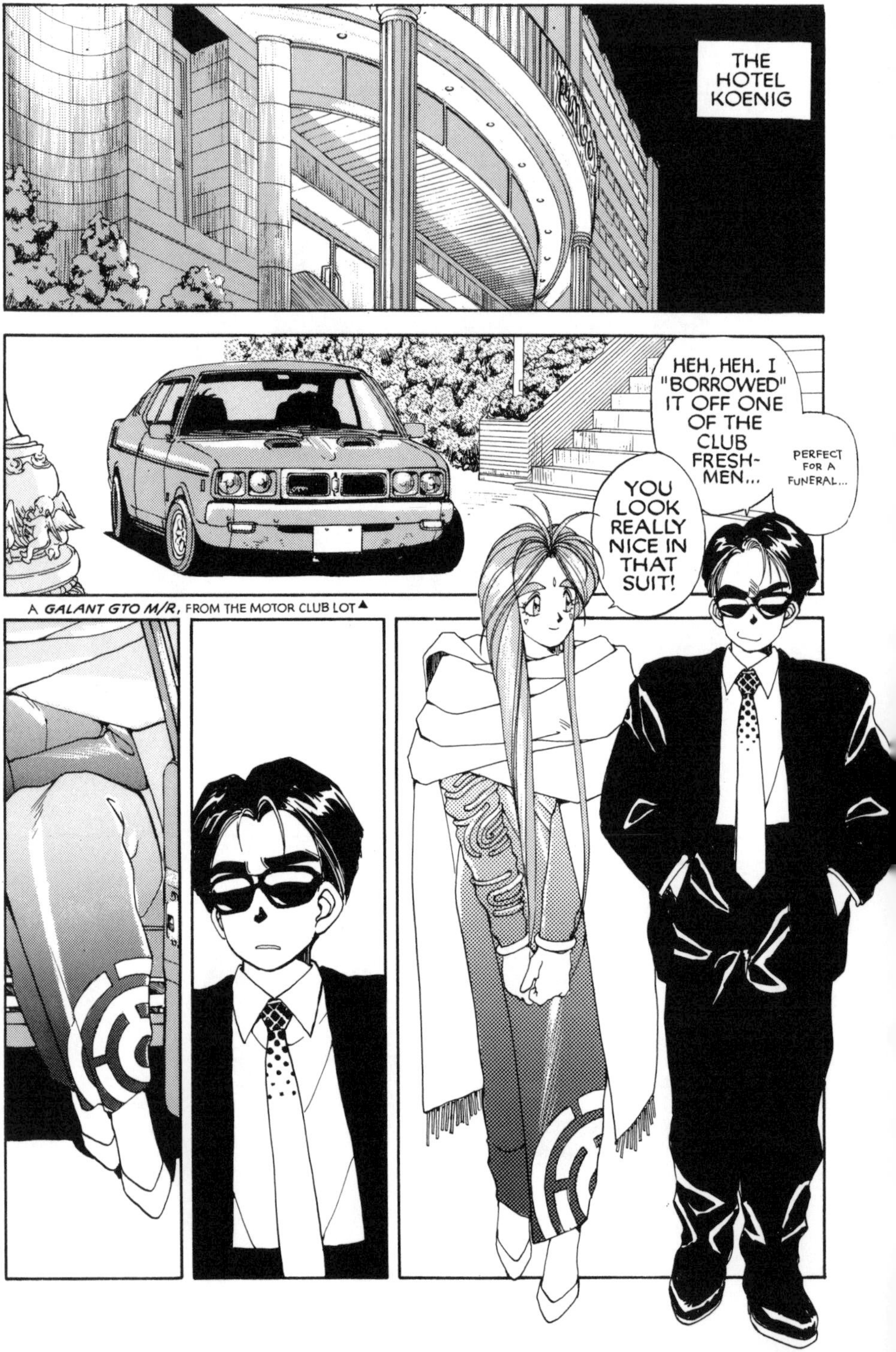
THE HOTEL KOENIG
HEH, HEH. I "BORROWED" IT OFF ONE OF THE CLUB FRESHMEN...
PERFECT FOR A FUNERAL...
A GALANT GTO M/R, FROM THE MOTOR CLUB LOT▲
YOU LOOK REALLY NICE IN THAT SUIT!

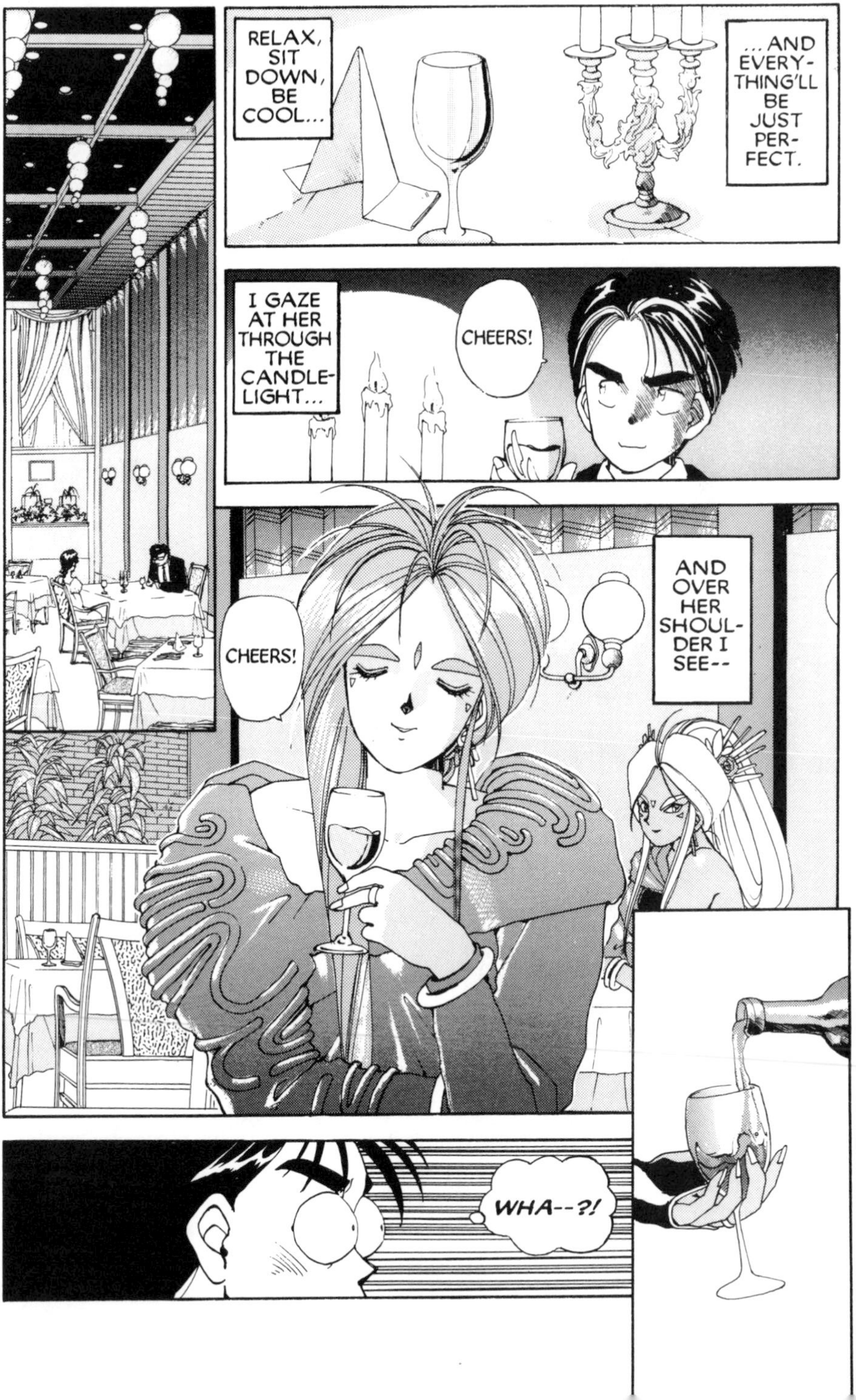
RELAX, SIT DOWN, BE COOL...
...AND EVERY-THING'LL BE JUST PER-FECT.
I GAZE AT HER THROUGH THE CANDLE-LIGHT...
CHEERS!
CHEERS!
AND OVER HER SHOUL-DER I SEE--
WHA--?!

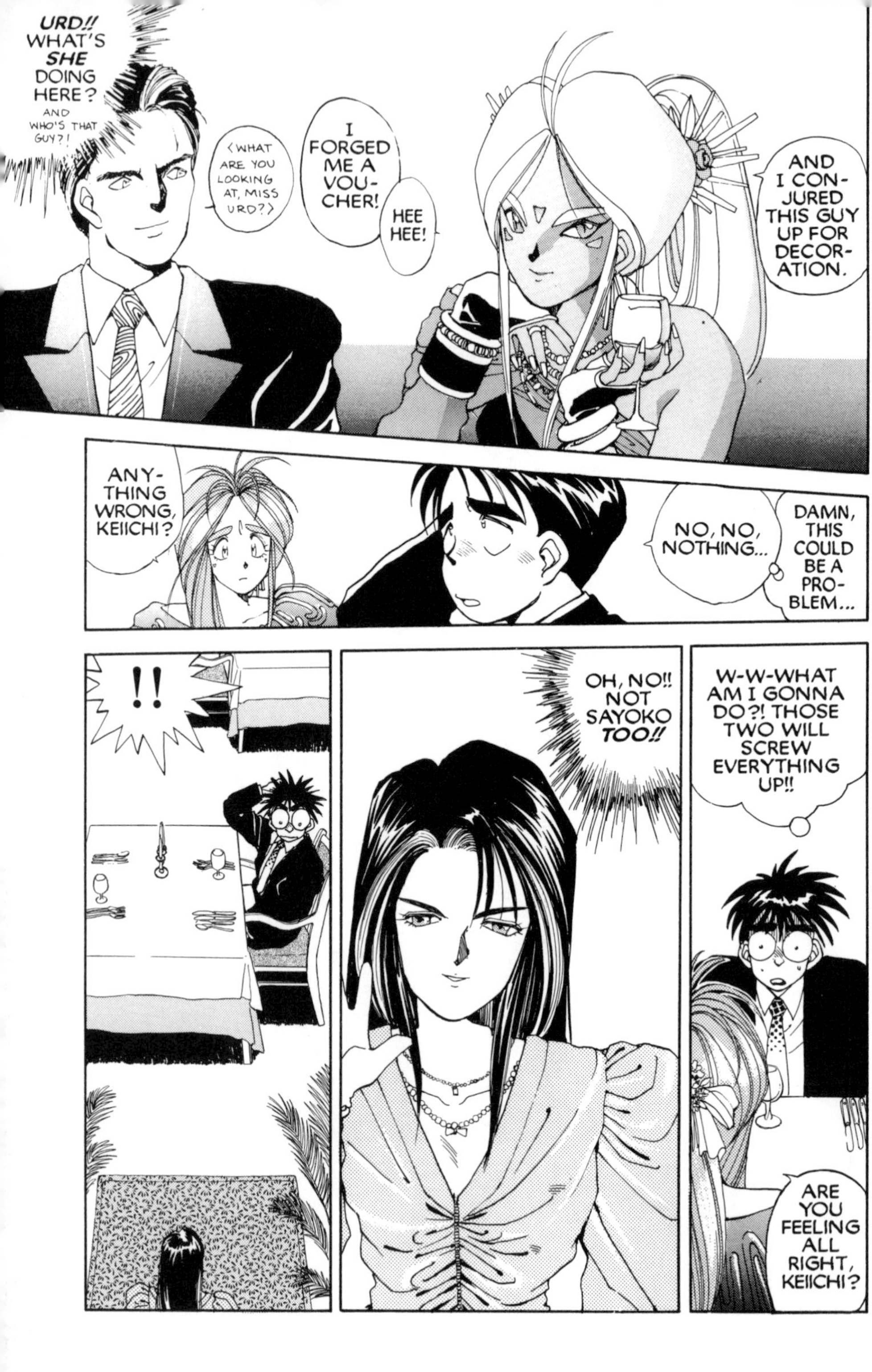
URD!! WHAT'S SHE DOING HERE?
AND WHO'S THAT GUY?!
<WHAT ARE YOU LOOKING AT, MISS URD?>
I FORGED ME A VOUCHER!
HEE HEE!
AND I CONJURED THIS GUY UP FOR DECORATION.
ANYTHING WRONG, KEIICHI?
NO, NO, NOTHING...
DAMN, THIS COULD BE A PROBLEM...
!!
OH, NO!! NOT SAYOKO TOO!!
W-W-WHAT AM I GONNA DO?! THOSE TWO WILL SCREW EVERYTHING UP!!
ARE YOU FEELING ALL RIGHT, KEIICHI?

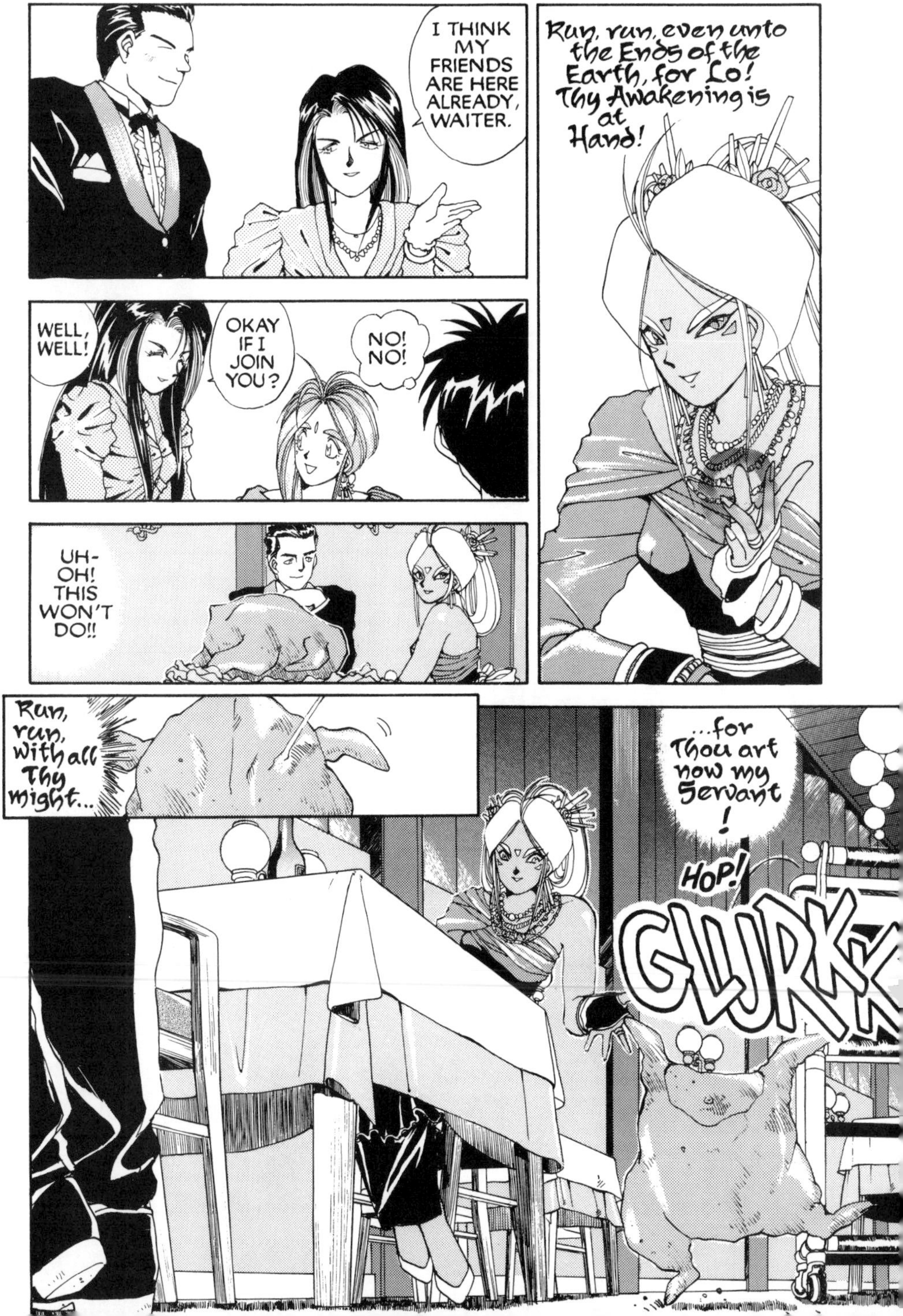
I THINK MY FRIENDS ARE HERE ALREADY, WAITER.
WELL, WELL!
OKAY IF I JOIN YOU?
NO! NO!
UH-OH! THIS WON'T DO!!
Run, run, even unto the Ends of the Earth, for Lo! Thy Awakening is at Hand!
Run, run, with all Thy might...
...for Thou art now my Servant!
HOP!
GLURK

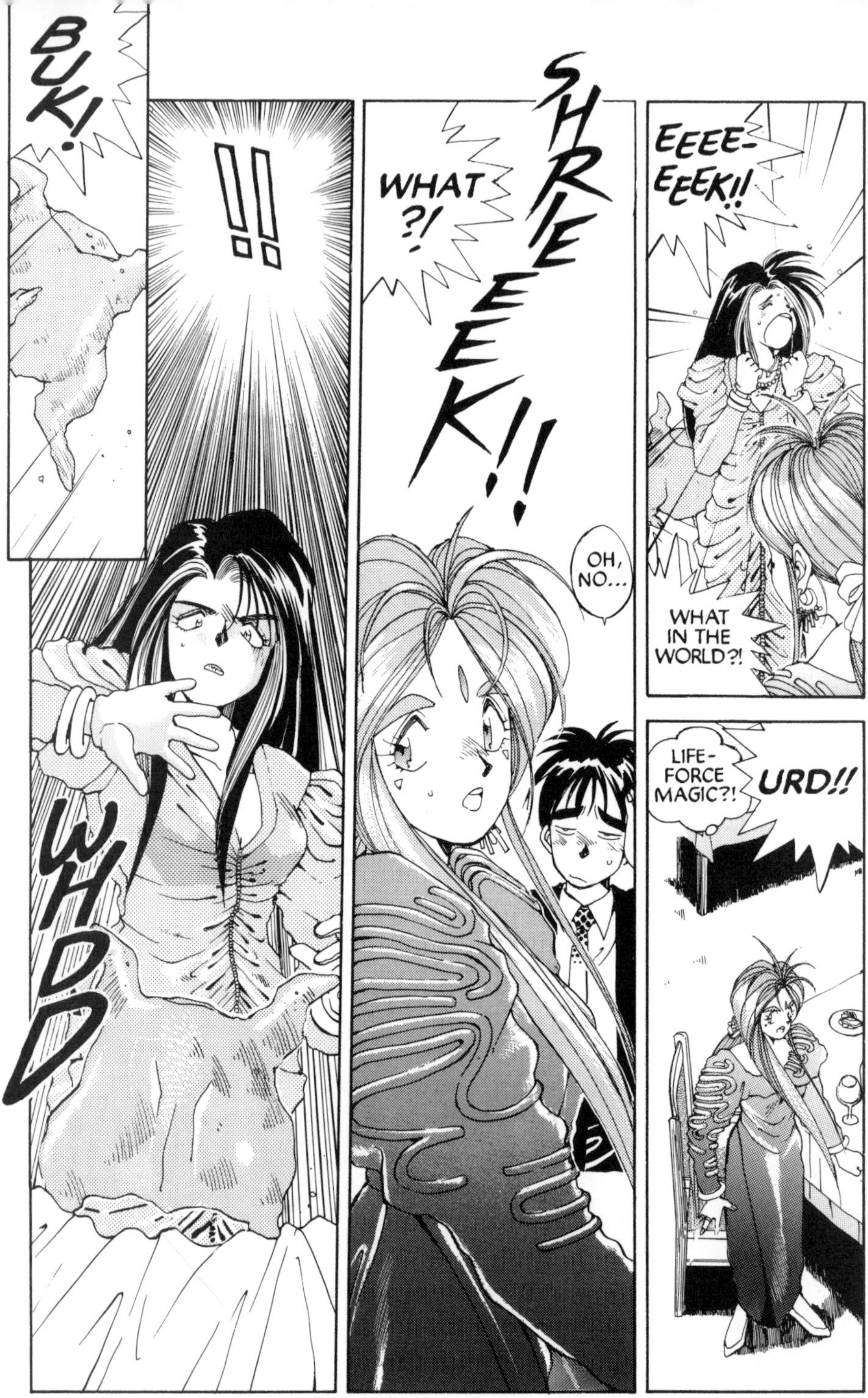
BUKI!
!!
WHDD
WHAT ?!
SHRIEEEEK!!
OH, NO...
EEEE-EEEK!!
WHAT IN THE WORLD?!
LIFE-FORCE MAGIC?!
URD!!

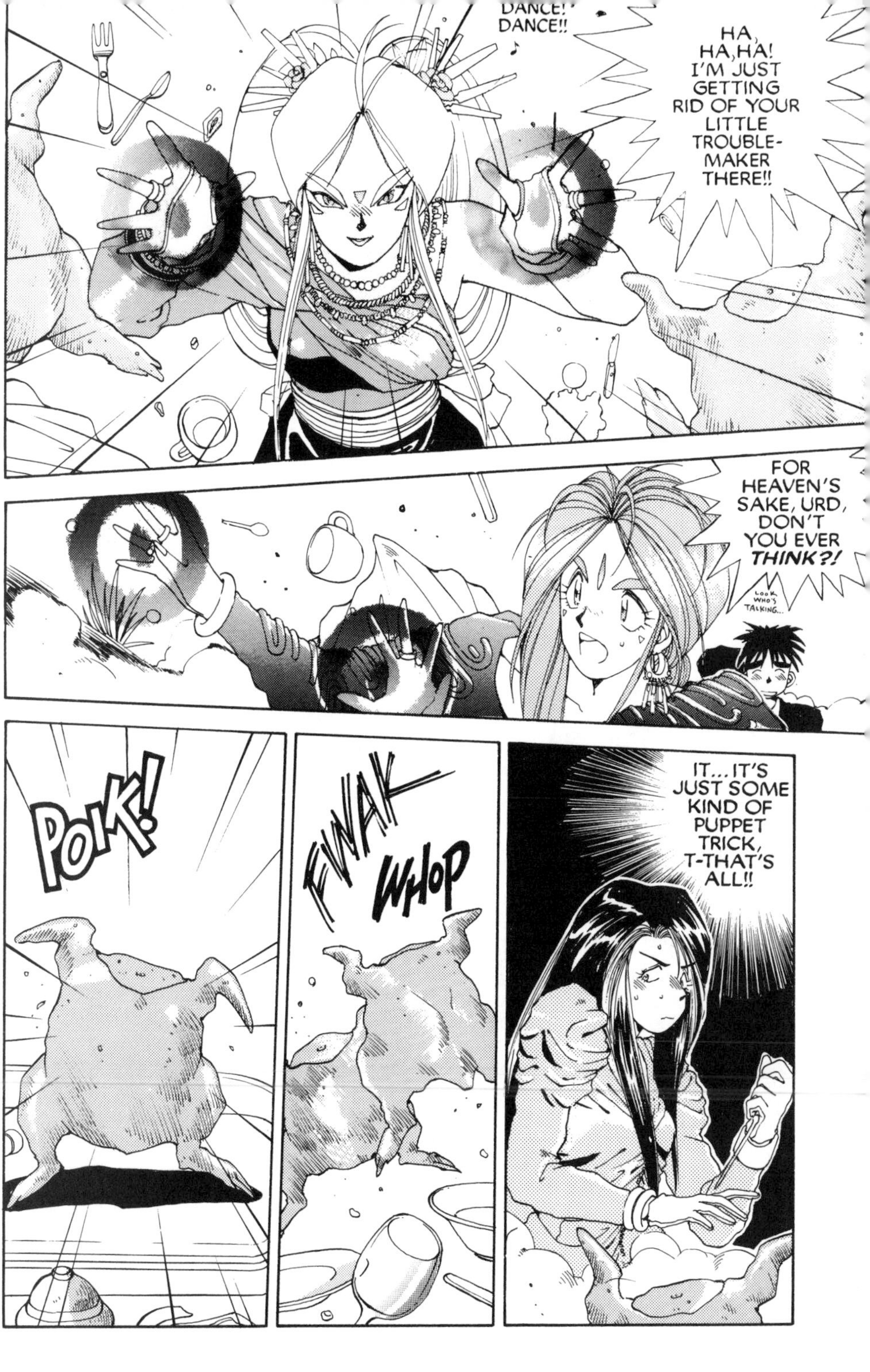
DANCE! DANCE!! ♪
HA, HA,HA! I'M JUST GETTING RID OF YOUR LITTLE TROUBLE-MAKER THERE!!
FOR HEAVEN'S SAKE, URD, DON'T YOU EVER *THINK?!*
LOOK WHO'S TALKING...
POIK!
FWAK
WHOP
IT...IT'S JUST SOME KIND OF PUPPET TRICK, T-THAT'S ALL!!

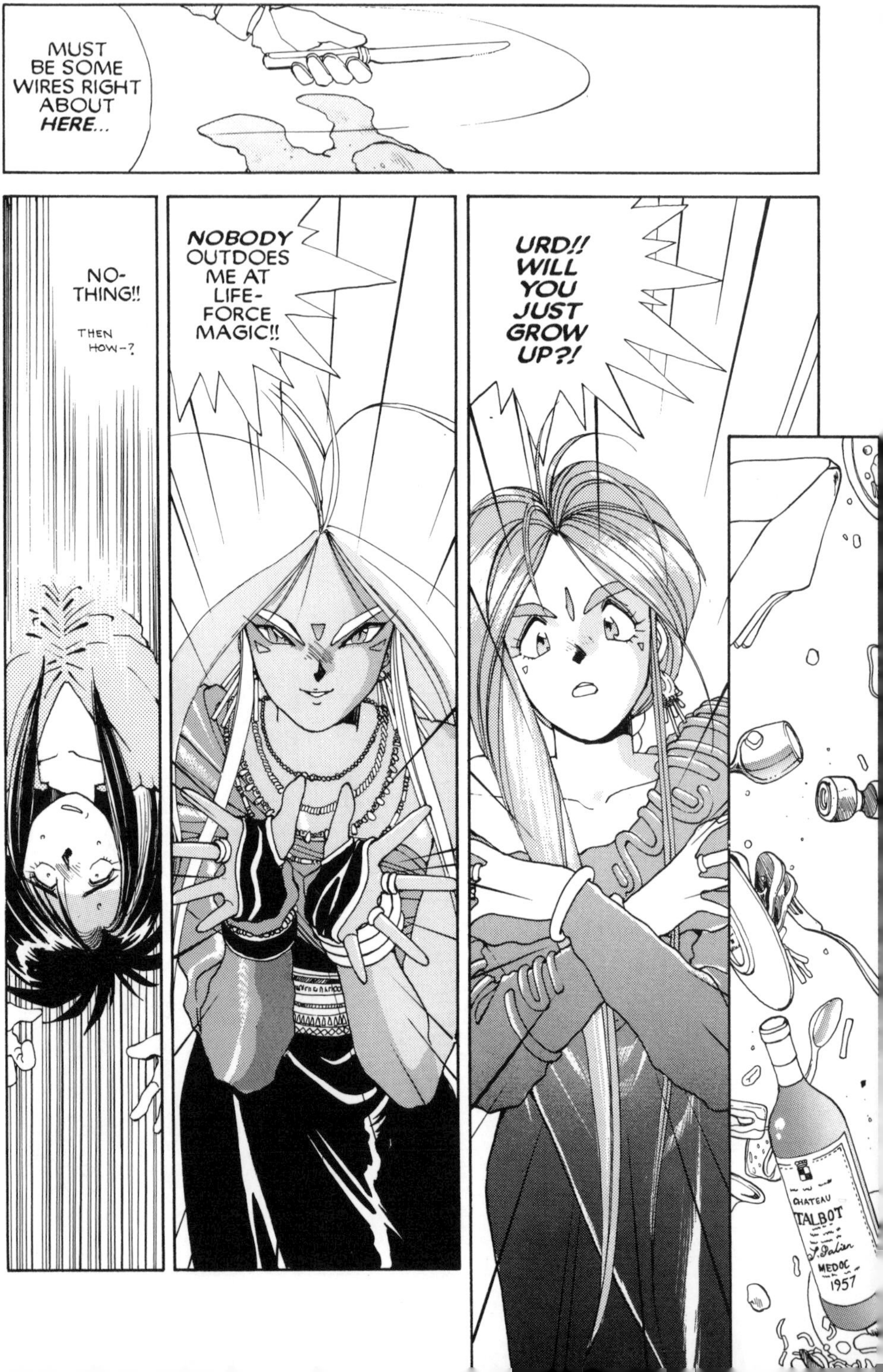
MUST BE SOME WIRES RIGHT ABOUT *HERE...*
NO-THING!!
THEN HOW-?
NOBODY OUTDOES ME AT LIFE-FORCE MAGIC!!
URD!! WILL YOU JUST GROW UP?!
CHATEAU
TALBOT
MEDOC
1957

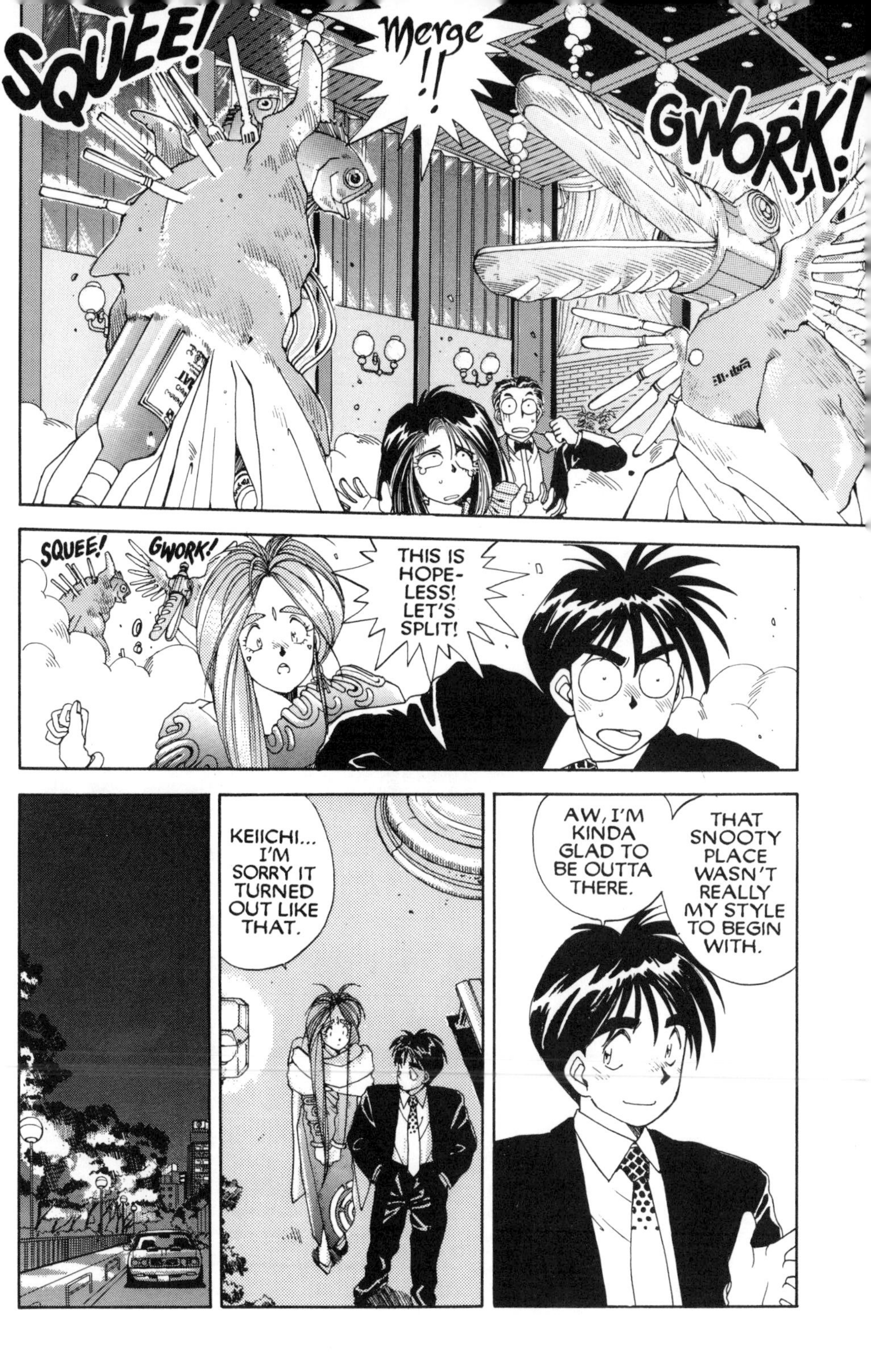
SQUEE!
Merge !!
GWORK!
SQUEE!
GWORK!
THIS IS HOPE-LESS! LET'S SPLIT!
KEIICHI... I'M SORRY IT TURNED OUT LIKE THAT.
AW, I'M KINDA GLAD TO BE OUTTA THERE.
THAT SNOOTY PLACE WASN'T REALLY MY STYLE TO BEGIN WITH.

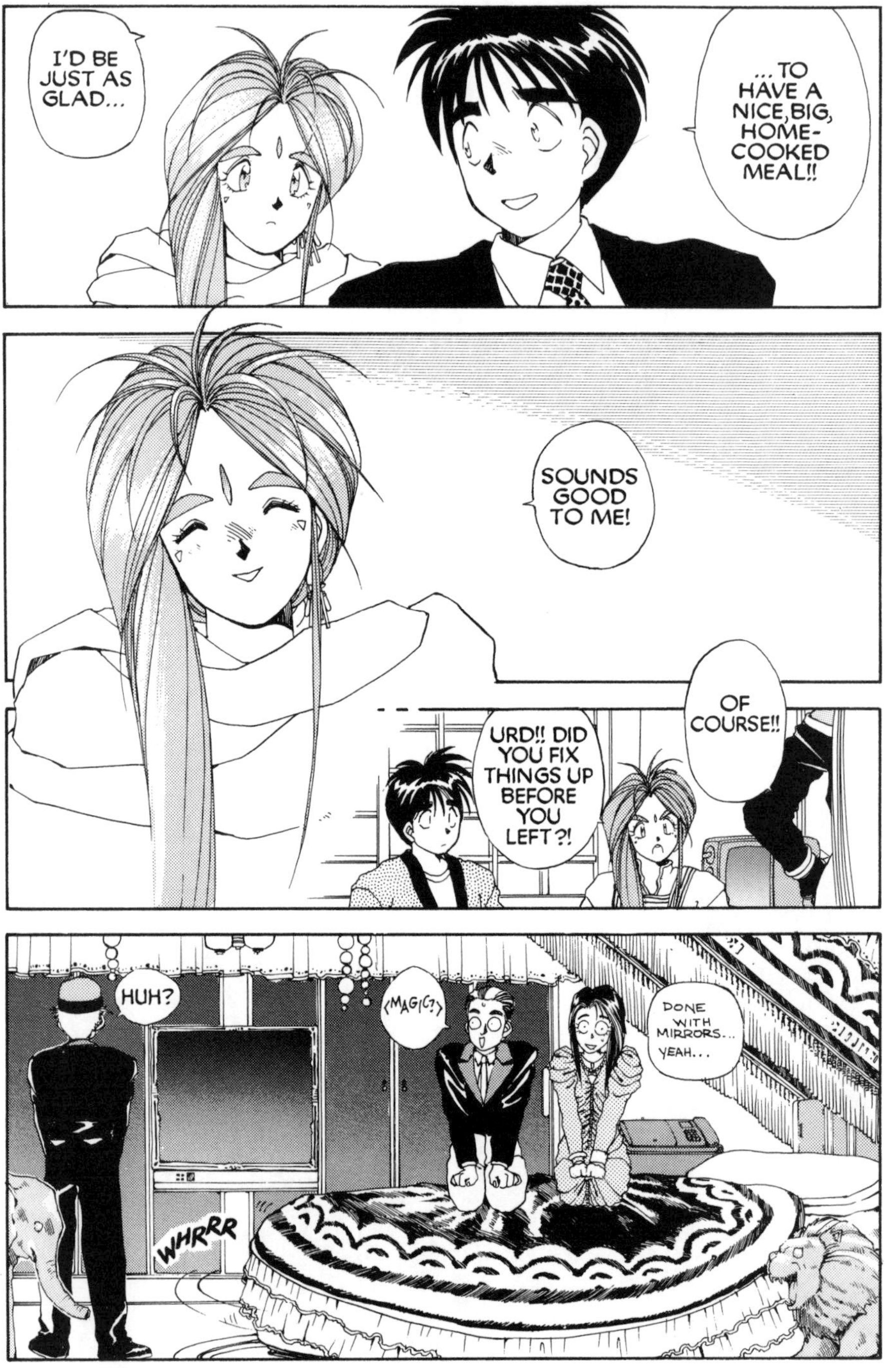

I'D BE JUST AS GLAD...
...TO HAVE A NICE, BIG, HOME-COOKED MEAL!!
SOUNDS GOOD TO ME!
URD!! DID YOU FIX THINGS UP BEFORE YOU LEFT?!
OF COURSE!!
HUH?
‹MAGIC?›
DONE WITH MIRRORS... YEAH...
WHRRR

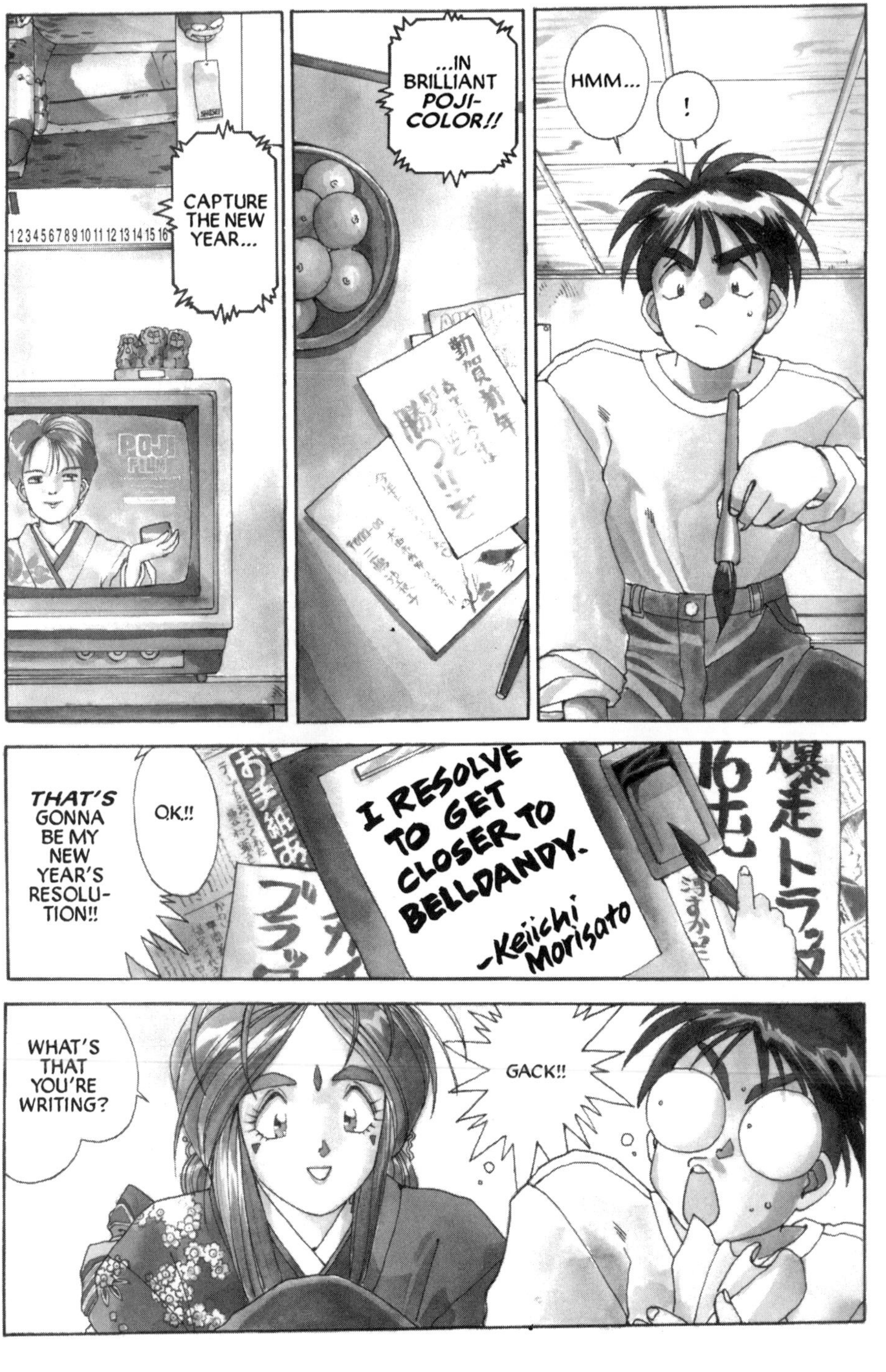

1 2 3 4 5 6 7 8 9 10 11 12 13 14 15 16
CAPTURE THE NEW YEAR...
...IN BRILLIANT POJI-COLOR!!
HMM...
!
THAT'S GONNA BE MY NEW YEAR'S RESOLUTION!!
O.K.!!
I RESOLVE TO GET CLOSER TO BELLDANDY.
-Keiichi Morisato
WHAT'S THAT YOU'RE WRITING?
GACK!!

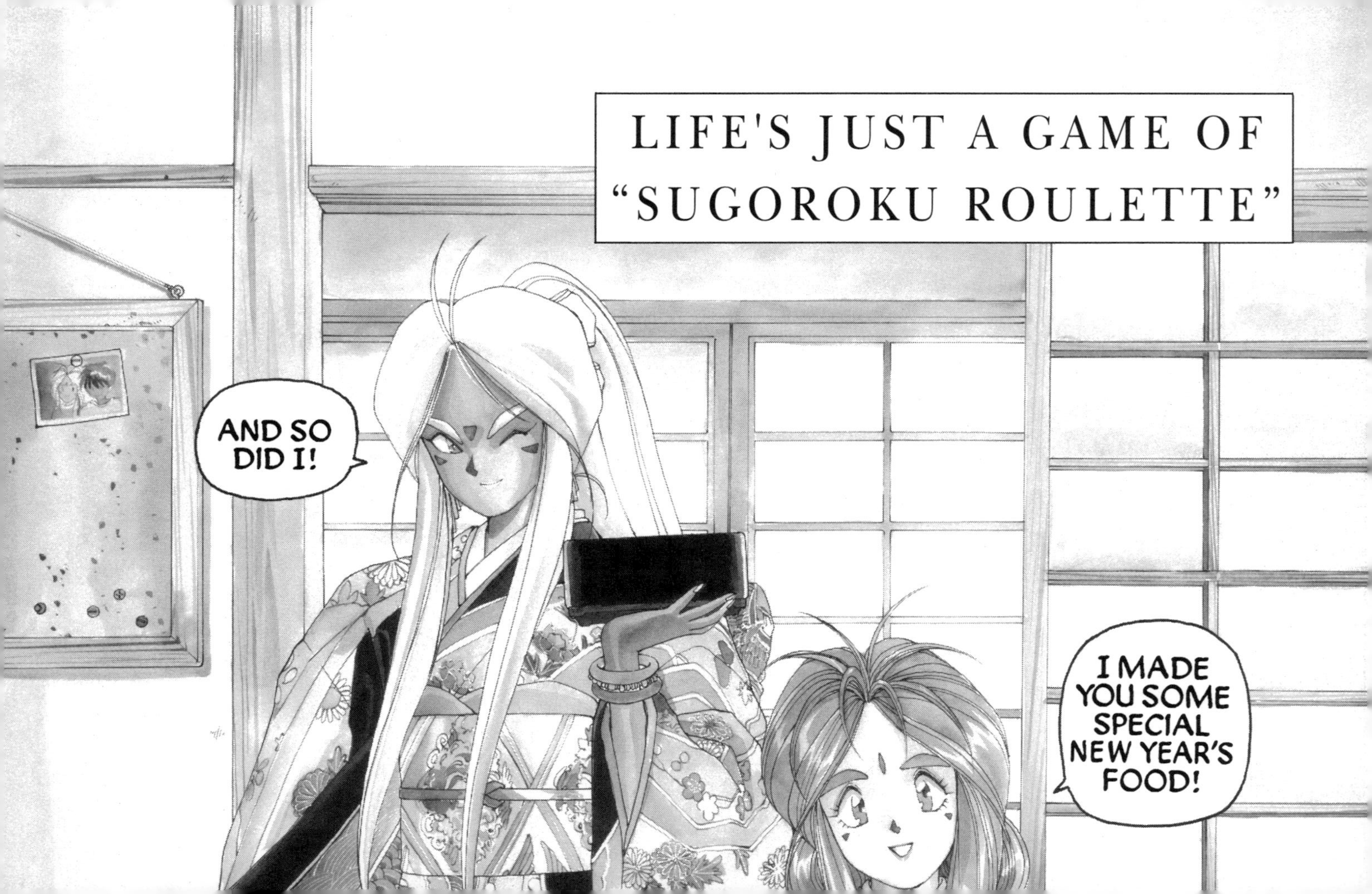
LIFE'S JUST A GAME OF "SUGOROKU ROULETTE"
I MADE YOU SOME SPECIAL NEW YEAR'S FOOD!
AND SO DID I!

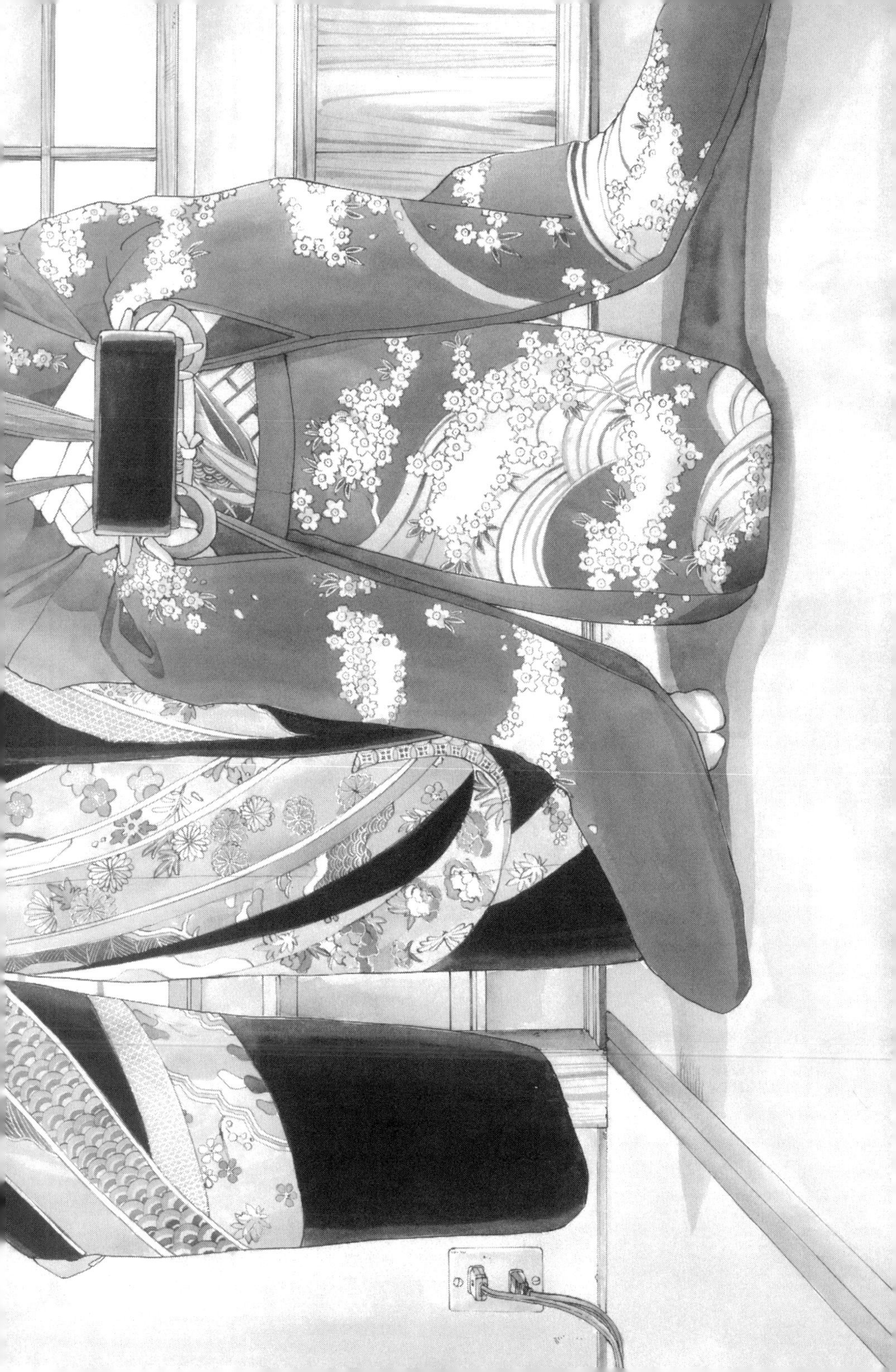

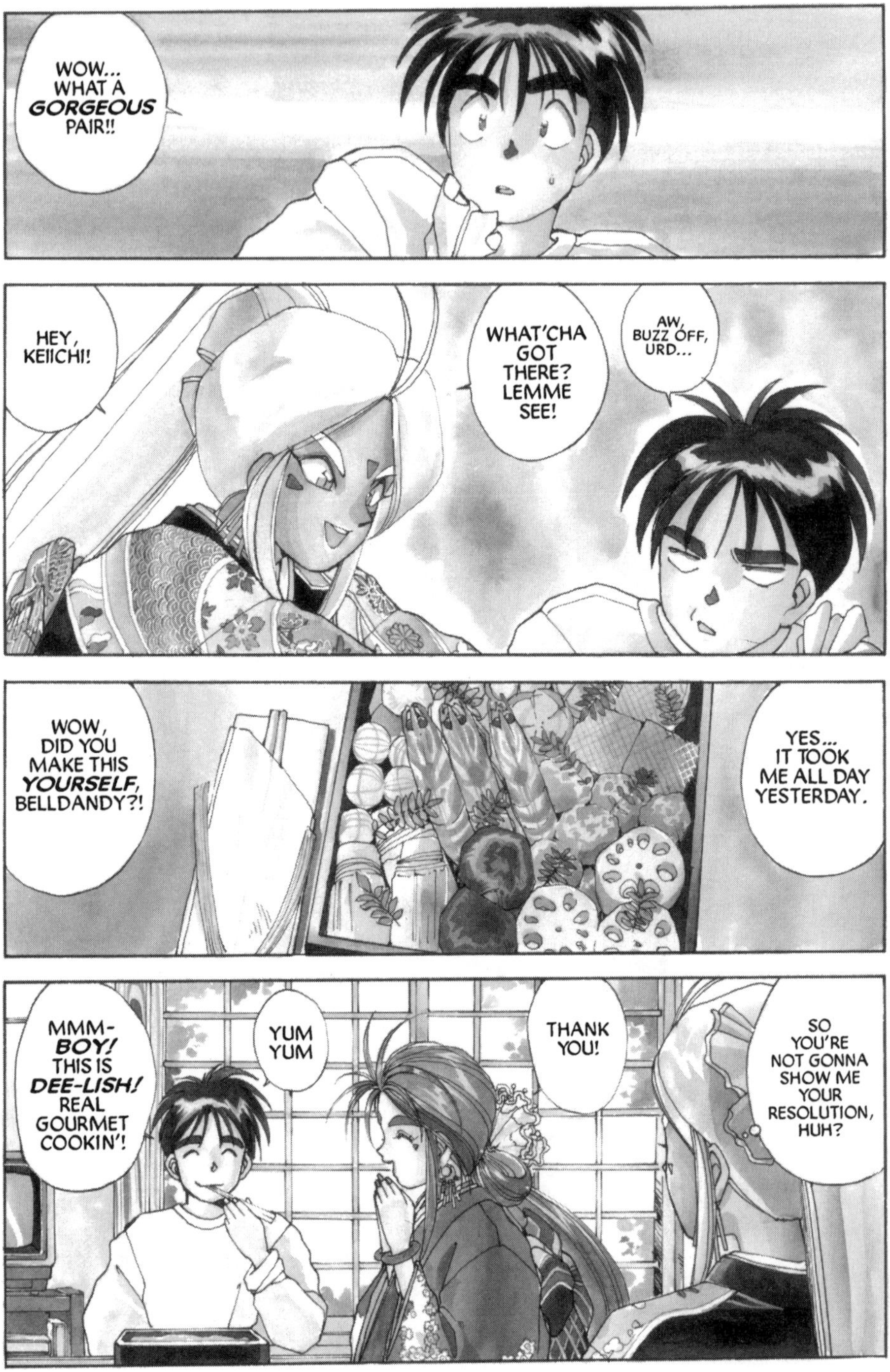
WOW... WHAT A GORGEOUS PAIR!!
HEY, KEIICHI!
WHAT'CHA GOT THERE? LEMME SEE!
AW, BUZZ OFF, URD...
WOW, DID YOU MAKE THIS YOURSELF, BELLDANDY?!
YES... IT TOOK ME ALL DAY YESTERDAY.
MMM-BOY! THIS IS DEE-LISH! REAL GOURMET COOKIN'!
YUM YUM
THANK YOU!
SO YOU'RE NOT GONNA SHOW ME YOUR RESOLUTION, HUH?

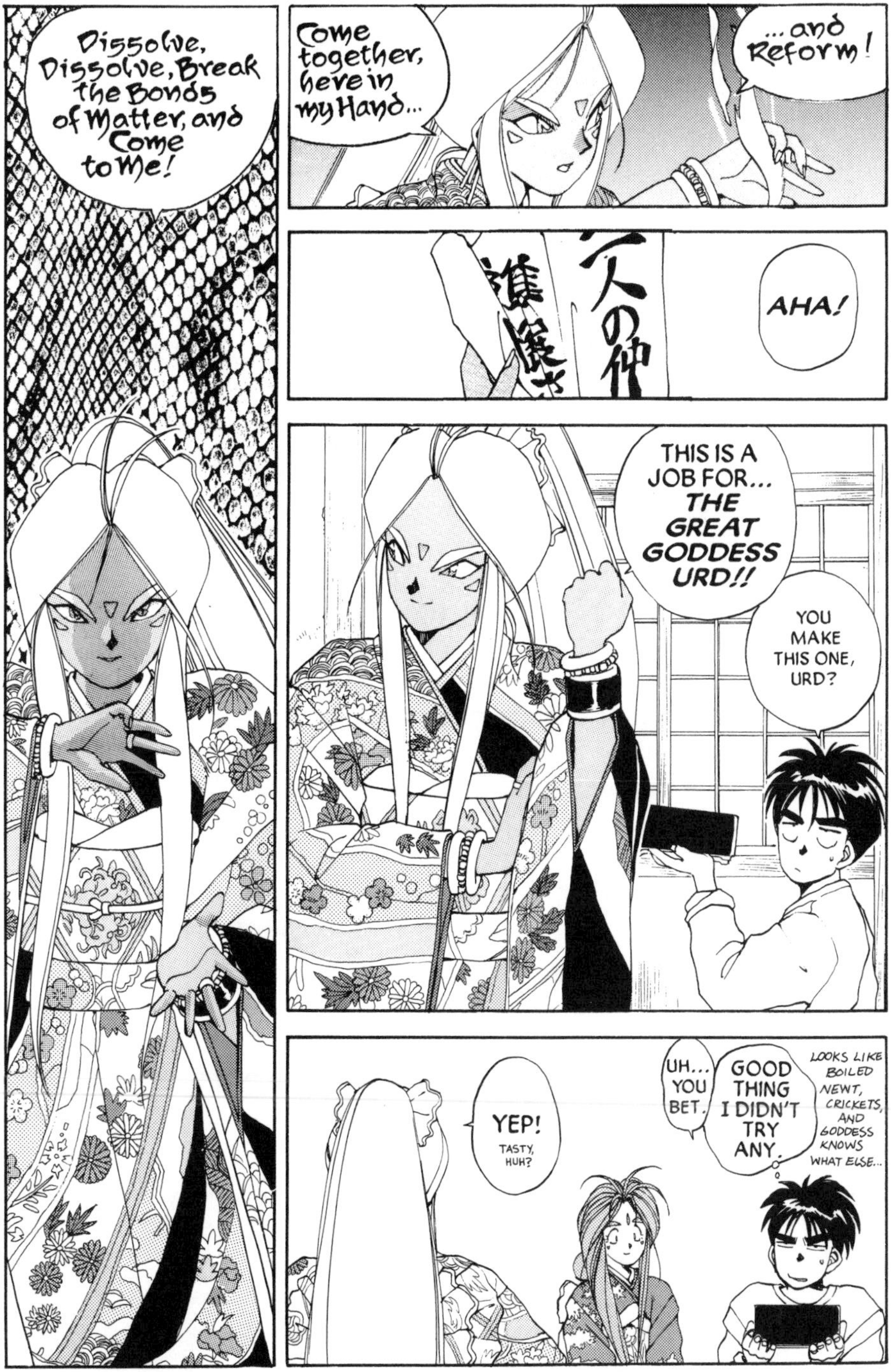
Dissolve, Dissolve, Break the Bonds of Matter, and Come to Me!
Come together, here in my Hand...
...and Reform!
AHA!
THIS IS A JOB FOR... THE GREAT GODDESS URD!!
YOU MAKE THIS ONE, URD?
YEP! TASTY, HUH?
UH... YOU BET.
GOOD THING I DIDN'T TRY ANY.
LOOKS LIKE BOILED NEWT, CRICKETS, AND GODDESS KNOWS WHAT ELSE...

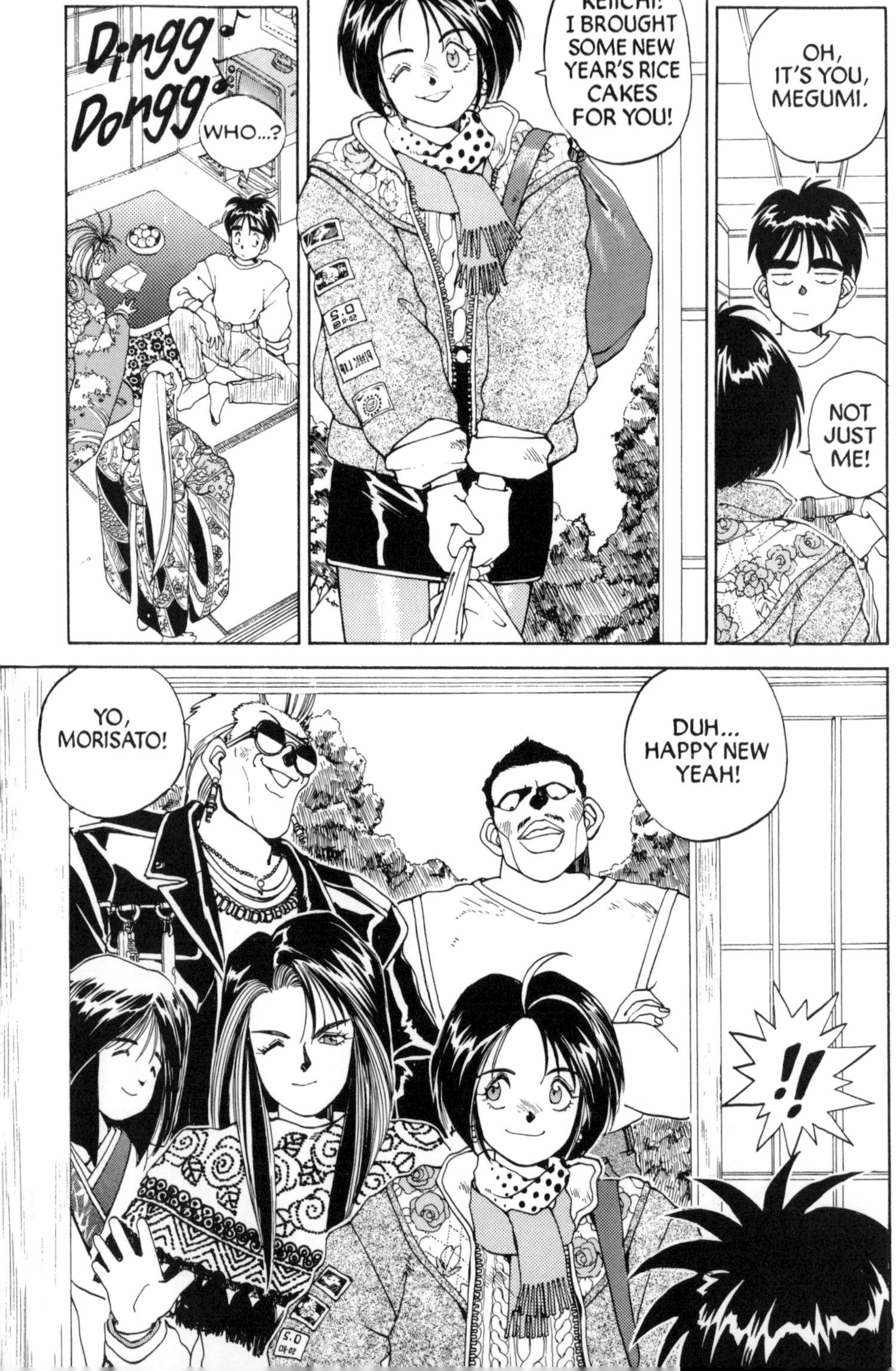
Dingg Dongg
WHO...?
HI, KEIICHI! I BROUGHT SOME NEW YEAR'S RICE CAKES FOR YOU!
OH, IT'S YOU, MEGUMI.
NOT JUST ME!
YO, MORISATO!
DUH... HAPPY NEW YEAH!
!!

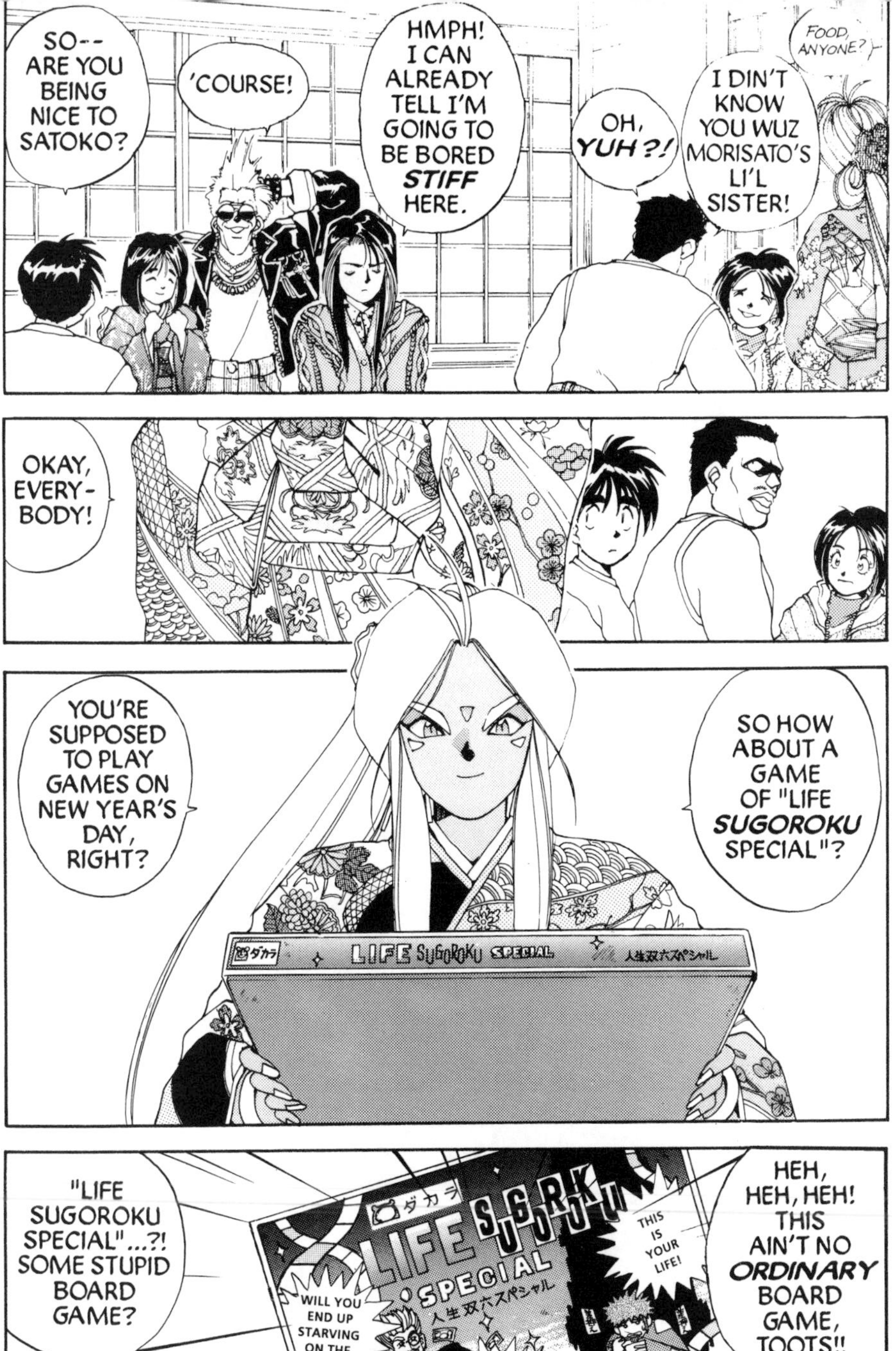
SO-- ARE YOU BEING NICE TO SATOKO?
'COURSE!
HMPH! I CAN ALREADY TELL I'M GOING TO BE BORED *STIFF* HERE.
OH, *YUH?!*
I DIN'T KNOW YOU WUZ MORISATO'S LI'L SISTER!
FOOD, ANYONE?
OKAY, EVERY-BODY!
YOU'RE SUPPOSED TO PLAY GAMES ON NEW YEAR'S DAY, RIGHT?
SO HOW ABOUT A GAME OF "LIFE *SUGOROKU* SPECIAL"?
ダカラ LIFE SUGOROKU SPECIAL 人生双六スペシャル
"LIFE SUGOROKU SPECIAL"...?! SOME STUPID BOARD GAME?
ダカラ
LIFE
SPECIAL
人生双六スペシャル
THIS IS YOUR LIFE!
WILL YOU END UP STARVING ON THE STREET?
OR LAUGH ALL THE WAY TO THE BANK??
HEH, HEH, HEH! THIS AIN'T NO *ORDINARY* BOARD GAME, TOOTS!!

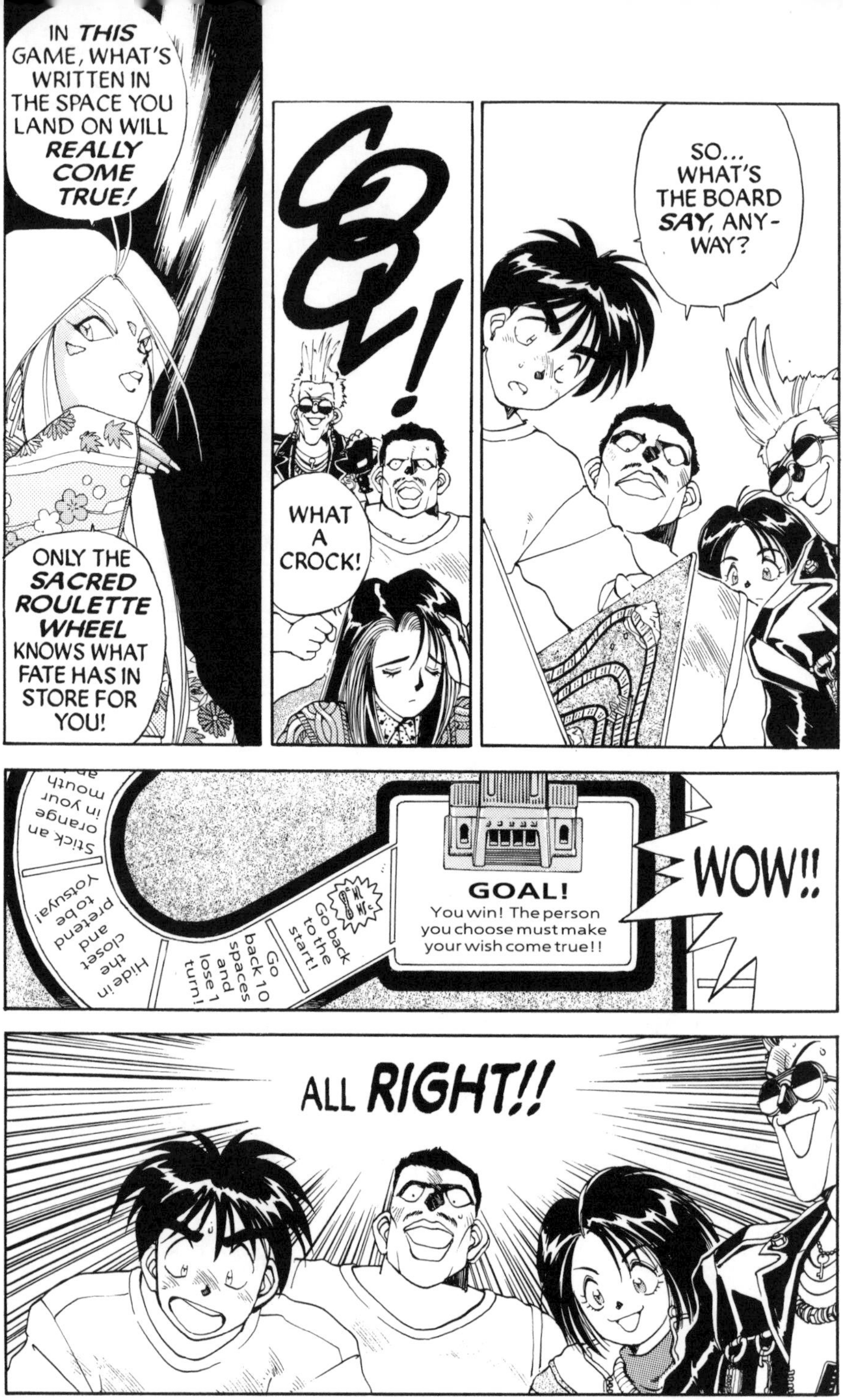
IN THIS GAME, WHAT'S WRITTEN IN THE SPACE YOU LAND ON WILL REALLY COME TRUE!
ONLY THE SACRED ROULETTE WHEEL KNOWS WHAT FATE HAS IN STORE FOR YOU!
WHAT A CROCK!
SO... WHAT'S THE BOARD SAY, ANY-WAY?
Stick an orange in your mouth
Hide in the closet and pretend to be Yotsuya!
Go back 10 spaces and lose 1 turn!
Go back to the start!
GOAL!
You win! The person you choose must make your wish come true!!
WOW!!
ALL RIGHT!!

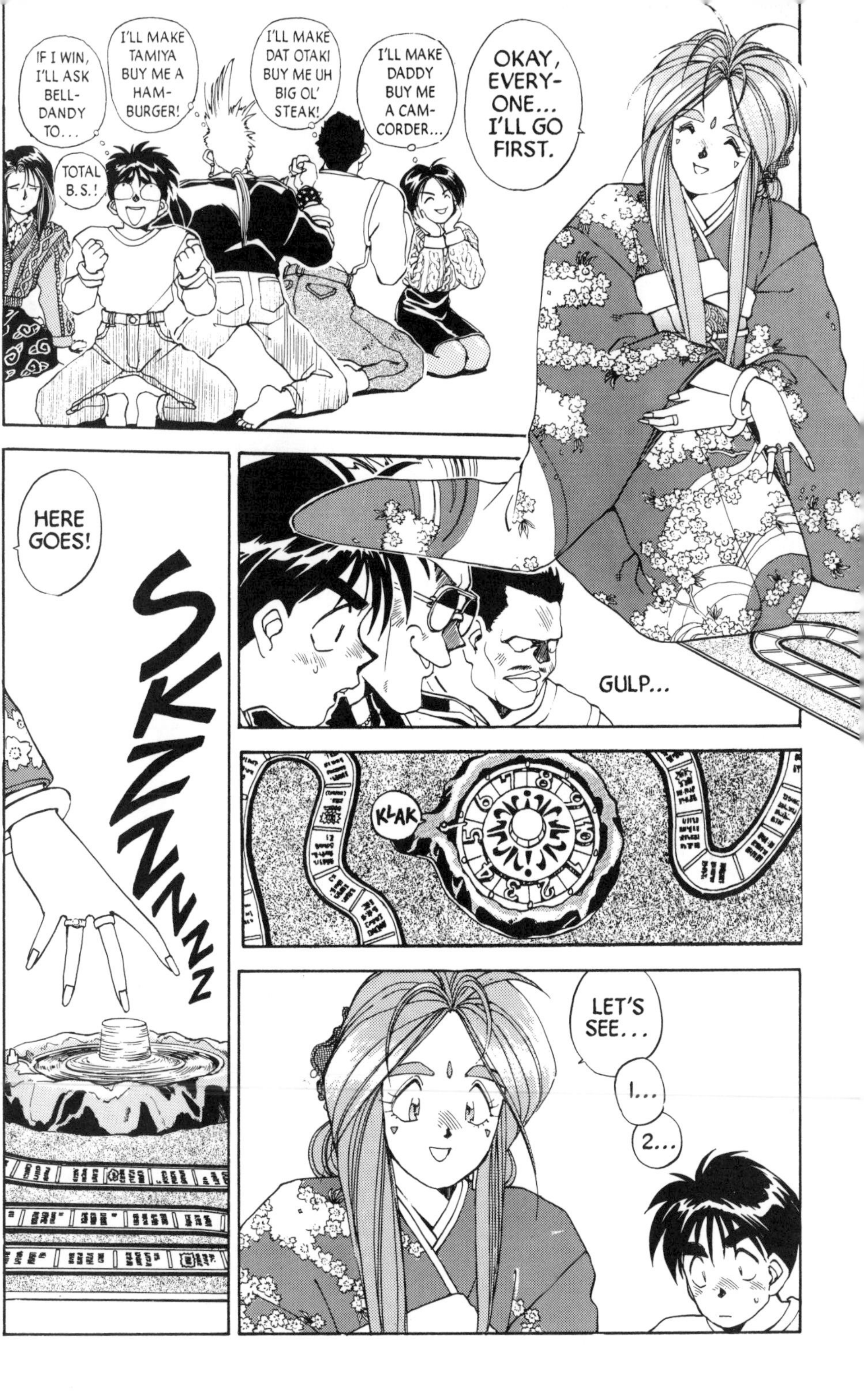

IF I WIN, I'LL ASK BELL-DANDY TO...
TOTAL B.S.!
I'LL MAKE TAMIYA BUY ME A HAM-BURGER!
I'LL MAKE DAT OTAKI BUY ME UH BIG OL' STEAK!
I'LL MAKE DADDY BUY ME A CAM-CORDER...
OKAY, EVERY-ONE... I'LL GO FIRST.
HERE GOES!
SKZZNNNNN
GULP...
KLAK
LET'S SEE...
1...
2...

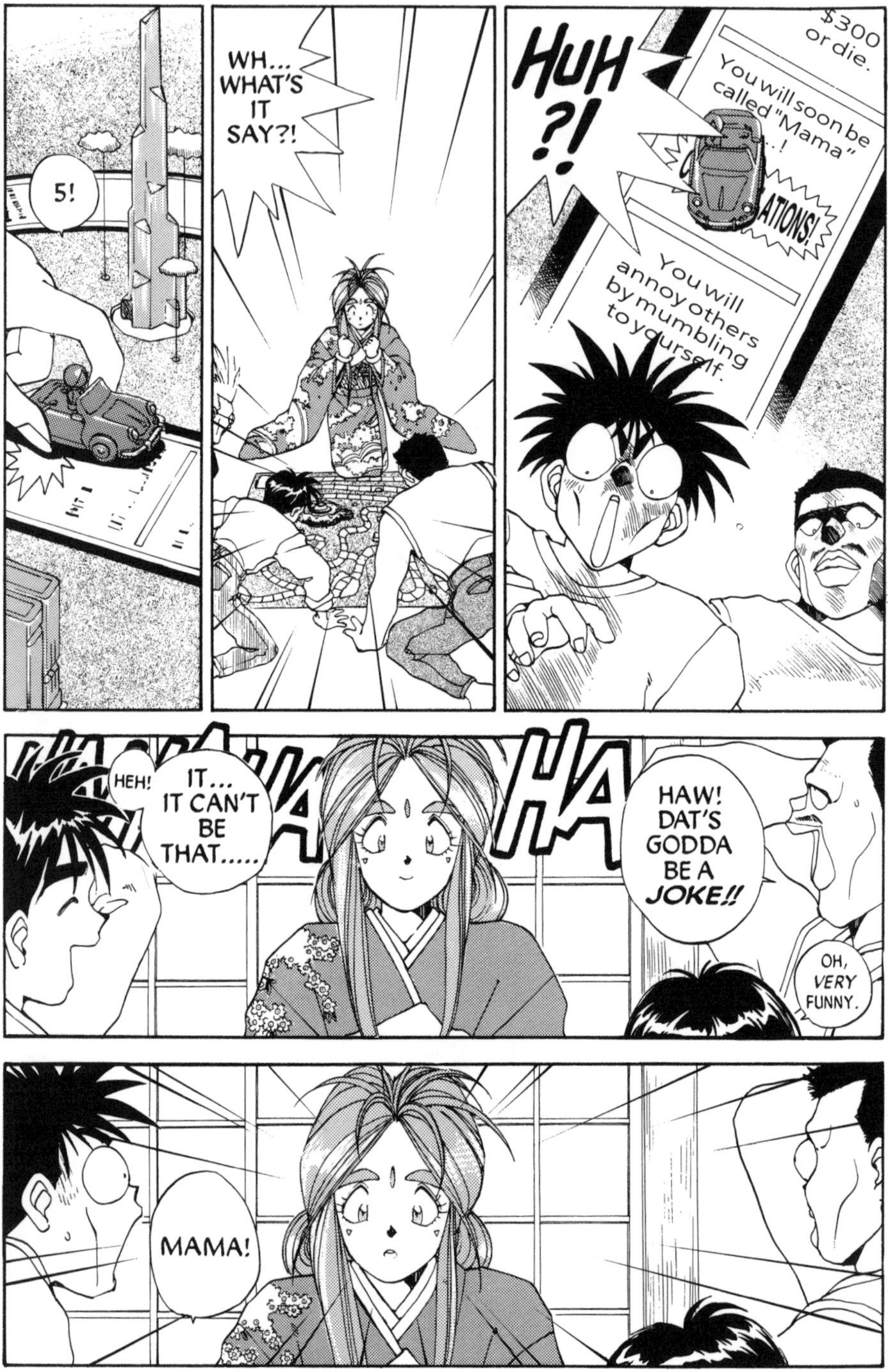
5!
WH... WHAT'S IT SAY?!
HUH ?!
$300 or die.
You will soon be called "Mama" ...!
You will annoy others by mumbling to yourself.
HEH!
IT... IT CAN'T BE THAT.....
HAW! DAT'S GODDA BE A JOKE!!
OH, VERY FUNNY.
MAMA!

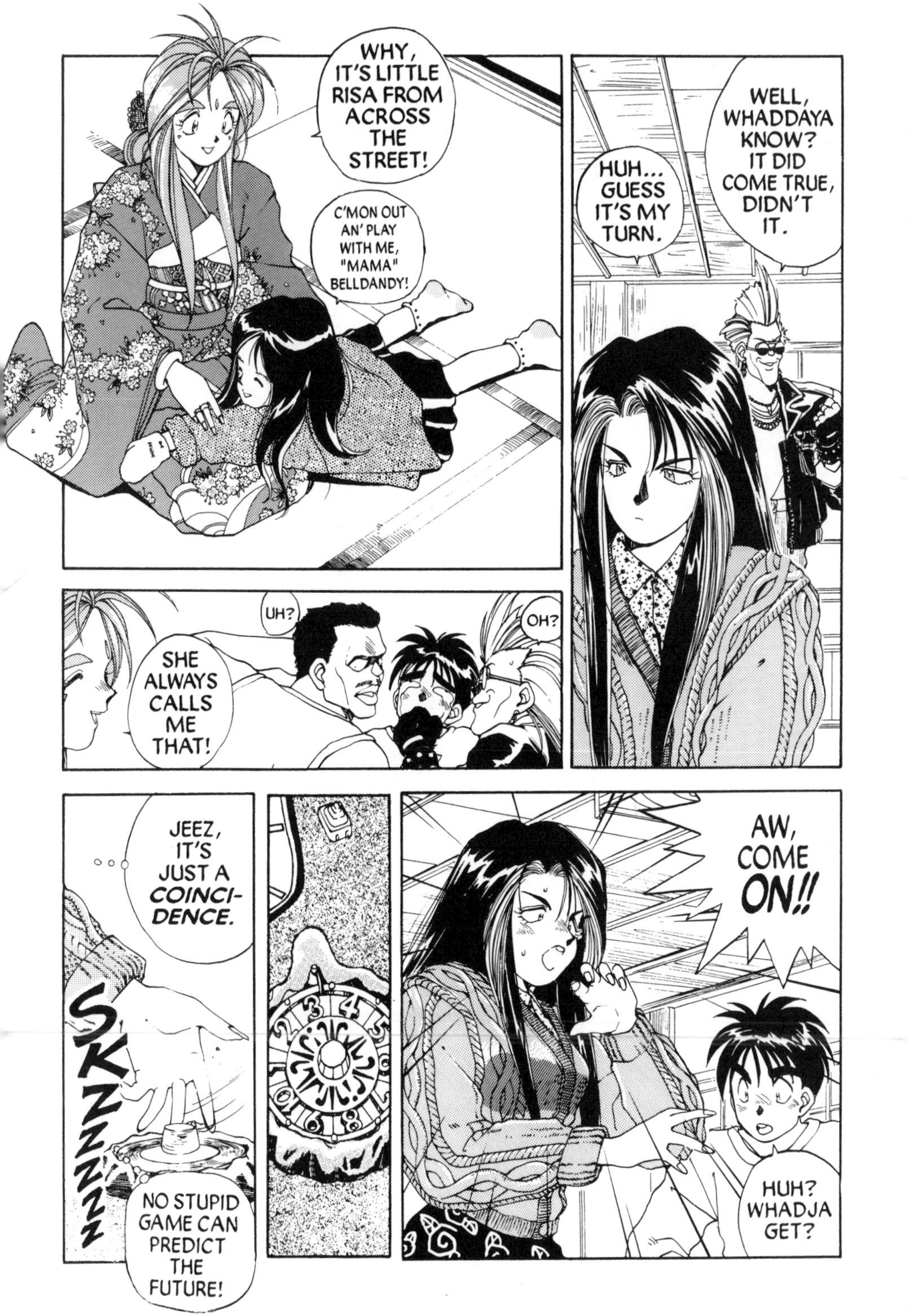
WHY, IT'S LITTLE RISA FROM ACROSS THE STREET!
C'MON OUT AN' PLAY WITH ME, "MAMA" BELLDANDY!
SHE ALWAYS CALLS ME THAT!
UH?
OH?
HUH... GUESS IT'S MY TURN.
WELL, WHADDAYA KNOW? IT DID COME TRUE, DIDN'T IT.
JEEZ, IT'S JUST A *COINCIDENCE.*
SKZZZZZ
NO STUPID GAME CAN PREDICT THE FUTURE!
AW, COME **ON!!**
HUH? WHADJA GET?

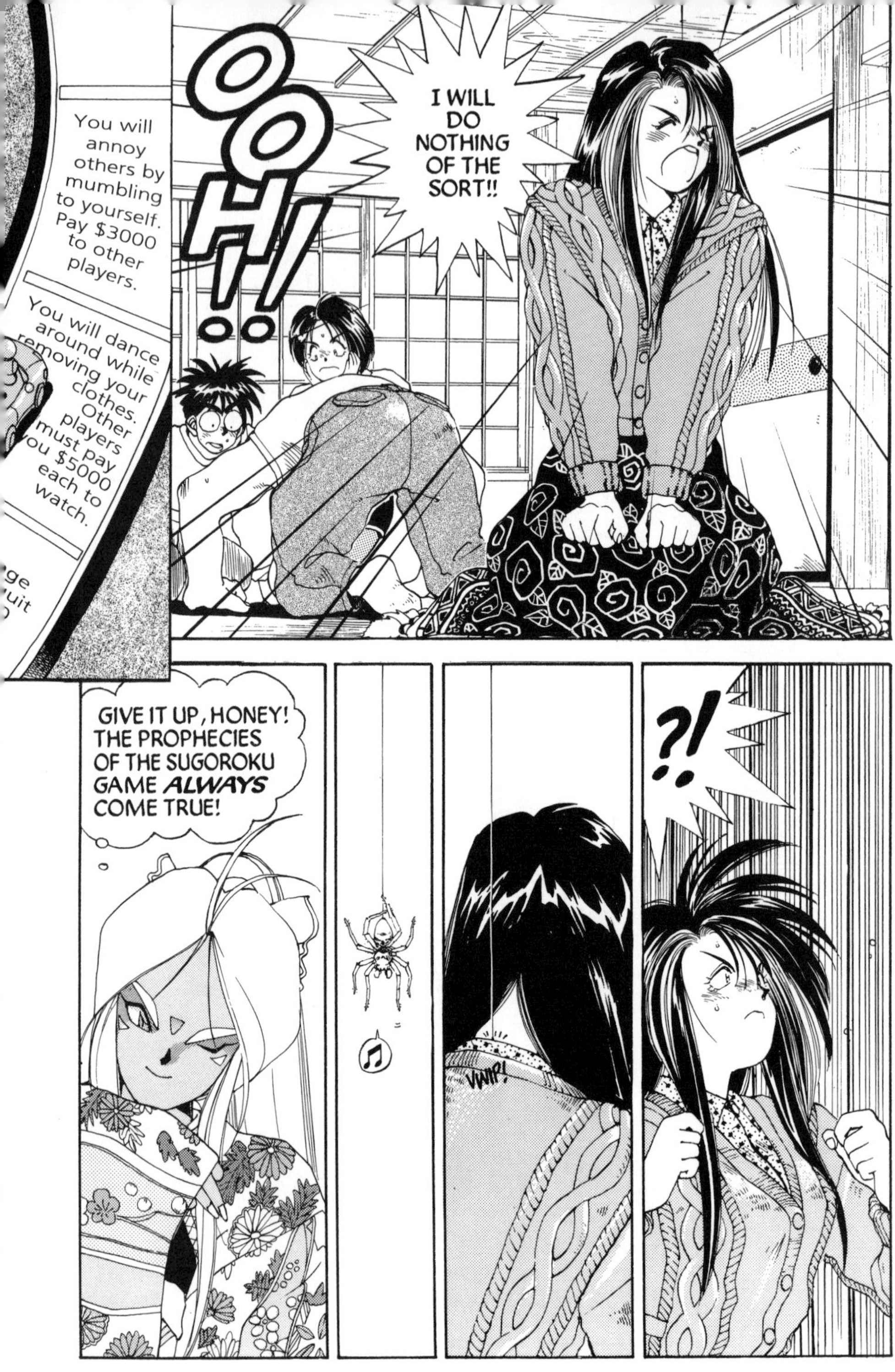

You will annoy others by mumbling to yourself. Pay $3000 to other players.
You will dance around while removing your clothes. Other players must pay you $5000 each to watch.
OOH!!
I WILL DO NOTHING OF THE SORT!!
GIVE IT UP, HONEY! THE PROPHECIES OF THE SUGOROKU GAME *ALWAYS* COME TRUE!
♪
VWIP!
?!

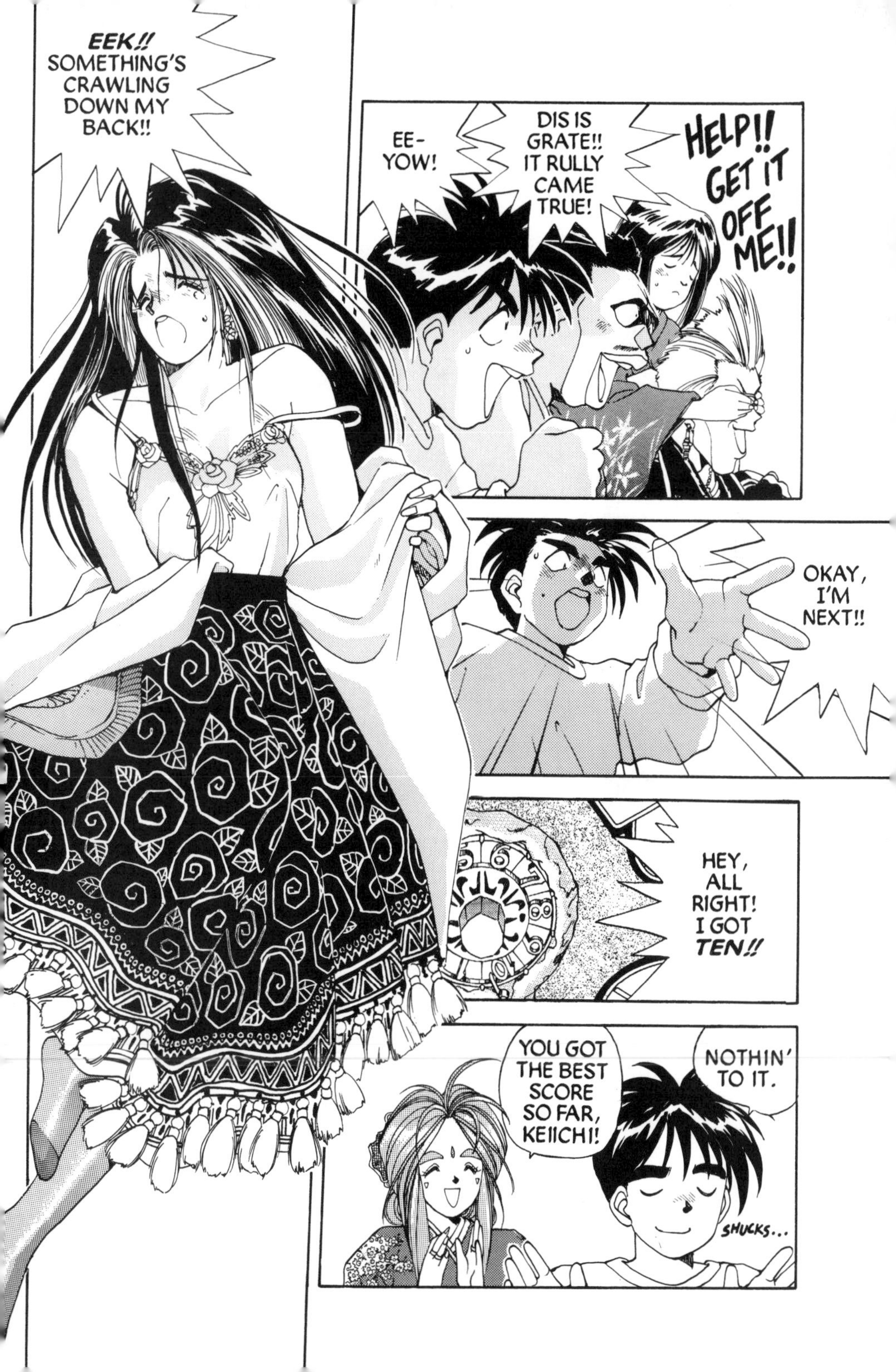
EEK!! SOMETHING'S CRAWLING DOWN MY BACK!!
EE- YOW!
DIS IS GRATE!! IT RULLY CAME TRUE!
HELP!! GET IT OFF ME!!
OKAY, I'M NEXT!!
HEY, ALL RIGHT! I GOT TEN!!
YOU GOT THE BEST SCORE SO FAR, KEIICHI!
NOTHIN' TO IT.
SHUCKS...

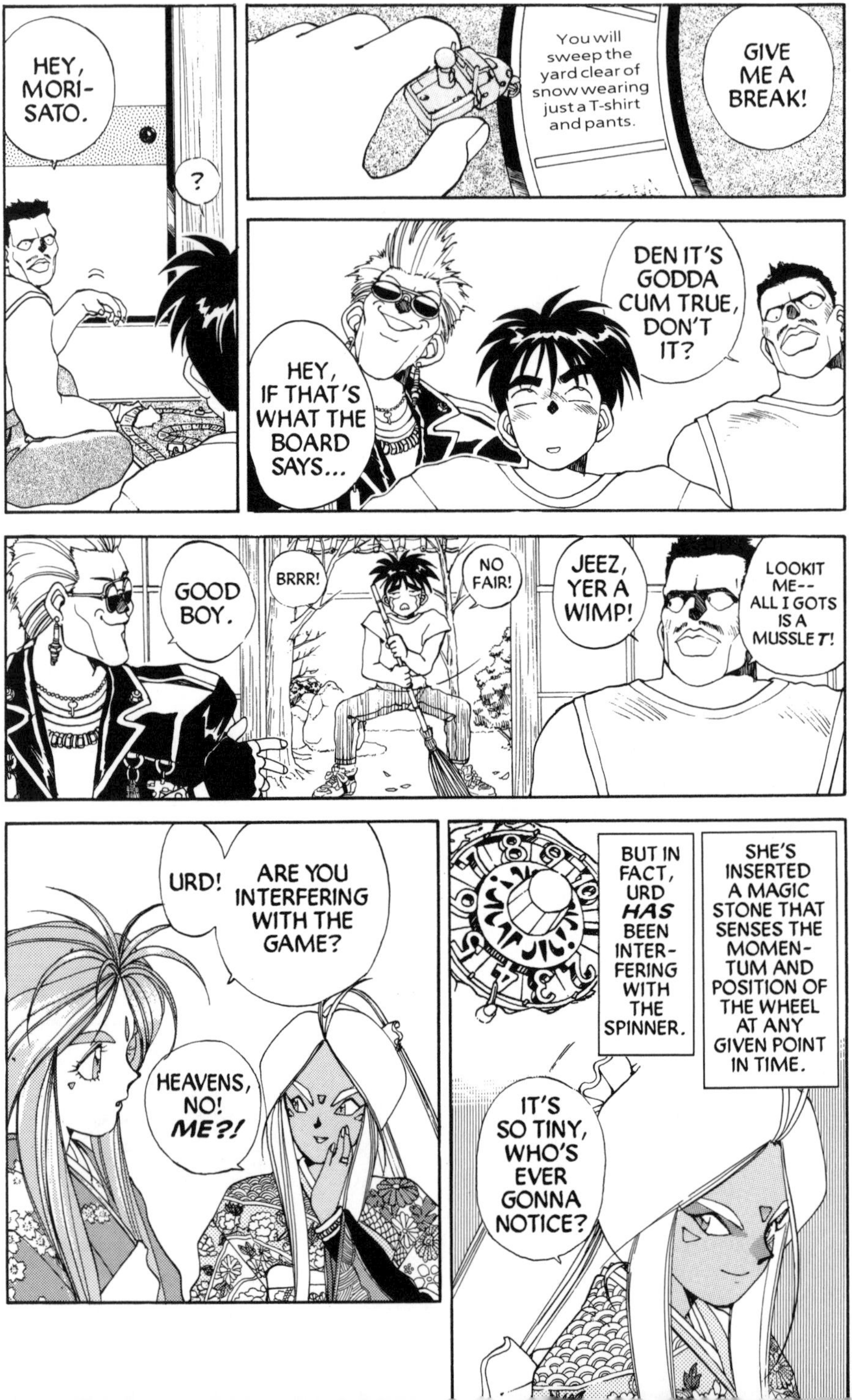
HEY, MORI-SATO.
?
You will sweep the yard clear of snow wearing just a T-shirt and pants.
GIVE ME A BREAK!
HEY, IF THAT'S WHAT THE BOARD SAYS...
DEN IT'S GODDA CUM TRUE, DON'T IT?
GOOD BOY.
BRRR!
NO FAIR!
JEEZ, YER A WIMP!
LOOKIT ME-- ALL I GOTS IS A MUSSLE T!
URD!
ARE YOU INTERFERING WITH THE GAME?
HEAVENS, NO! ME?!
BUT IN FACT, URD HAS BEEN INTER-FERING WITH THE SPINNER.
SHE'S INSERTED A MAGIC STONE THAT SENSES THE MOMEN-TUM AND POSITION OF THE WHEEL AT ANY GIVEN POINT IN TIME.
IT'S SO TINY, WHO'S EVER GONNA NOTICE?

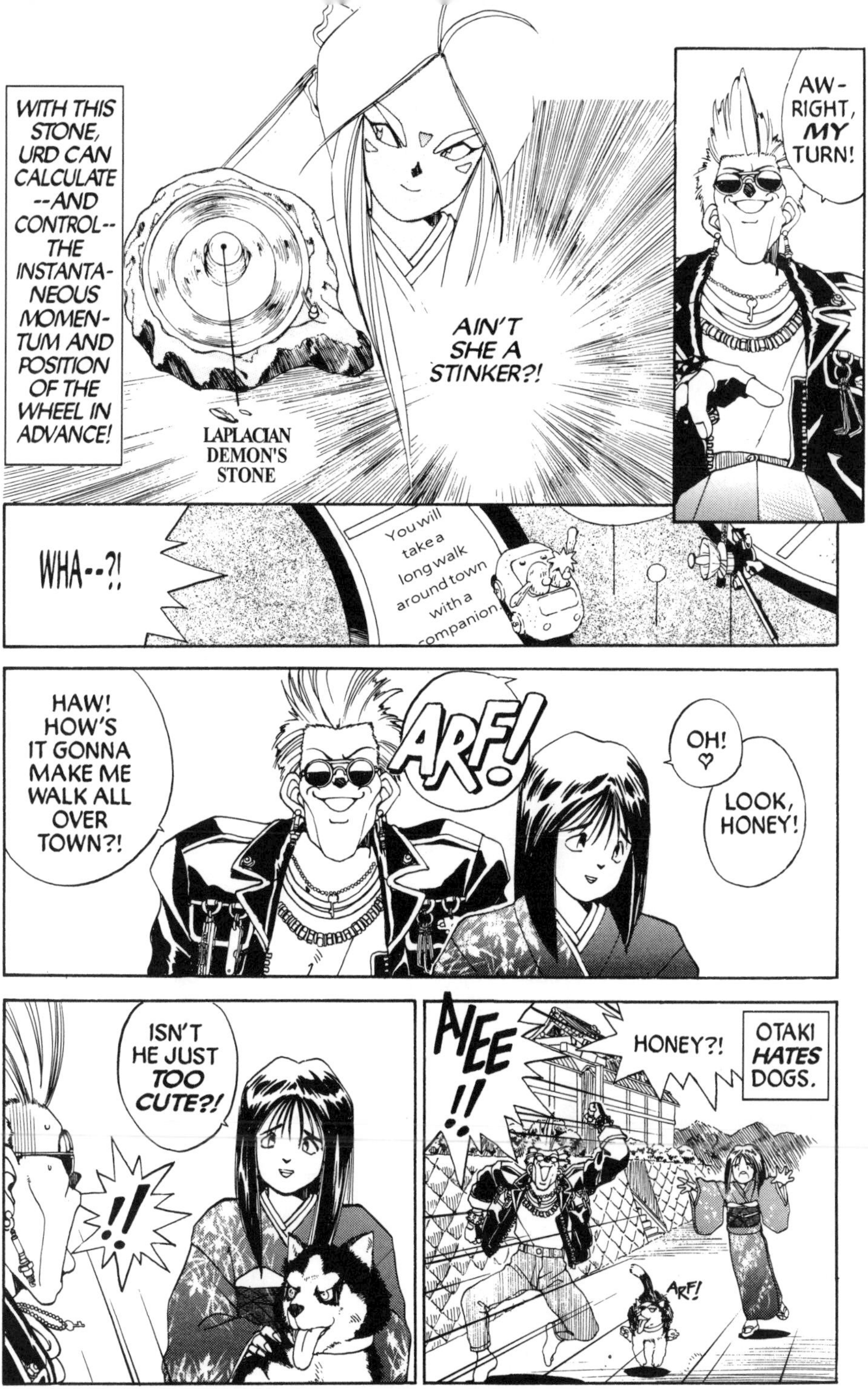
WITH THIS STONE, URD CAN CALCULATE --AND CONTROL-- THE INSTANTANEOUS MOMENTUM AND POSITION OF THE WHEEL IN ADVANCE!
LAPLACIAN DEMON'S STONE
AIN'T SHE A STINKER?!
AW-RIGHT, MY TURN!
WHA--?!
You will take a long walk around town with a companion.
HAW! HOW'S IT GONNA MAKE ME WALK ALL OVER TOWN?!
ARF!
OH! ♡
LOOK, HONEY!
ISN'T HE JUST TOO CUTE?!
!!
AIEE!!
HONEY?!
OTAKI HATES DOGS.
ARF!

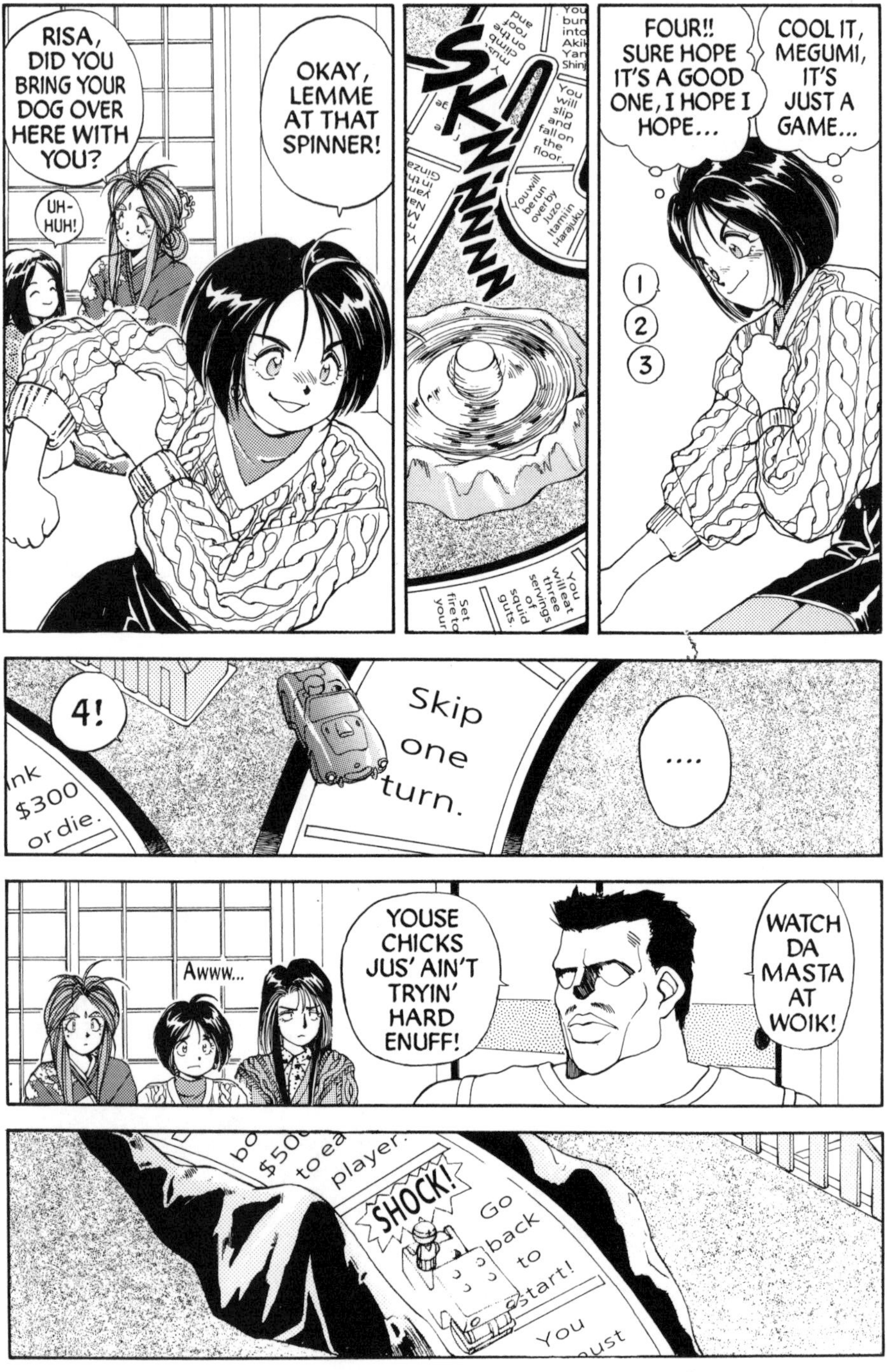
RISA, DID YOU BRING YOUR DOG OVER HERE WITH YOU?
UH-HUH!
OKAY, LEMME AT THAT SPINNER!
You will slip and fall on the floor.
You will be run over by Juzo Itami in Harajuku.
You will eat three servings of squid guts.
FOUR!! SURE HOPE IT'S A GOOD ONE, I HOPE I HOPE...
COOL IT, MEGUMI, IT'S JUST A GAME...
1
2
3
4!
Skip one turn.
....
Awww...
YOUSE CHICKS JUS' AIN'T TRYIN' HARD ENUFF!
WATCH DA MASTA AT WOIK!
player.
SHOCK!
Go back to start!
You

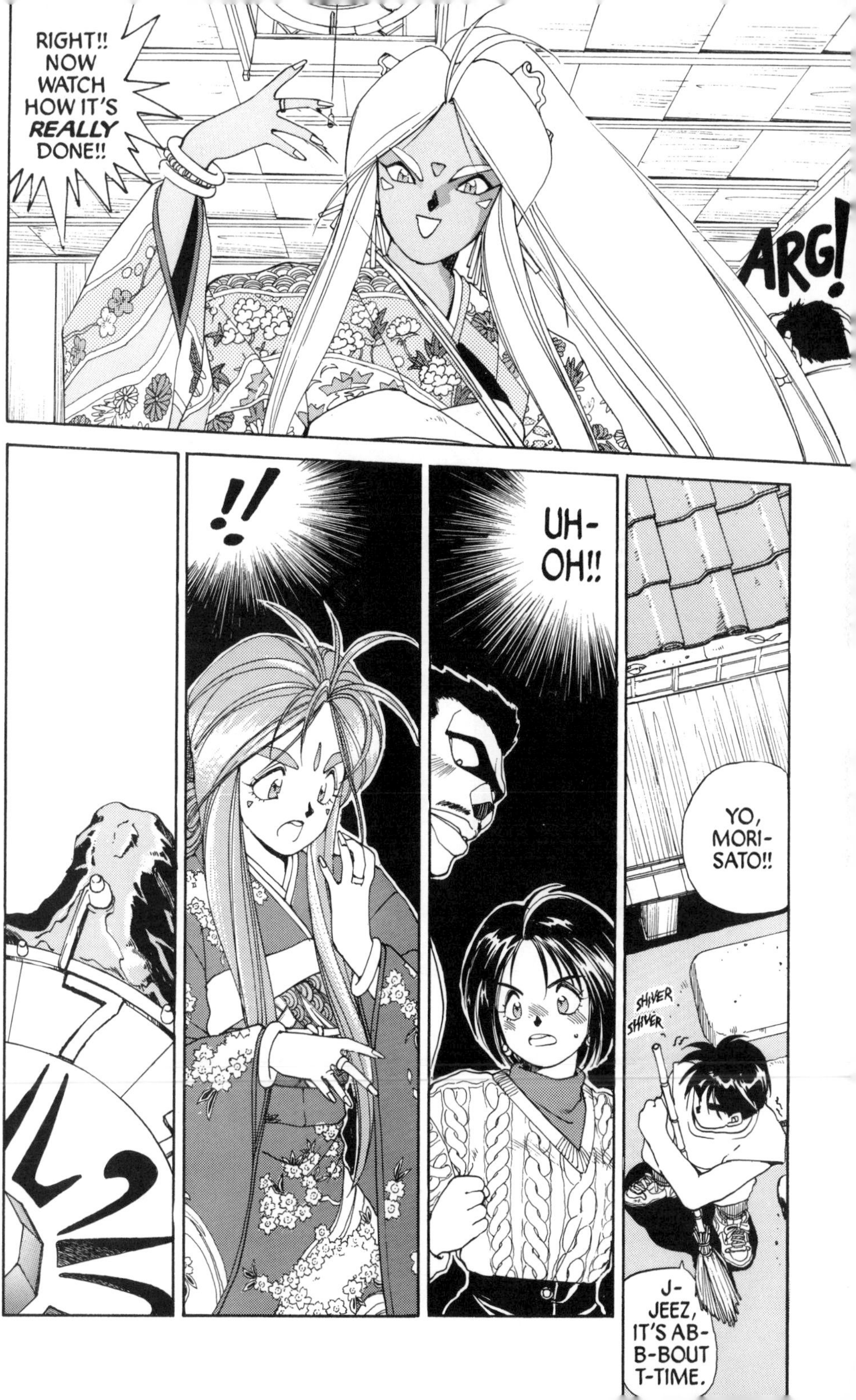
RIGHT!! NOW WATCH HOW IT'S *REALLY* DONE!!
ARG!
!!
UH-OH!!
YO, MORI-SATO!!
SHIVER
SHIVER
J-JEEZ, IT'S AB-B-BOUT T-TIME.

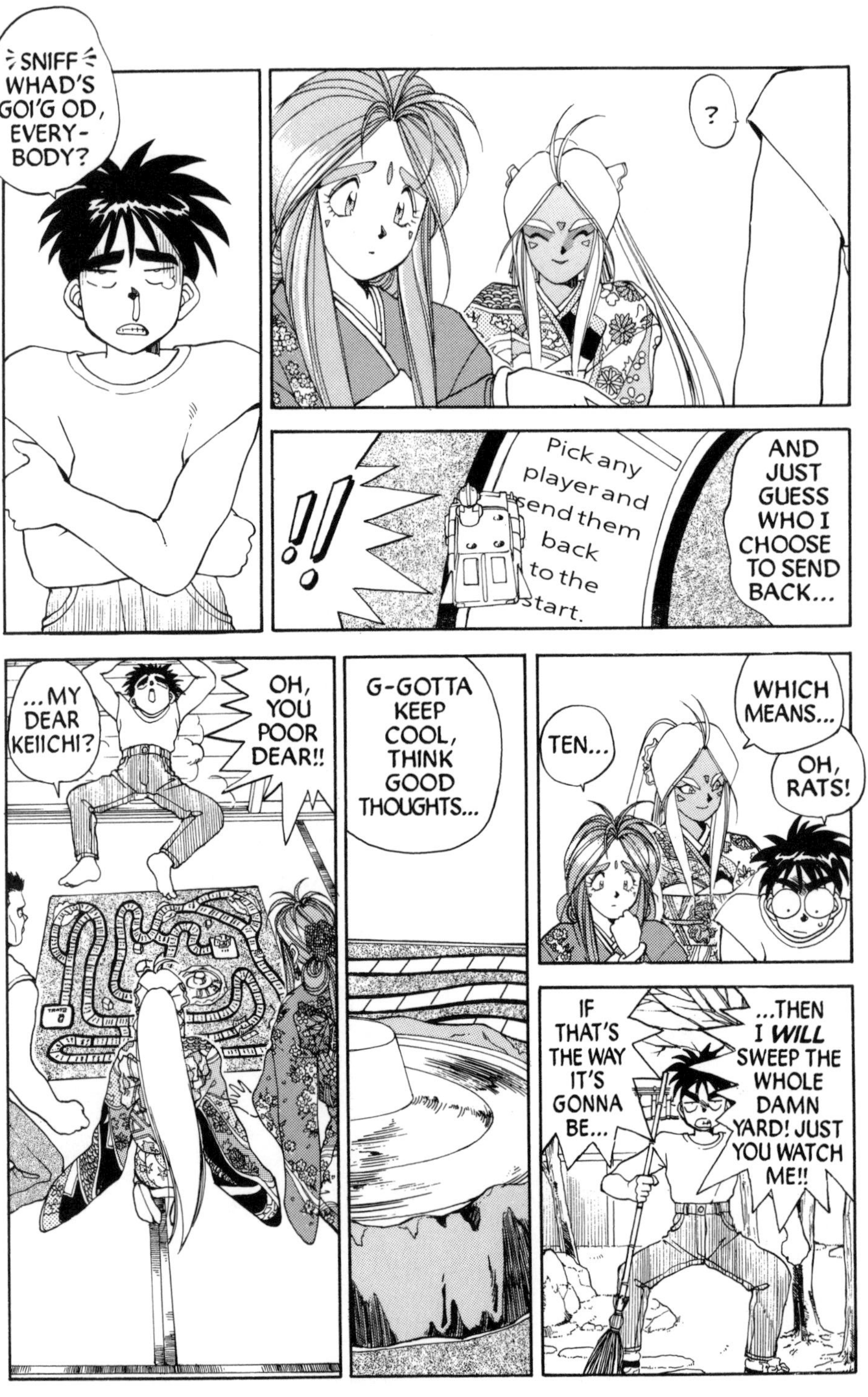
SNIFF WHAD'S GOI'G OD, EVERY-BODY?
?
!!
Pick any player and send them back to the start.
AND JUST GUESS WHO I CHOOSE TO SEND BACK...
...MY DEAR KEIICHI?
OH, YOU POOR DEAR!!
G-GOTTA KEEP COOL, THINK GOOD THOUGHTS...
TEN...
WHICH MEANS...
OH, RATS!
IF THAT'S THE WAY IT'S GONNA BE...
...THEN I *WILL* SWEEP THE WHOLE DAMN YARD! JUST YOU WATCH ME!!

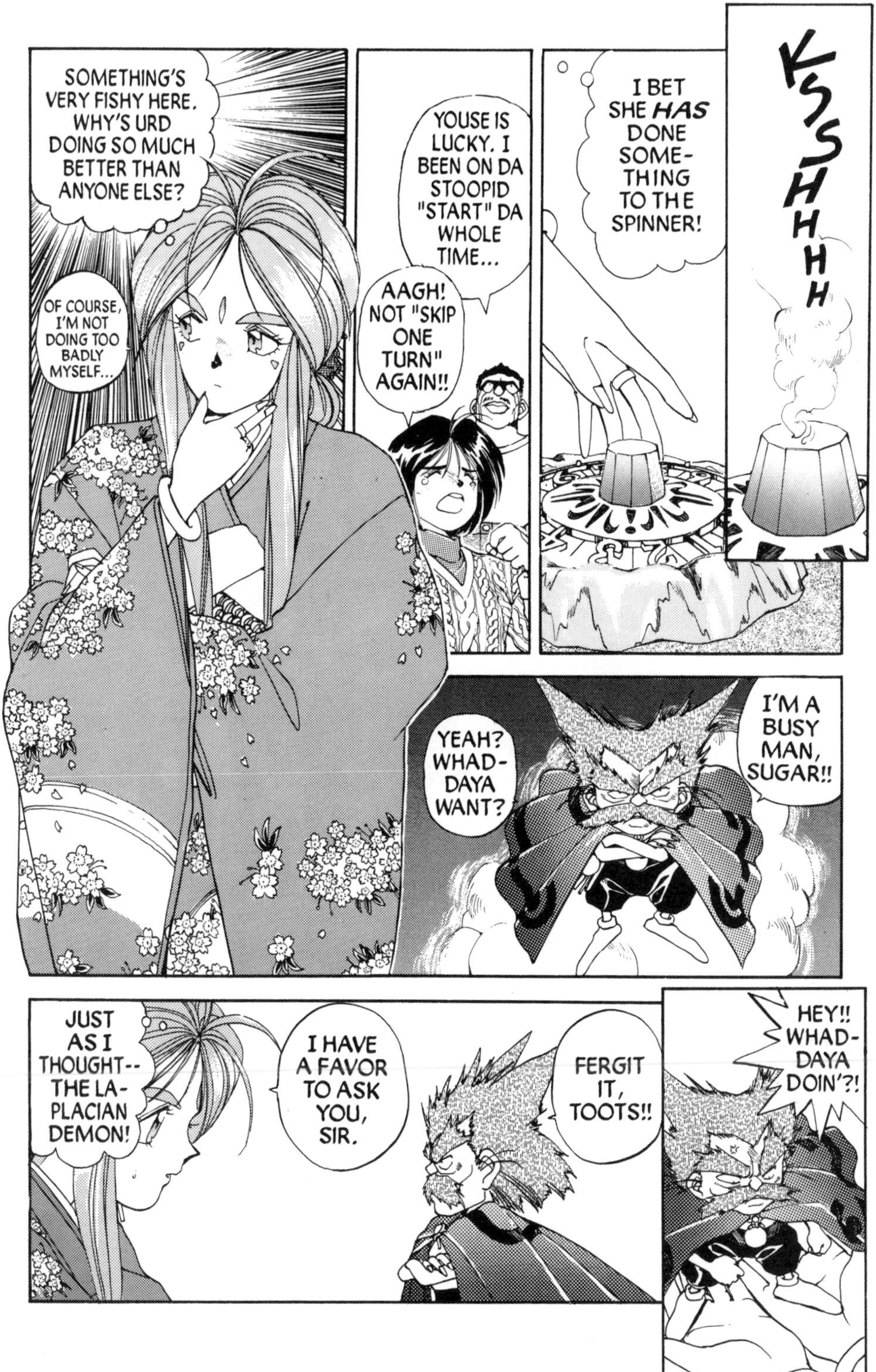
SOMETHING'S VERY FISHY HERE. WHY'S URD DOING SO MUCH BETTER THAN ANYONE ELSE?
OF COURSE, I'M NOT DOING TOO BADLY MYSELF...
YOUSE IS LUCKY. I BEEN ON DA STOOPID "START" DA WHOLE TIME...
AAGH! NOT "SKIP ONE TURN" AGAIN!!
I BET SHE HAS DONE SOME-THING TO THE SPINNER!
KSSHHHH
YEAH? WHAD-DAYA WANT?
I'M A BUSY MAN, SUGAR!!
JUST AS I THOUGHT-- THE LA-PLACIAN DEMON!
I HAVE A FAVOR TO ASK YOU, SIR.
FERGIT IT, TOOTS!!
HEY!! WHAD-DAYA DOIN'?!

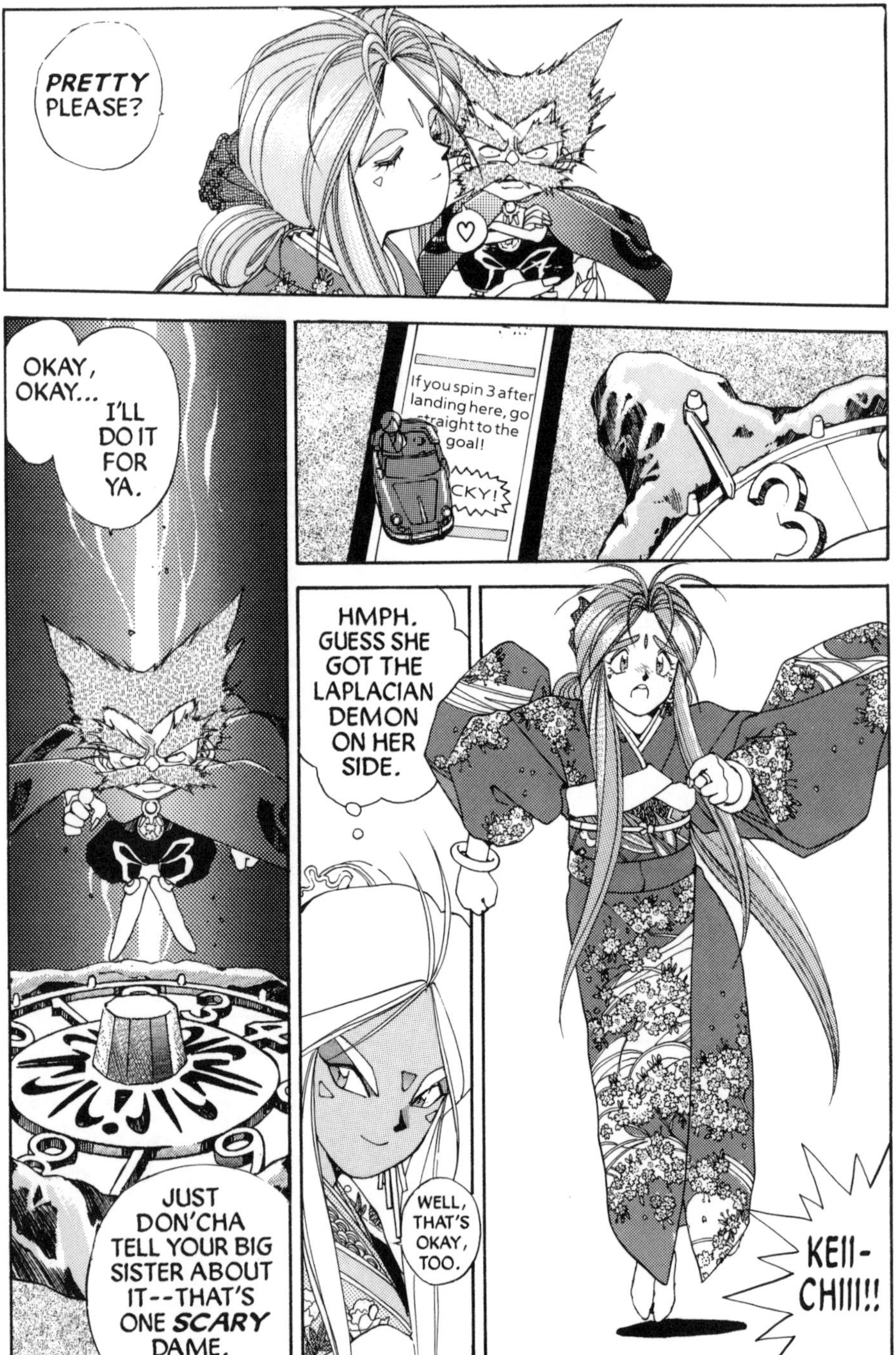
PRETTY PLEASE?
OKAY, OKAY...
I'LL DO IT FOR YA.
JUST DON'CHA TELL YOUR BIG SISTER ABOUT IT--THAT'S ONE SCARY DAME.
If you spin 3 after landing here, go straight to the goal!
CKY!
HMPH. GUESS SHE GOT THE LAPLACIAN DEMON ON HER SIDE.
WELL, THAT'S OKAY, TOO.
KEII-CHIIII!!

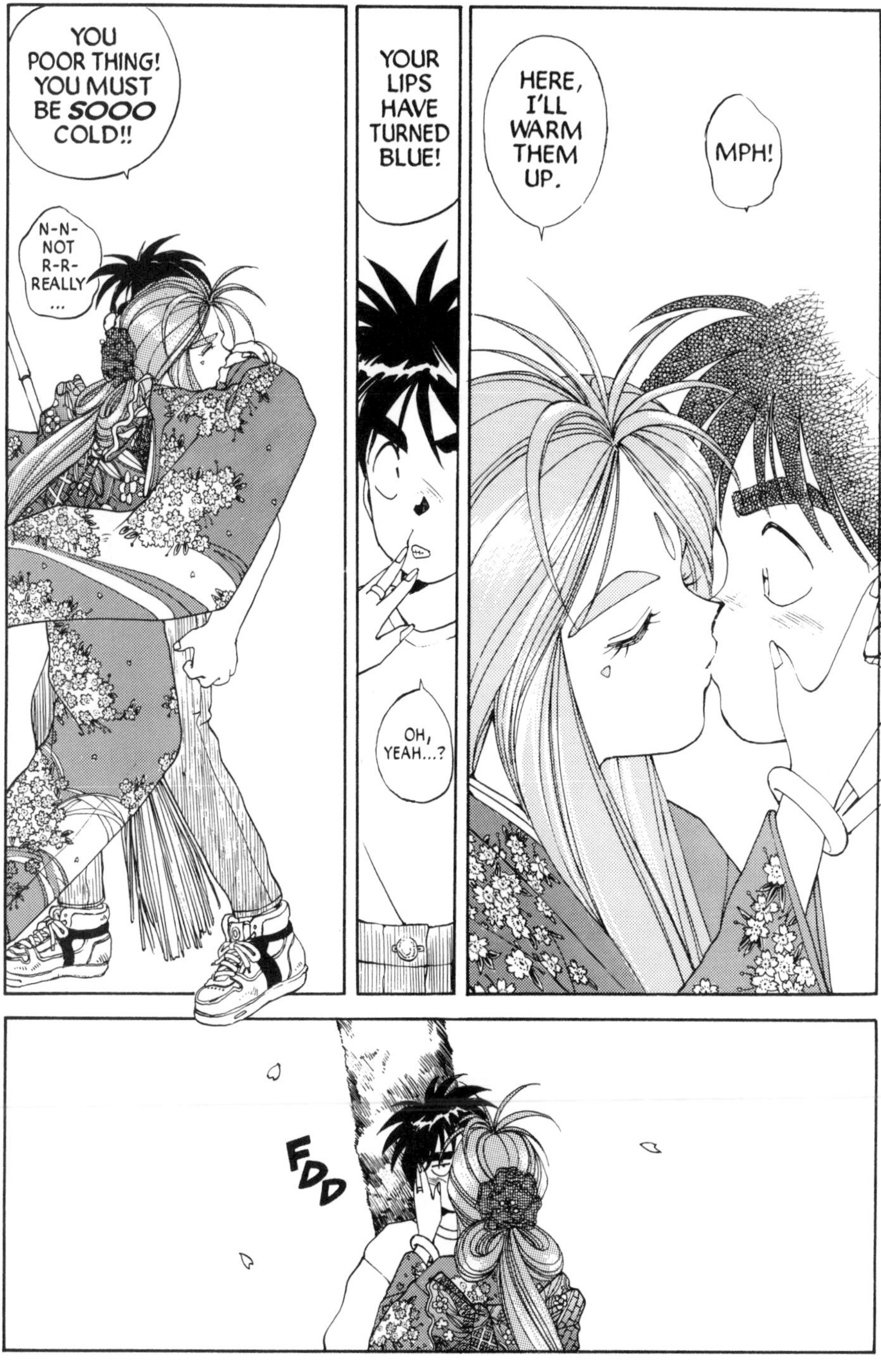
YOU POOR THING! YOU MUST BE SOOO COLD!!
N-N-NOT R-R-REALLY...
YOUR LIPS HAVE TURNED BLUE!
OH, YEAH...?
HERE, I'LL WARM THEM UP.
MPH!
FDD

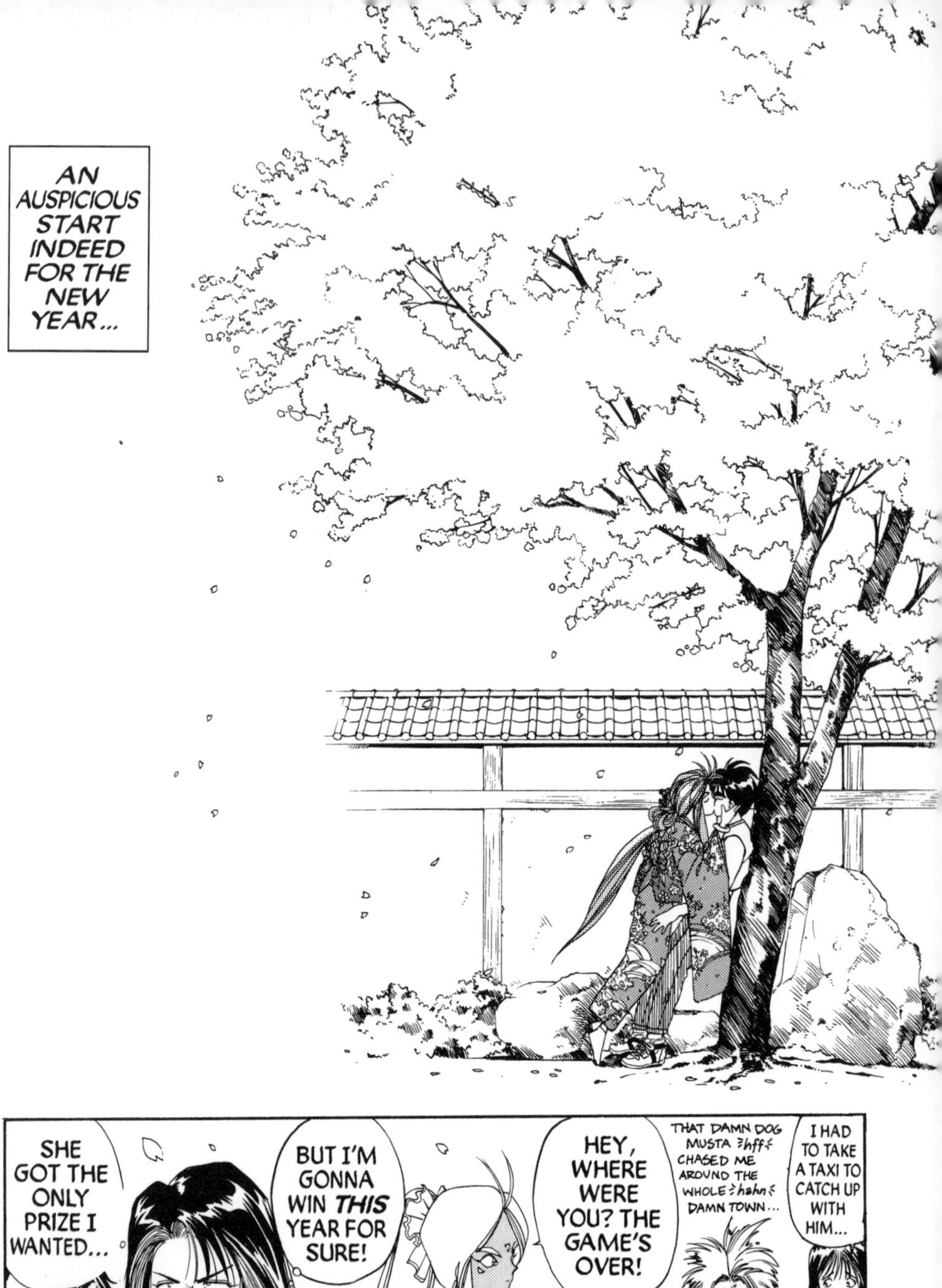
AN AUSPICIOUS START INDEED FOR THE NEW YEAR...

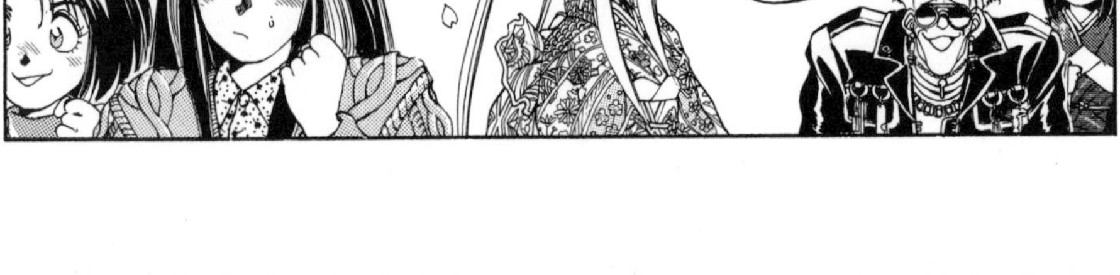
SHE GOT THE ONLY PRIZE I WANTED...
BUT I'M GONNA WIN *THIS* YEAR FOR SURE!
HEY, WHERE WERE YOU? THE GAME'S OVER!
THAT DAMN DOG MUSTA *hff* CHASED ME AROUND THE WHOLE *hahn* DAMN TOWN...
I HAD TO TAKE A TAXI TO CATCH UP WITH HIM...

FINAL EXAM

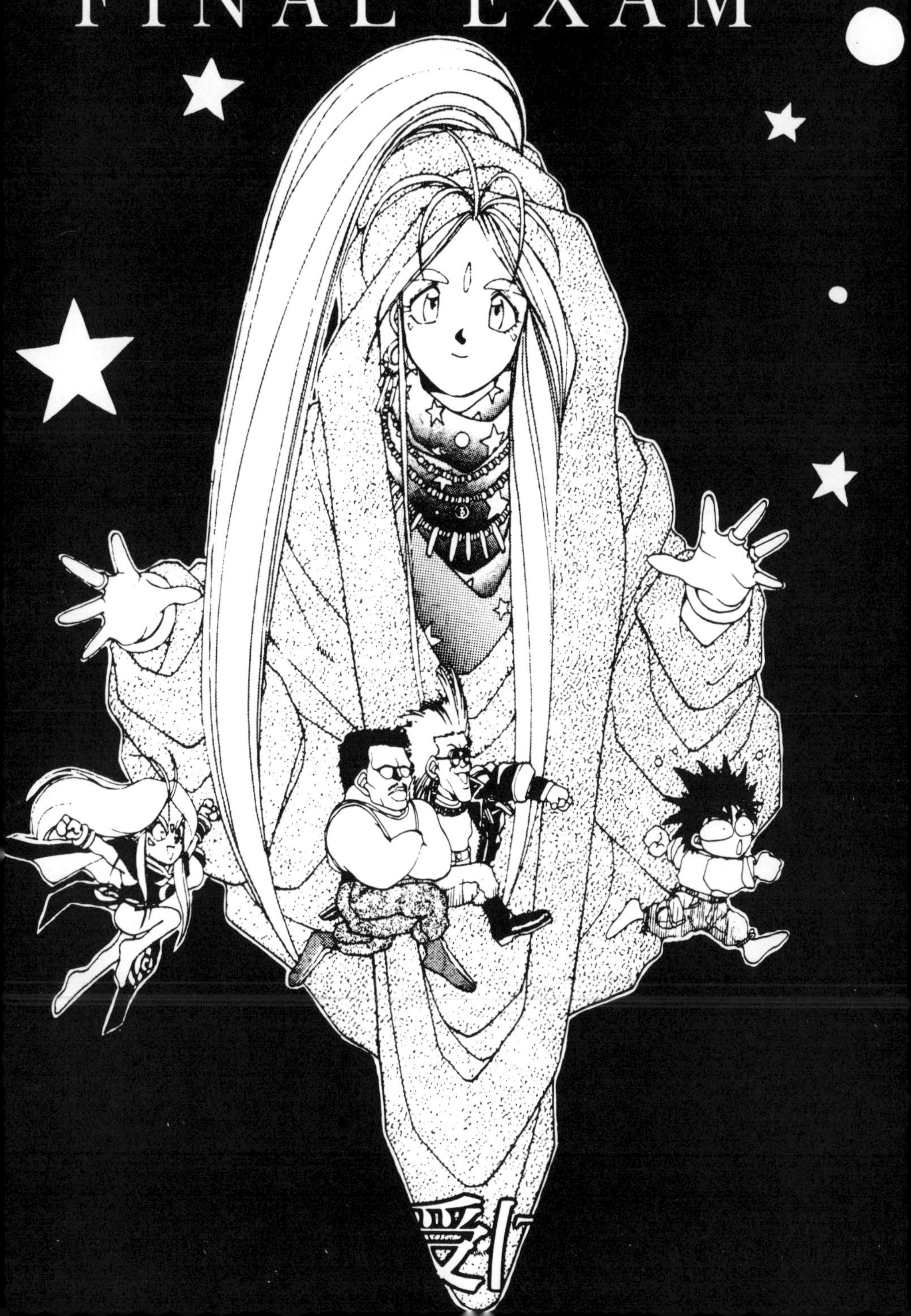

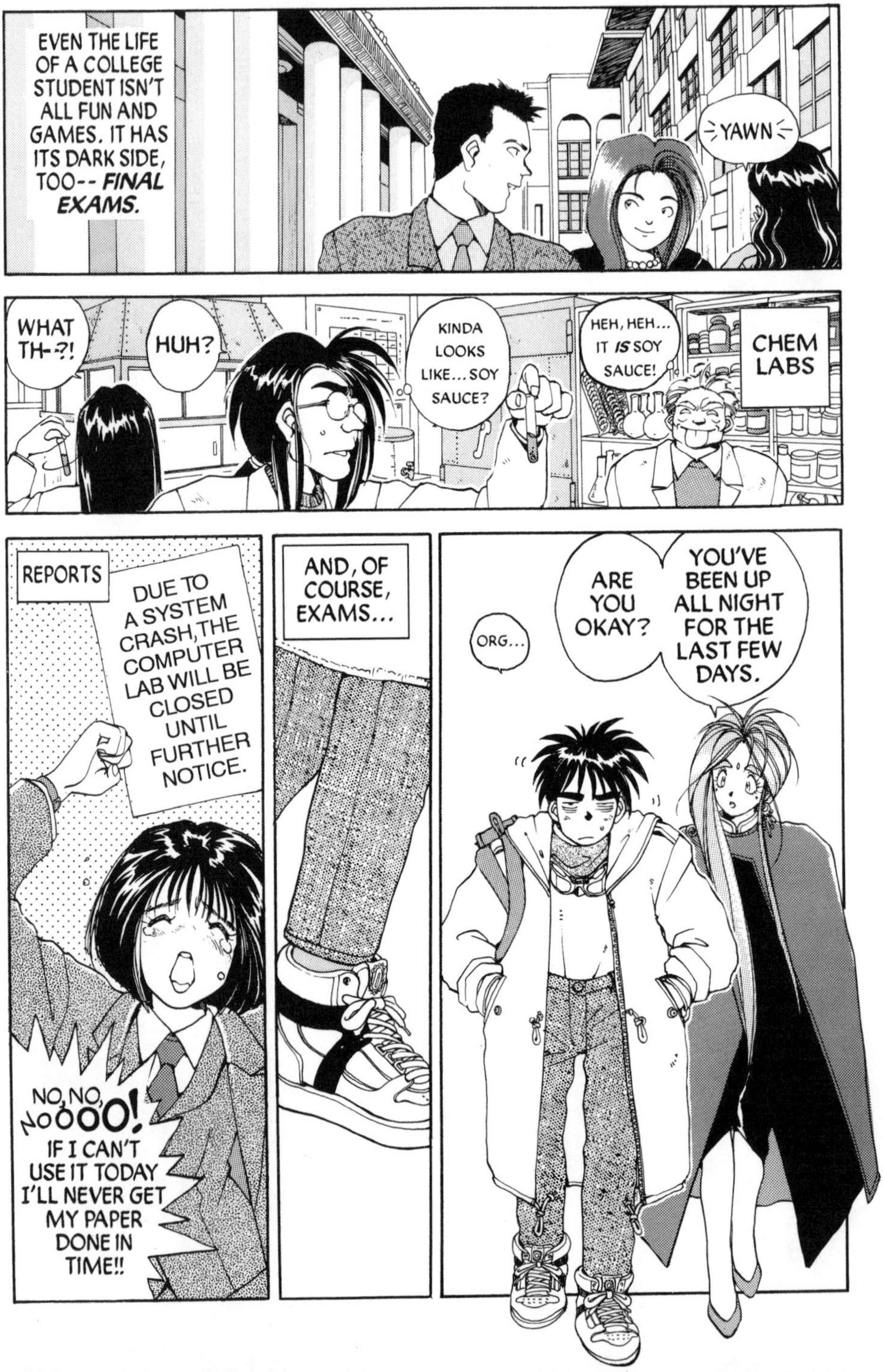

EVEN THE LIFE OF A COLLEGE STUDENT ISN'T ALL FUN AND GAMES. IT HAS ITS DARK SIDE, TOO-- *FINAL EXAMS.*
YAWN
WHAT TH-?!
HUH?
KINDA LOOKS LIKE... SOY SAUCE?
HEH, HEH... IT *IS* SOY SAUCE!
CHEM LABS
REPORTS
DUE TO A SYSTEM CRASH, THE COMPUTER LAB WILL BE CLOSED UNTIL FURTHER NOTICE.
NO, NO, NOOOOO!
IF I CAN'T USE IT TODAY I'LL NEVER GET MY PAPER DONE IN TIME!!
AND, OF COURSE, EXAMS...
ORG...
ARE YOU OKAY?
YOU'VE BEEN UP ALL NIGHT FOR THE LAST FEW DAYS.

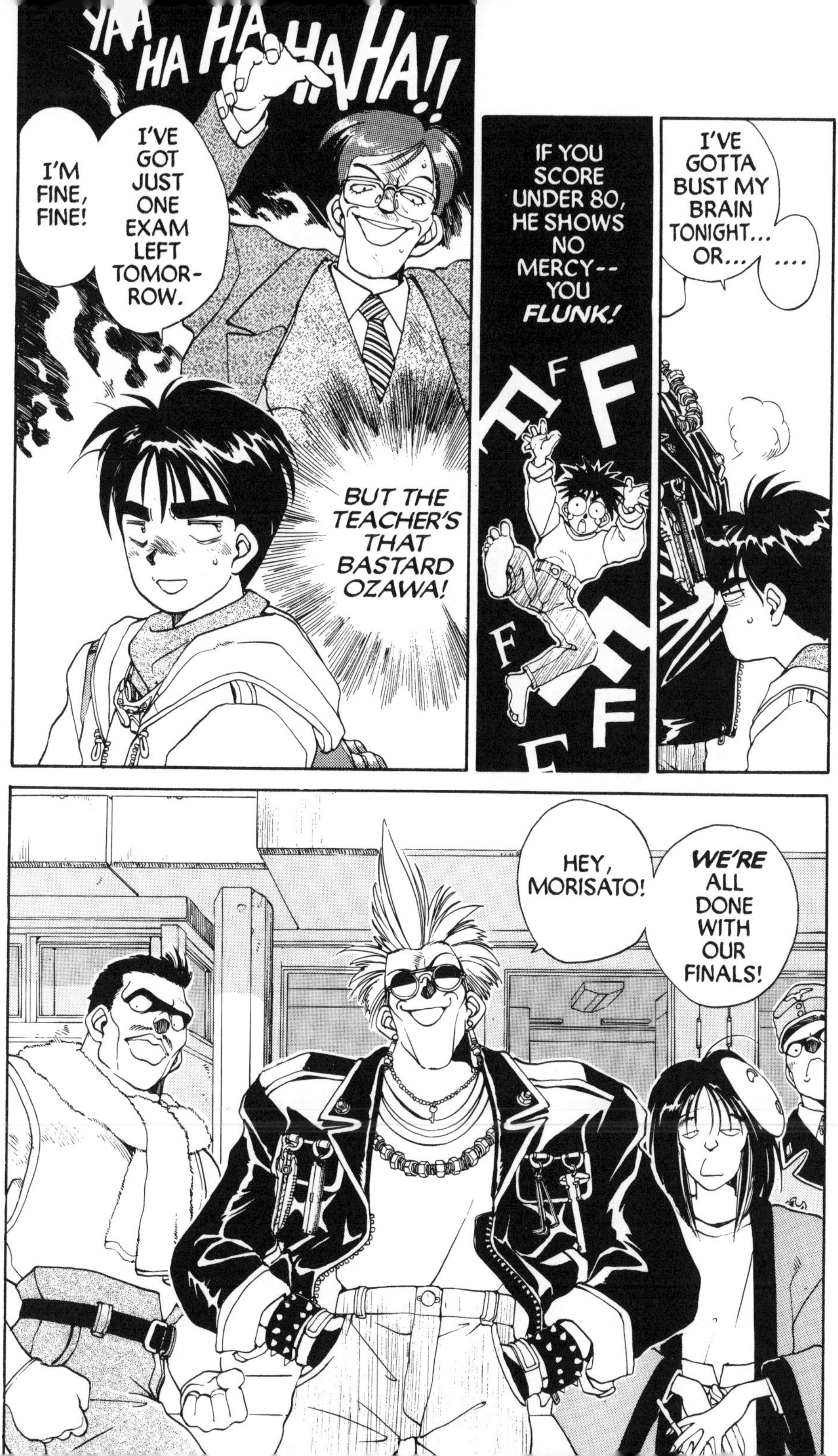
YAA HA HA HA HA HA!!
I'M FINE, FINE!
I'VE GOT JUST ONE EXAM LEFT TOMORROW.
BUT THE TEACHER'S THAT BASTARD OZAWA!
IF YOU SCORE UNDER 80, HE SHOWS NO MERCY-- YOU *FLUNK!*
F F F F F F
I'VE GOTTA BUST MY BRAIN TONIGHT... OR...
....
HEY, MORISATO!
WE'RE ALL DONE WITH OUR FINALS!

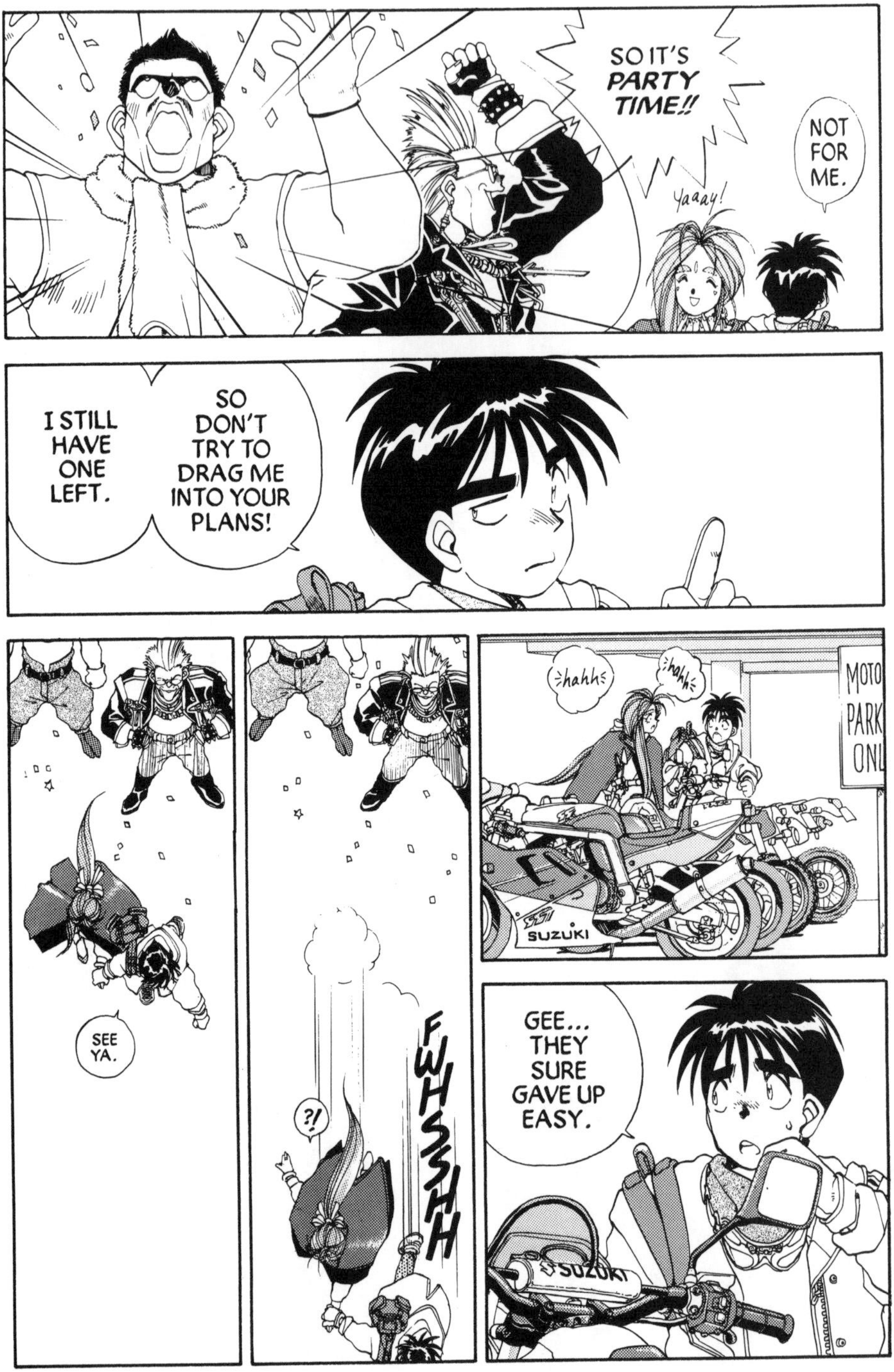
SO IT'S PARTY TIME!!
Yaaay!
NOT FOR ME.
I STILL HAVE ONE LEFT.
SO DON'T TRY TO DRAG ME INTO YOUR PLANS!
SEE YA.
?!
FWHSSHH
hahh
hahh
SUZUKI
GEE... THEY SURE GAVE UP EASY.
SUZUKI

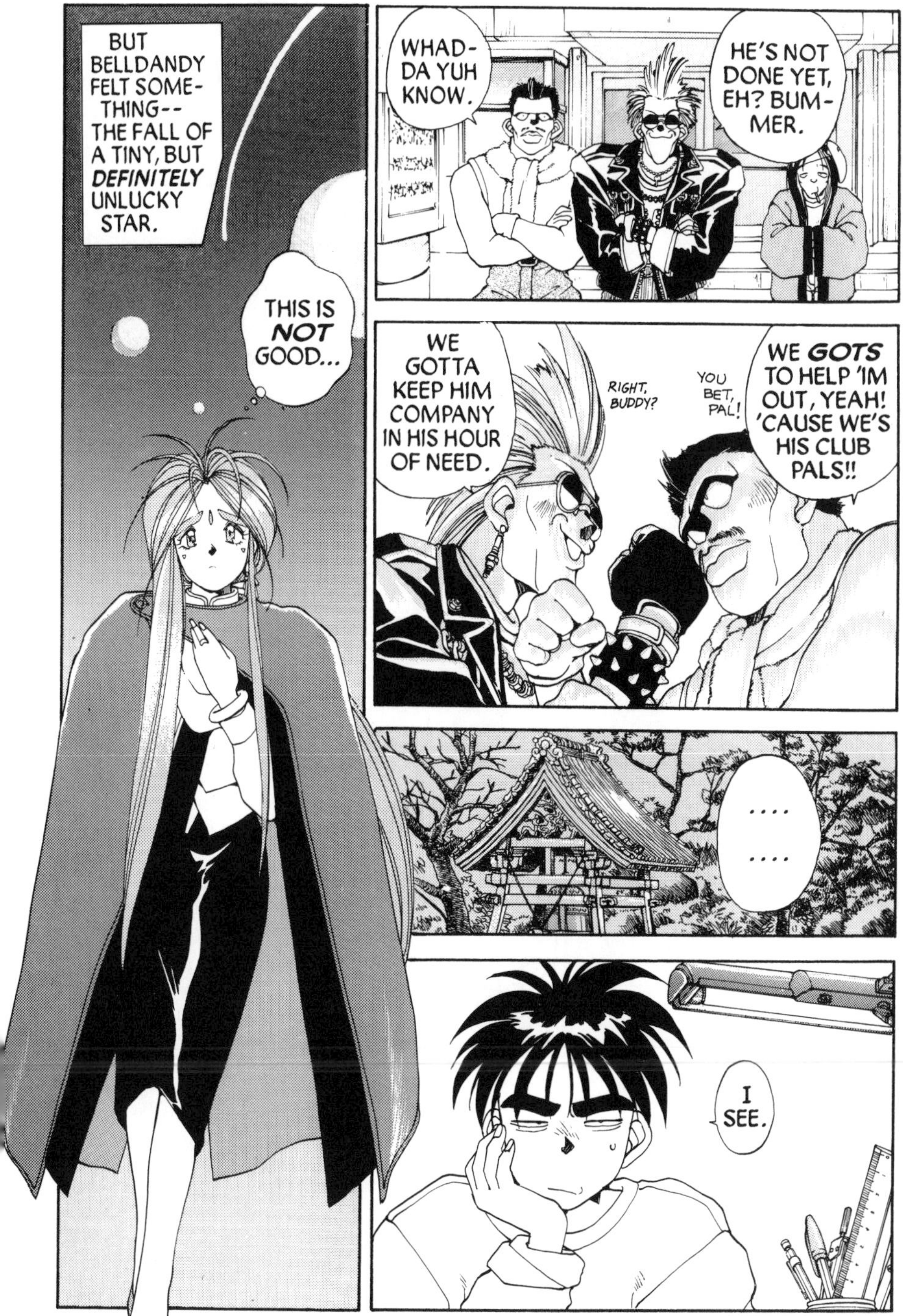
BUT BELLDANDY FELT SOMETHING-- THE FALL OF A TINY, BUT DEFINITELY UNLUCKY STAR.
THIS IS NOT GOOD...
WHADDA YUH KNOW.
HE'S NOT DONE YET, EH? BUMMER.
WE GOTTA KEEP HIM COMPANY IN HIS HOUR OF NEED.
RIGHT, BUDDY?
YOU BET, PAL!
WE GOTS TO HELP 'IM OUT, YEAH! 'CAUSE WE'S HIS CLUB PALS!!
....
I SEE.

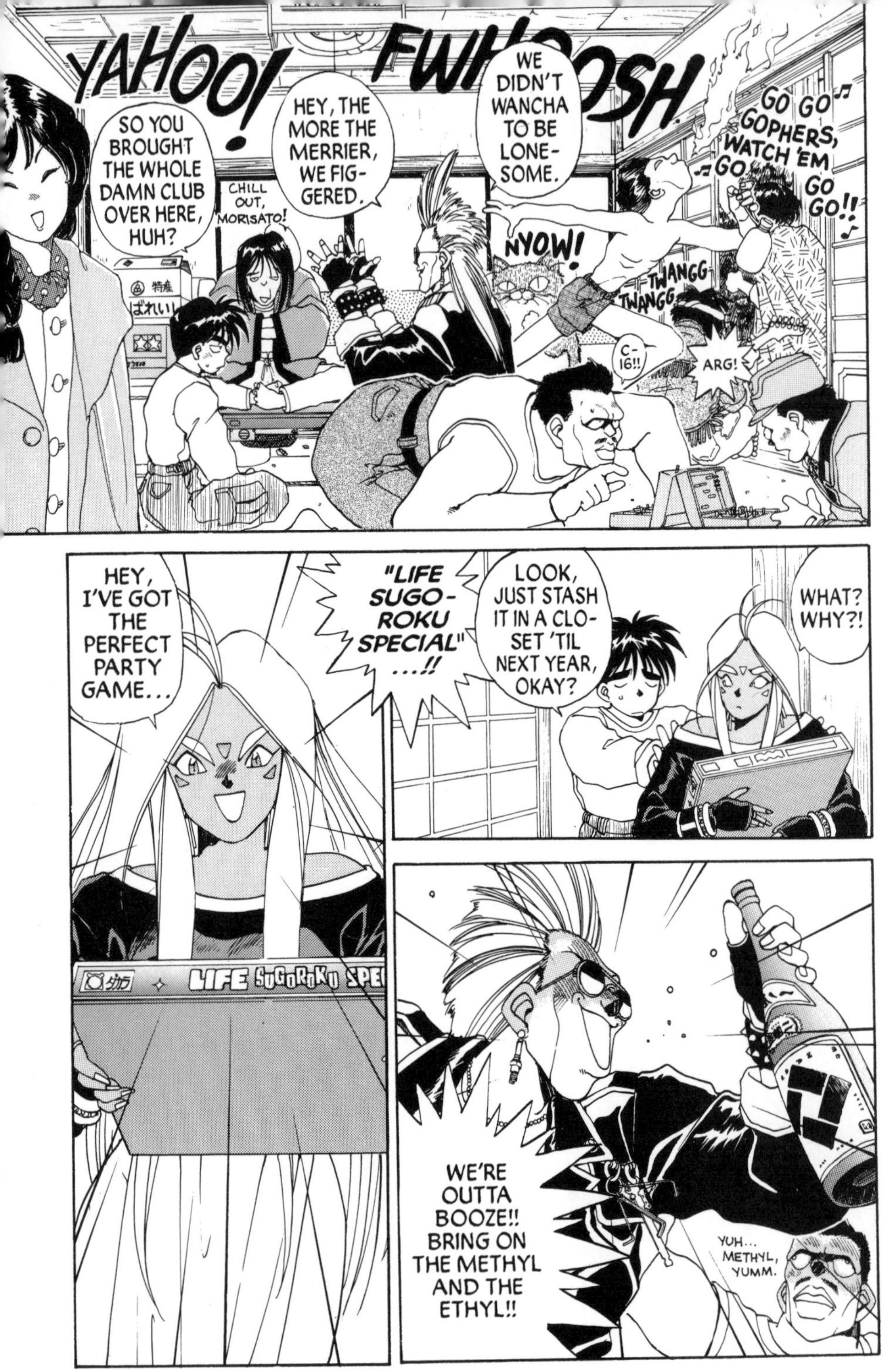
YAHOO!
FWHOOSH
SO YOU BROUGHT THE WHOLE DAMN CLUB OVER HERE, HUH?
CHILL OUT, MORISATO!
特産
HEY, THE MORE THE MERRIER, WE FIGGERED.
WE DIDN'T WANCHA TO BE LONESOME.
NYOW!
GO GO GOPHERS, WATCH 'EM GO GO GO!!
TWANGG TWANGG
C-16!!
ARG!
HEY, I'VE GOT THE PERFECT PARTY GAME...
"LIFE SUGOROKU SPECIAL"...!!
LOOK, JUST STASH IT IN A CLOSET 'TIL NEXT YEAR, OKAY?
WHAT? WHY?!
LIFE
WE'RE OUTTA BOOZE!! BRING ON THE METHYL AND THE ETHYL!!
YUH... METHYL, YUMM.

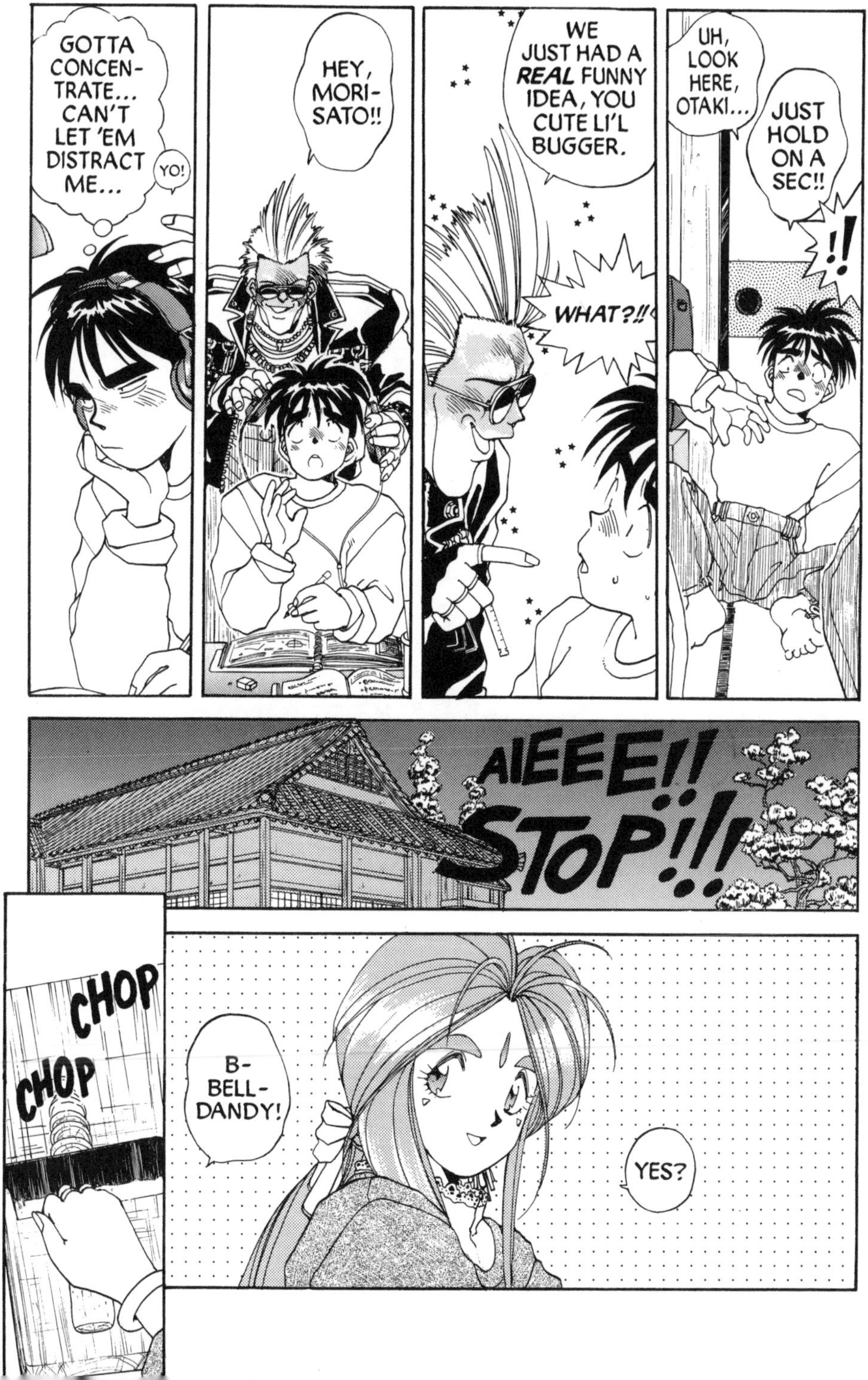
GOTTA CONCENTRATE... CAN'T LET 'EM DISTRACT ME...
YO!
HEY, MORI-SATO!!
WE JUST HAD A REAL FUNNY IDEA, YOU CUTE LI'L BUGGER.
WHAT?!!
UH, LOOK HERE, OTAKI...
JUST HOLD ON A SEC!!
!!
AIEEE!!
STOP!!!
CHOP
CHOP
B-BELL-DANDY!
YES?

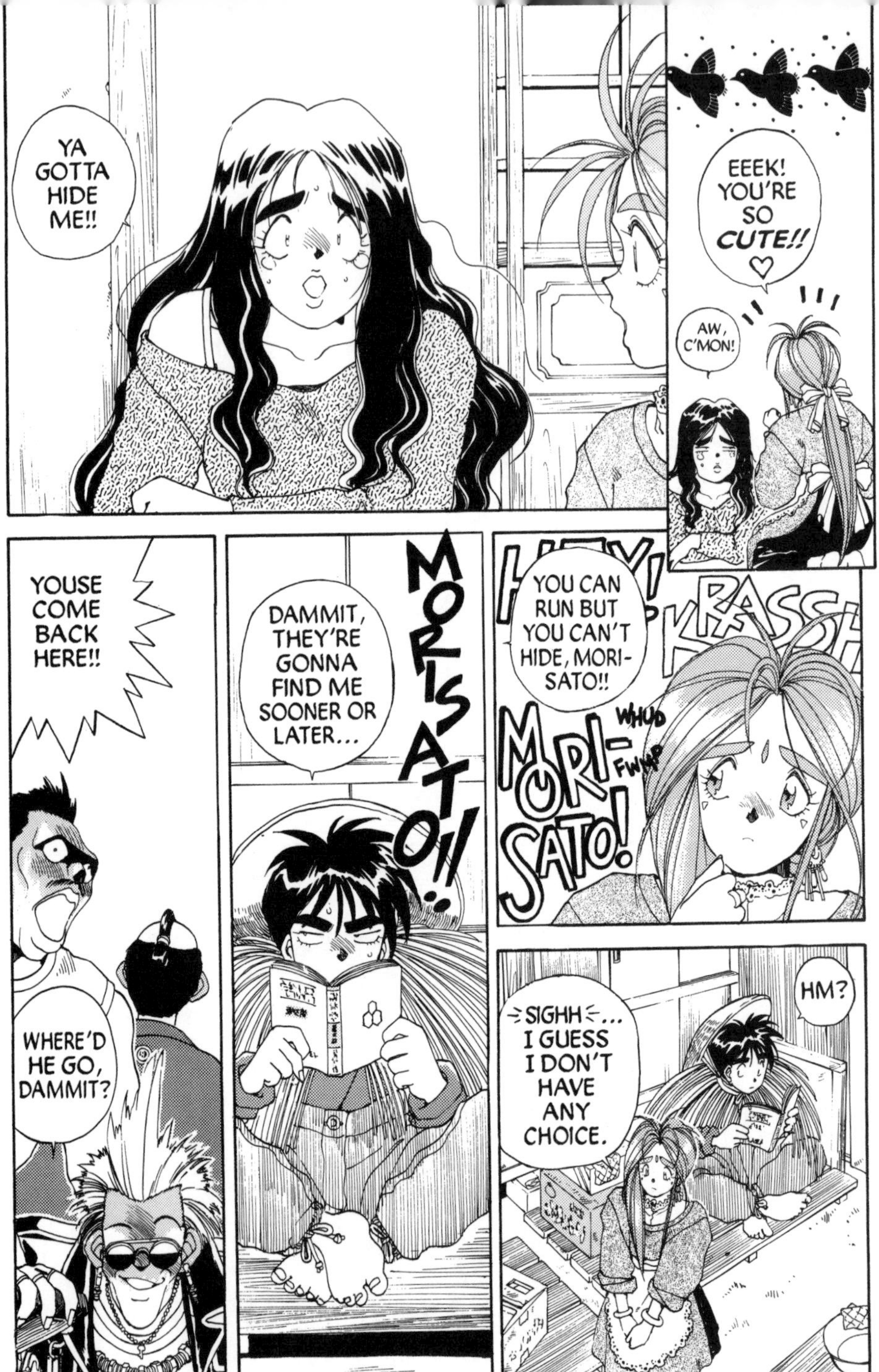
YA GOTTA HIDE ME!!
EEEK! YOU'RE SO CUTE!! ♡
AW, C'MON!
YOUSE COME BACK HERE!!
WHERE'D HE GO, DAMMIT?
MORISATO!!
DAMMIT, THEY'RE GONNA FIND ME SOONER OR LATER...
KRASSH
YOU CAN RUN BUT YOU CAN'T HIDE, MORI-SATO!!
MORI-SATO!
WHUD-FWMP
SIGHH... I GUESS I DON'T HAVE ANY CHOICE.
HM?

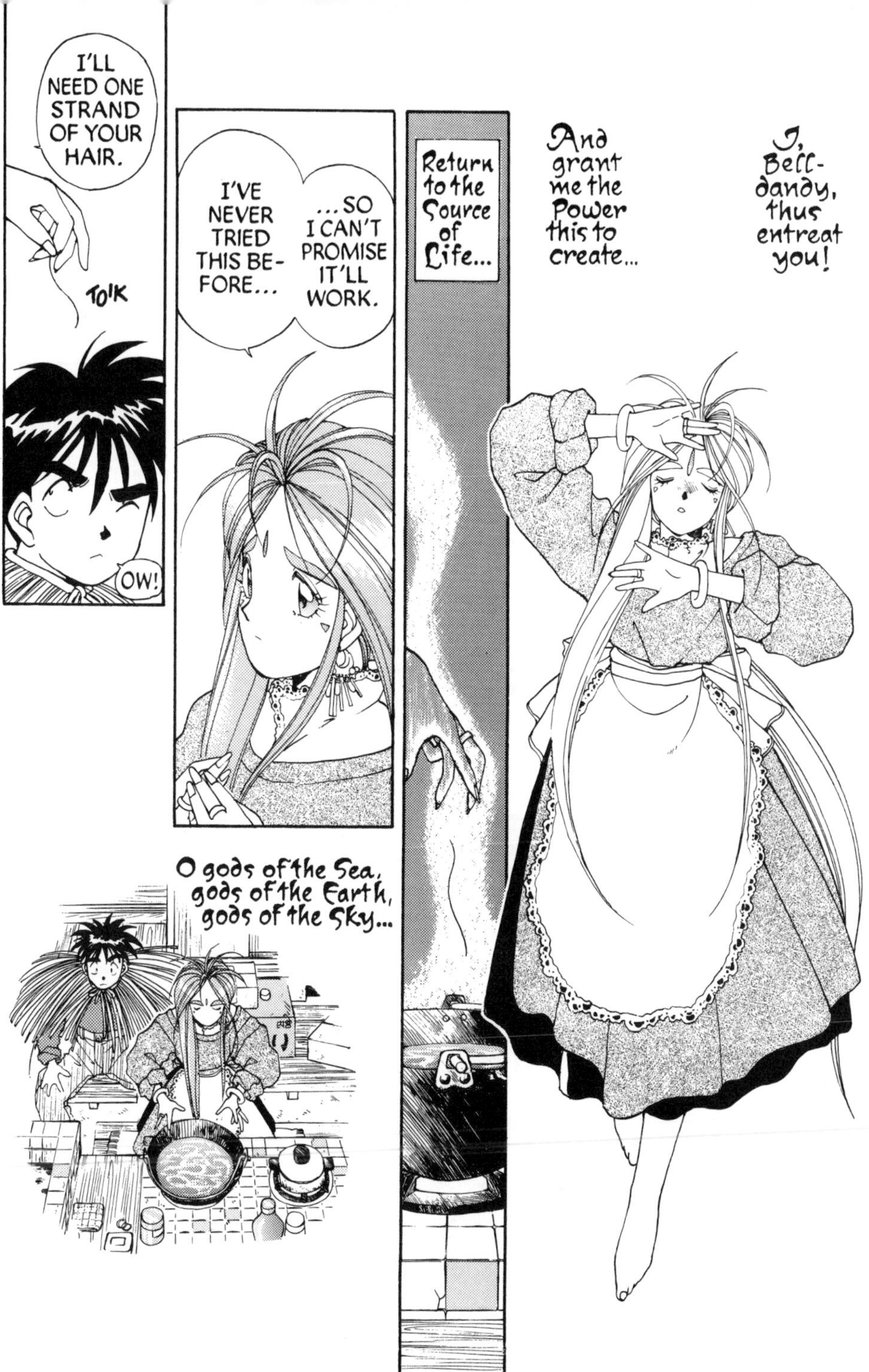
I'LL NEED ONE STRAND OF YOUR HAIR.
TO!K
OW!
I'VE NEVER TRIED THIS BEFORE...
...SO I CAN'T PROMISE IT'LL WORK.
O gods of the Sea, gods of the Earth, gods of the Sky...
Return to the Source of Life...
And grant me the Power this to create...
I, Belldandy, thus entreat you!

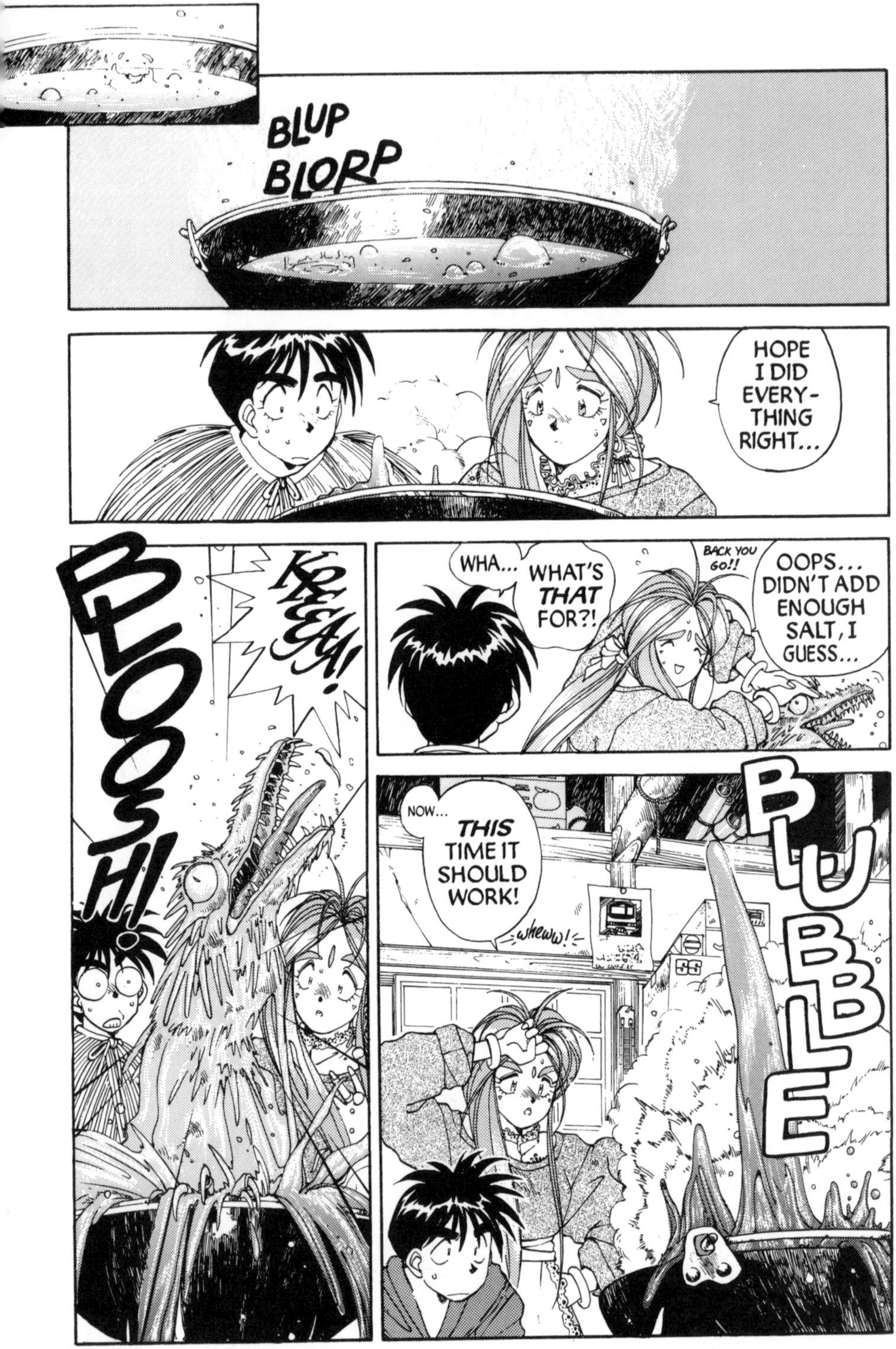
BLUP
BLORP
HOPE I DID EVERY-THING RIGHT...
BLOOSH!
KREEAA!
WHA...
WHAT'S *THAT* FOR?!
BACK YOU GO!!
OOPS... DIDN'T ADD ENOUGH SALT, I GUESS...
NOW...
THIS TIME IT SHOULD WORK!
whewww!
BLUBBLE

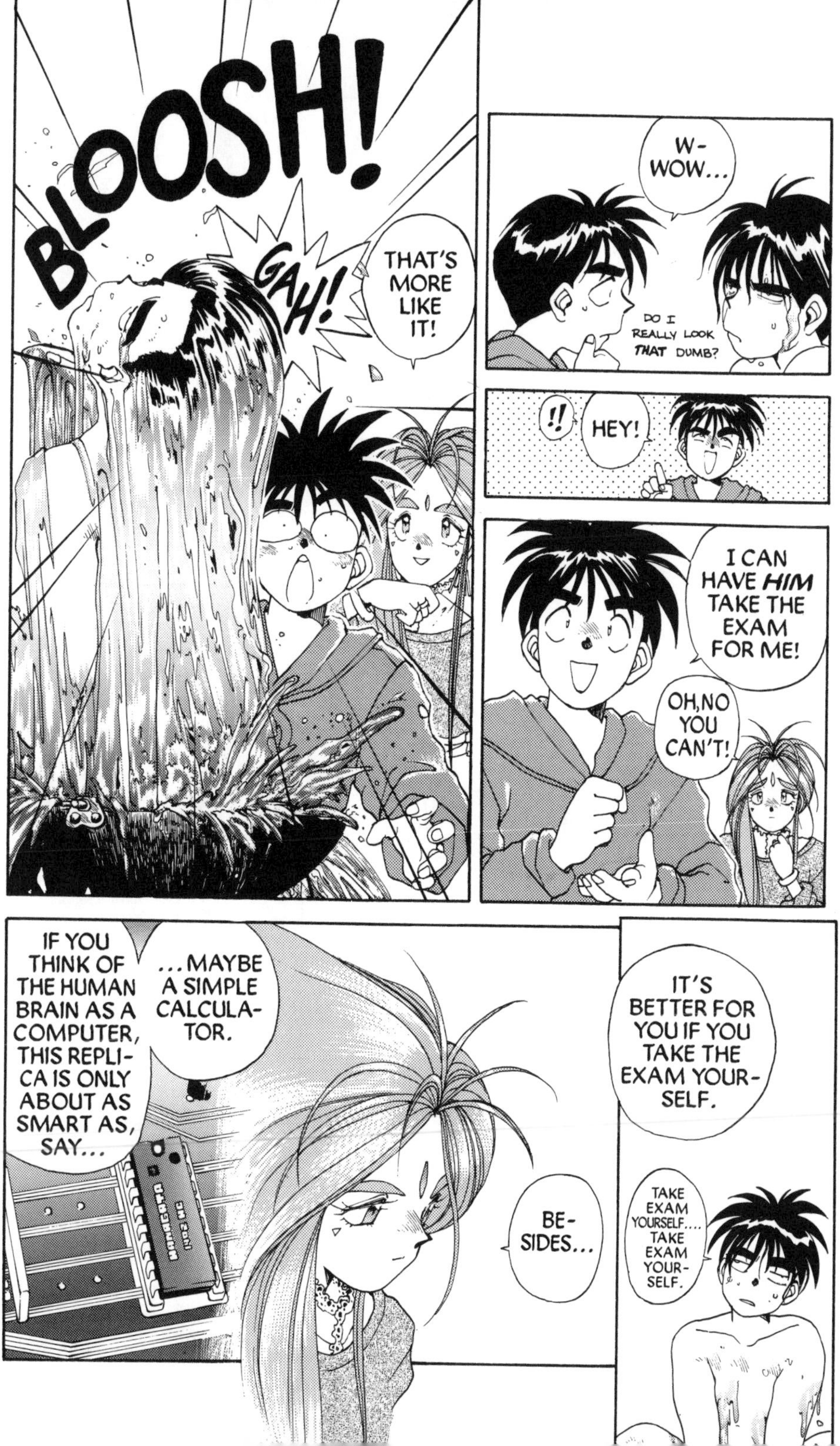
BLOOSH!
GAH!
THAT'S MORE LIKE IT!
W-WOW...
DO I REALLY LOOK THAT DUMB?
!!
HEY!
I CAN HAVE HIM TAKE THE EXAM FOR ME!
OH, NO YOU CAN'T!
IF YOU THINK OF THE HUMAN BRAIN AS A COMPUTER, THIS REPLICA IS ONLY ABOUT AS SMART AS, SAY...
...MAYBE A SIMPLE CALCULATOR.
BE-SIDES...
IT'S BETTER FOR YOU IF YOU TAKE THE EXAM YOUR-SELF.
TAKE EXAM YOURSELF.... TAKE EXAM YOUR-SELF.

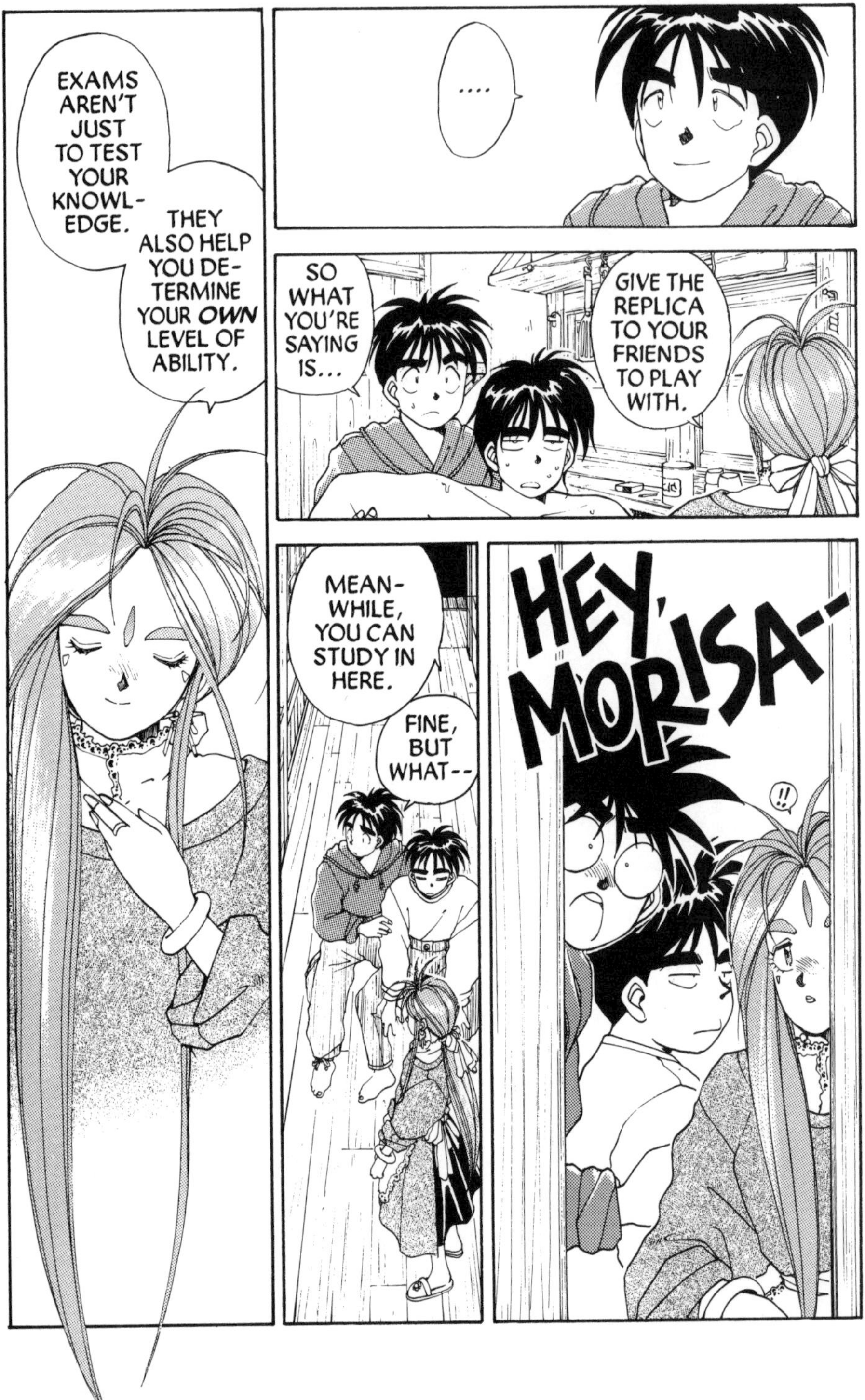
EXAMS AREN'T JUST TO TEST YOUR KNOWL-EDGE.
THEY ALSO HELP YOU DE-TERMINE YOUR *OWN* LEVEL OF ABILITY.
....
SO WHAT YOU'RE SAYING IS...
GIVE THE REPLICA TO YOUR FRIENDS TO PLAY WITH.
MEAN-WHILE, YOU CAN STUDY IN HERE.
FINE, BUT WHAT--
HEY, MORISA--
!!

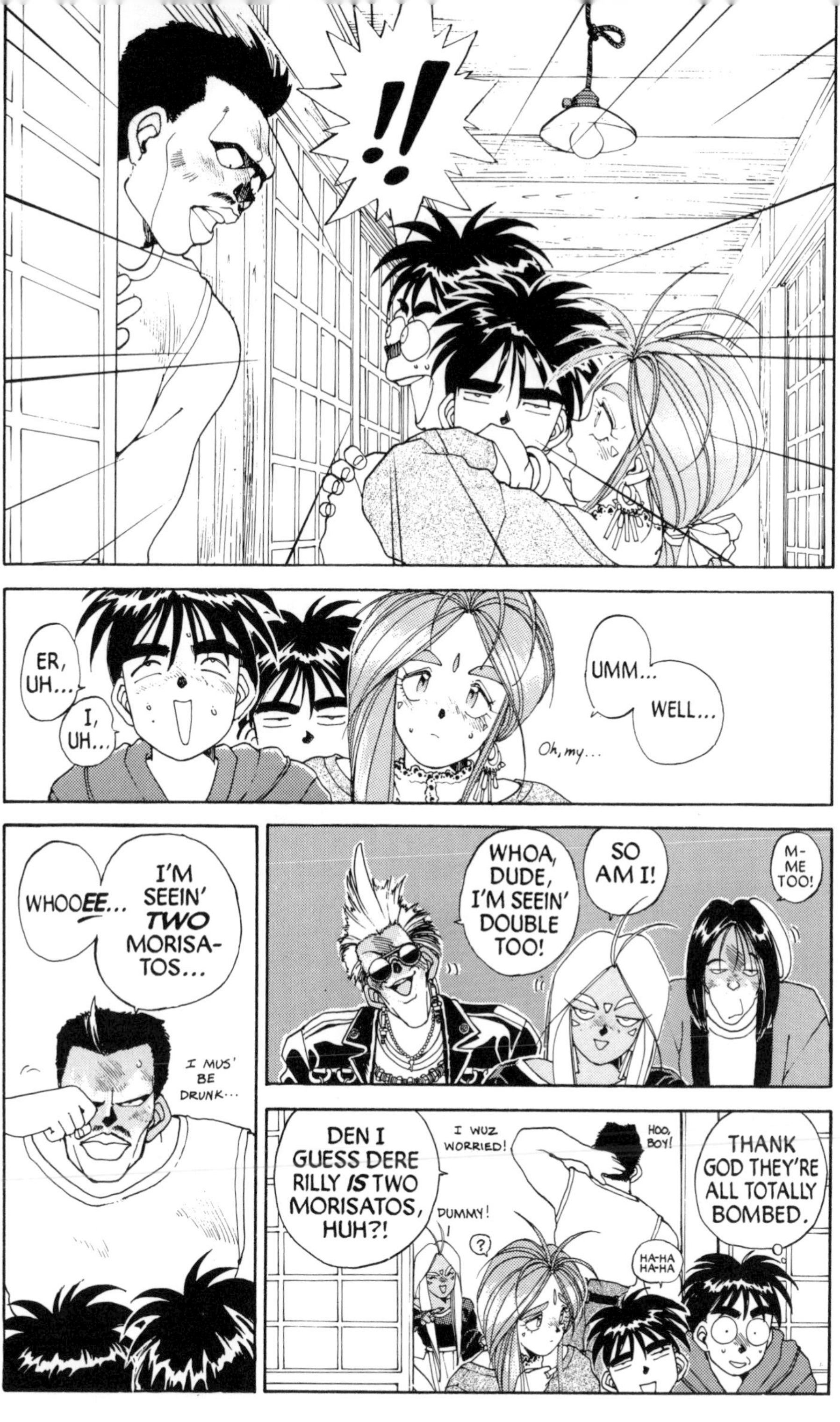
!!
ER, UH...
I, UH...
Oh, my...
UMM... WELL...
WHOOEE... I'M SEEIN' TWO MORISATOS...
I MUS' BE DRUNK...
WHOA, DUDE, I'M SEEIN' DOUBLE TOO!
SO AM I!
M-ME TOO!
DEN I GUESS DERE RILLY IS TWO MORISATOS, HUH?!
I WUZ WORRIED!
DUMMY!
?
HOO, BOY!
HA-HA HA-HA
THANK GOD THEY'RE ALL TOTALLY BOMBED.

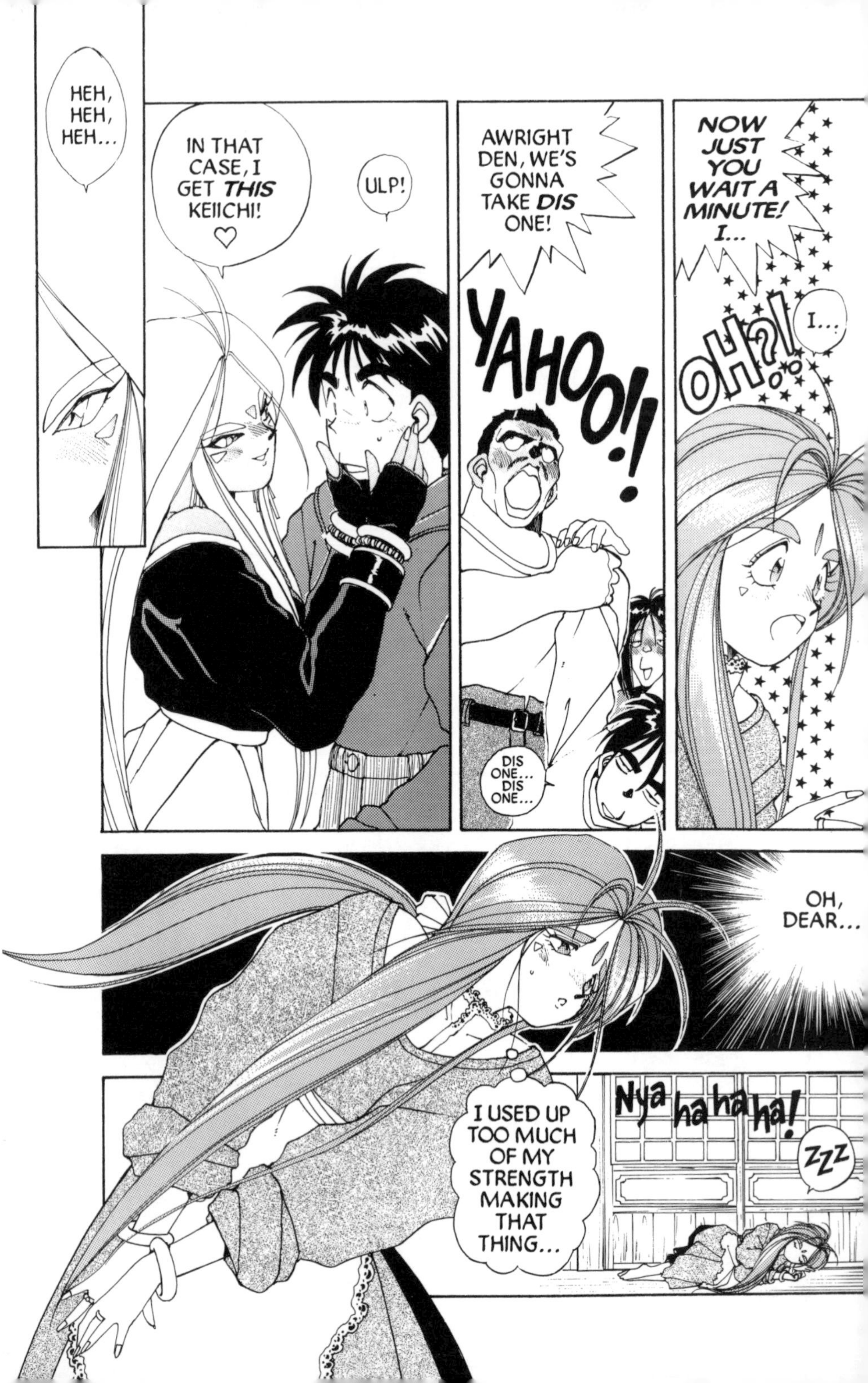
HEH, HEH, HEH...
IN THAT CASE, I GET THIS KEIICHI! ♡
ULP!
AWRIGHT DEN, WE'S GONNA TAKE DIS ONE!
YAHOO!!
DIS ONE... DIS ONE...
NOW JUST YOU WAIT A MINUTE! I...
OH?!
I...
OH, DEAR...
I USED UP TOO MUCH OF MY STRENGTH MAKING THAT THING...
Nya ha ha ha ha!
ZZZ

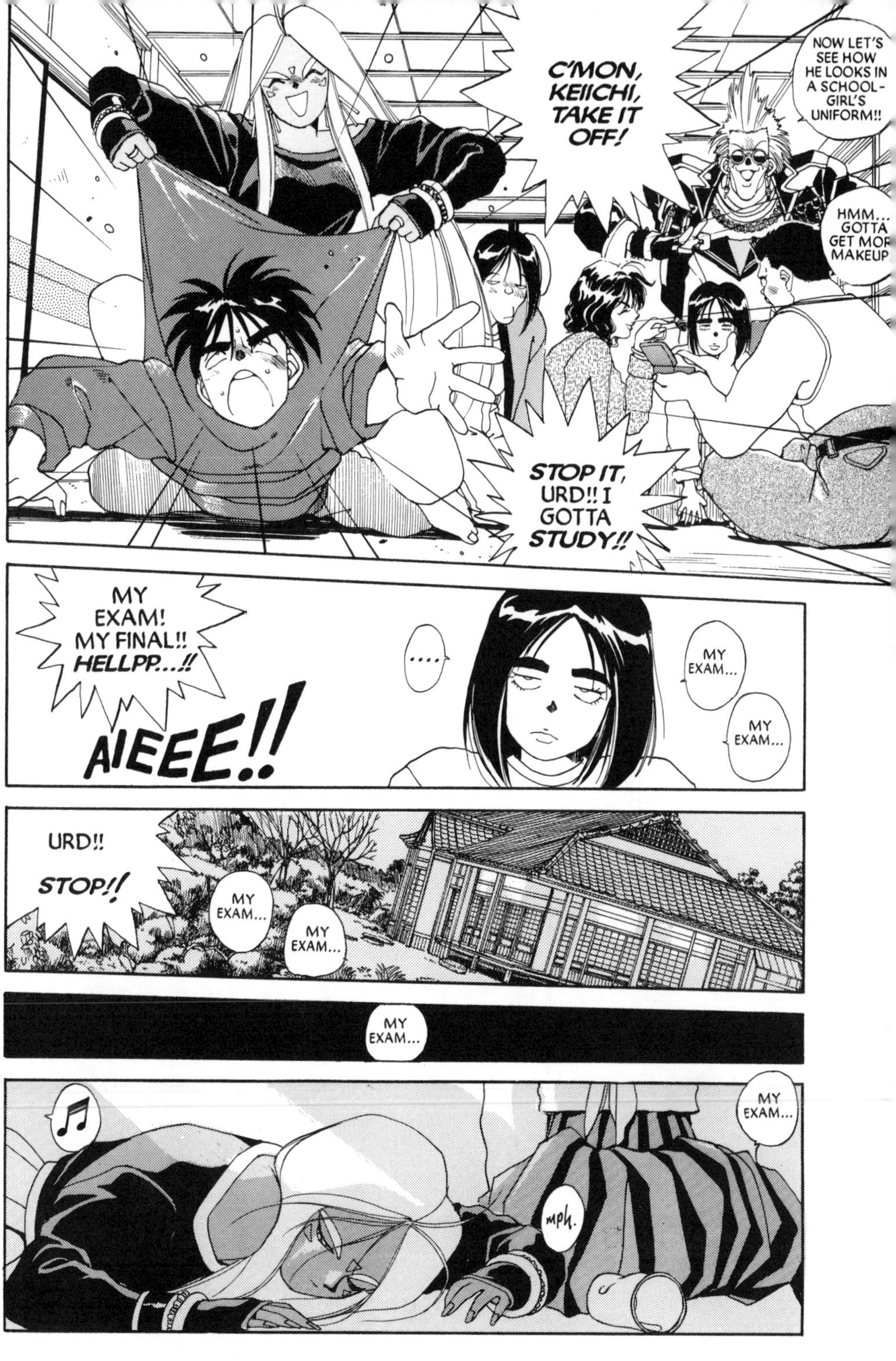
C'MON, KEIICHI, TAKE IT OFF!
NOW LET'S SEE HOW HE LOOKS IN A SCHOOL-GIRL'S UNIFORM!!
HMM... GOTTA GET MOR MAKEUP
STOP IT, URD!! I GOTTA STUDY!!
MY EXAM! MY FINAL!! HELLPP...!!
AIEEE!!
....
MY EXAM...
MY EXAM...
URD!!
STOP!!
MY EXAM...
MY EXAM...
MY EXAM...
MY EXAM...
mph.

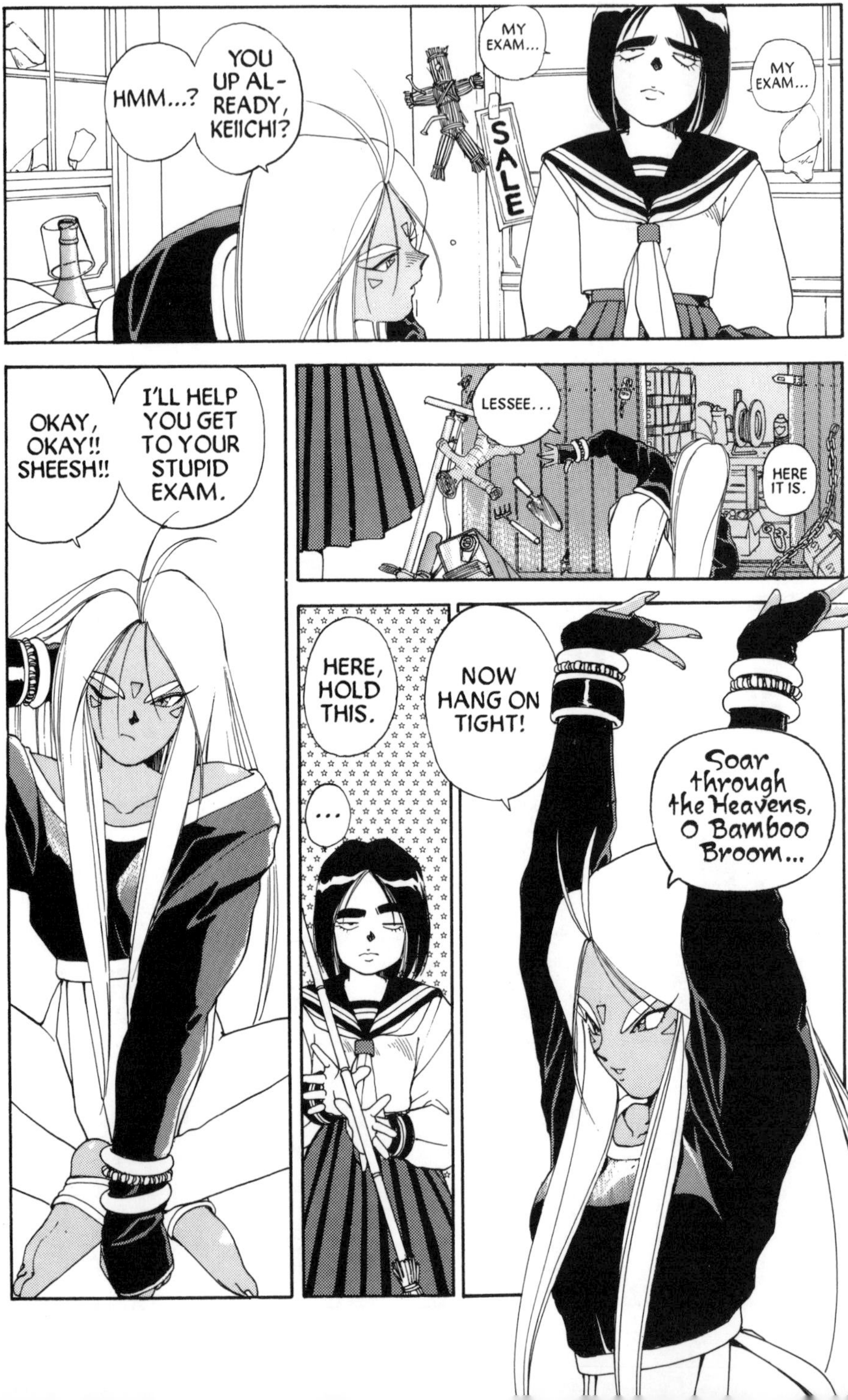
HMM...?
YOU UP AL-READY, KEIICHI?
MY EXAM...
SALE
MY EXAM...
OKAY, OKAY!! SHEESH!!
I'LL HELP YOU GET TO YOUR STUPID EXAM.
LESSEE...
HERE IT IS.
HERE, HOLD THIS.
...
NOW HANG ON TIGHT!
Soar through the Heavens, O Bamboo Broom...

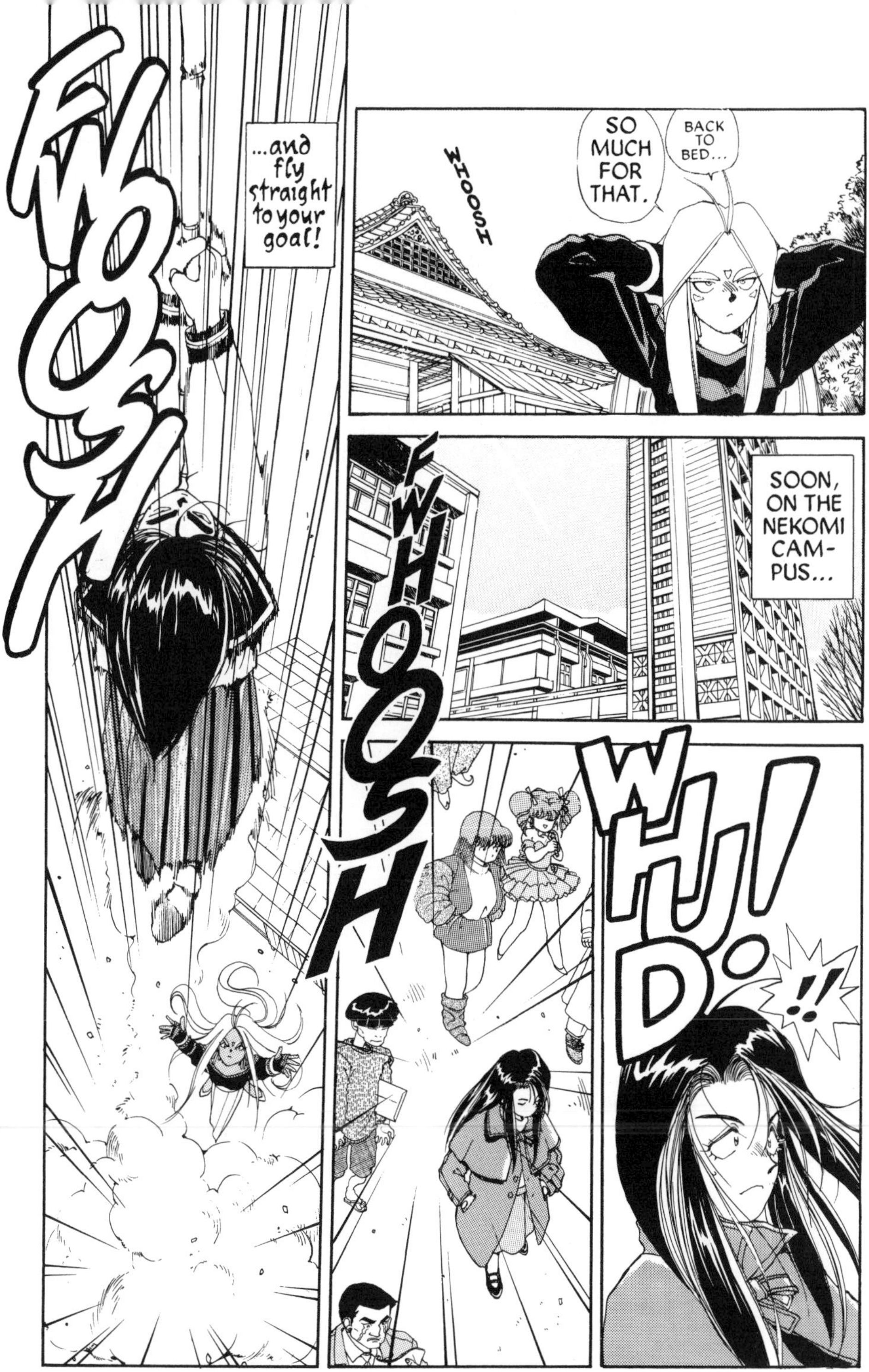
FWOOSH
...and fly straight to your goal!
WHOOSH
SO MUCH FOR THAT.
BACK TO BED...
FWHOOSH
SOON, ON THE NEKOMI CAMPUS...
WHUD!
!!

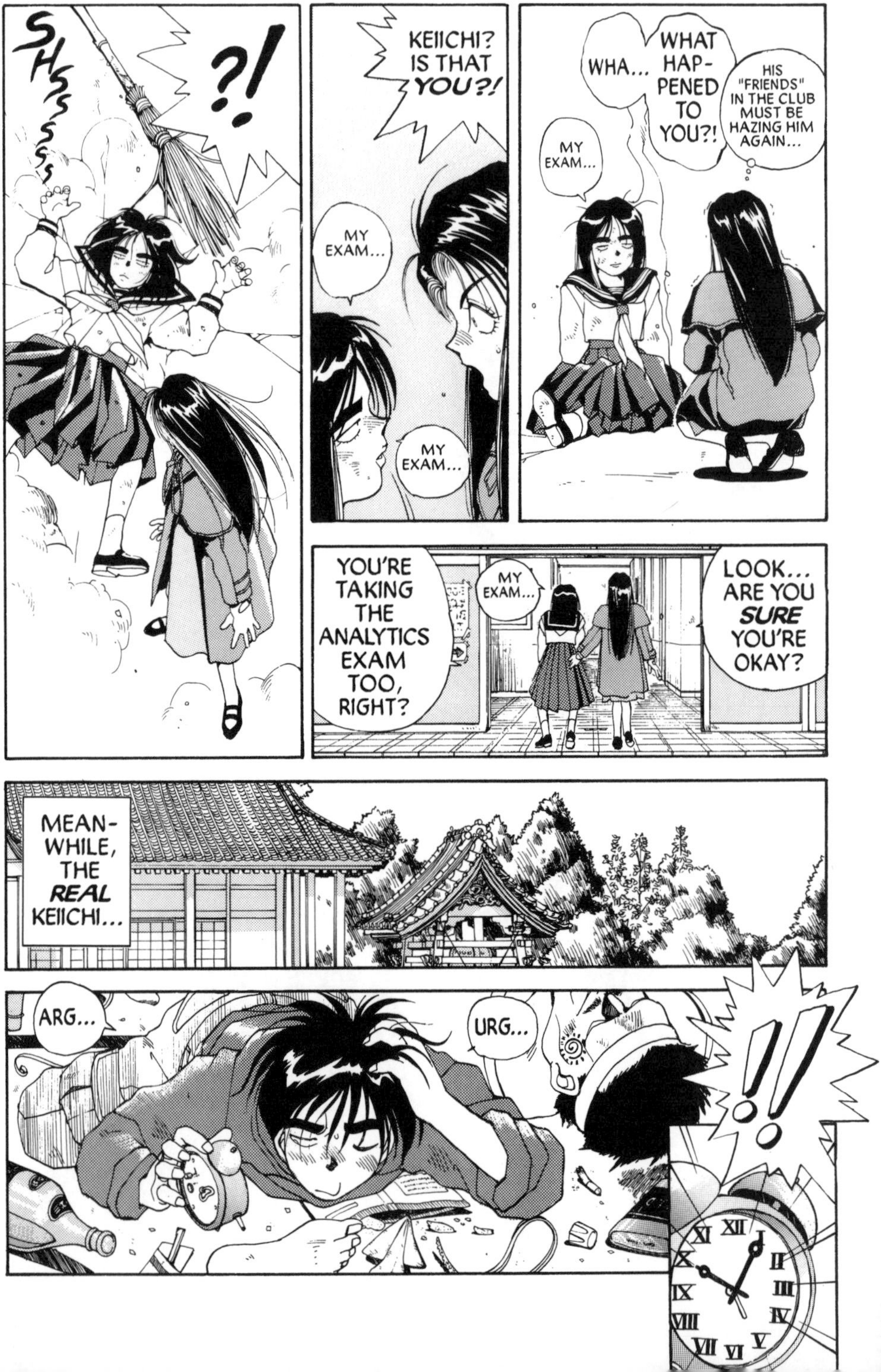
SHSSSSSSS
?!
KEIICHI? IS THAT YOU?!
MY EXAM...
MY EXAM...
WHA...
WHAT HAPPENED TO YOU?!
HIS "FRIENDS" IN THE CLUB MUST BE HAZING HIM AGAIN...
MY EXAM...
YOU'RE TAKING THE ANALYTICS EXAM TOO, RIGHT?
MY EXAM...
LOOK... ARE YOU SURE YOU'RE OKAY?
MEANWHILE, THE REAL KEIICHI...
ARG...
URG...
!!

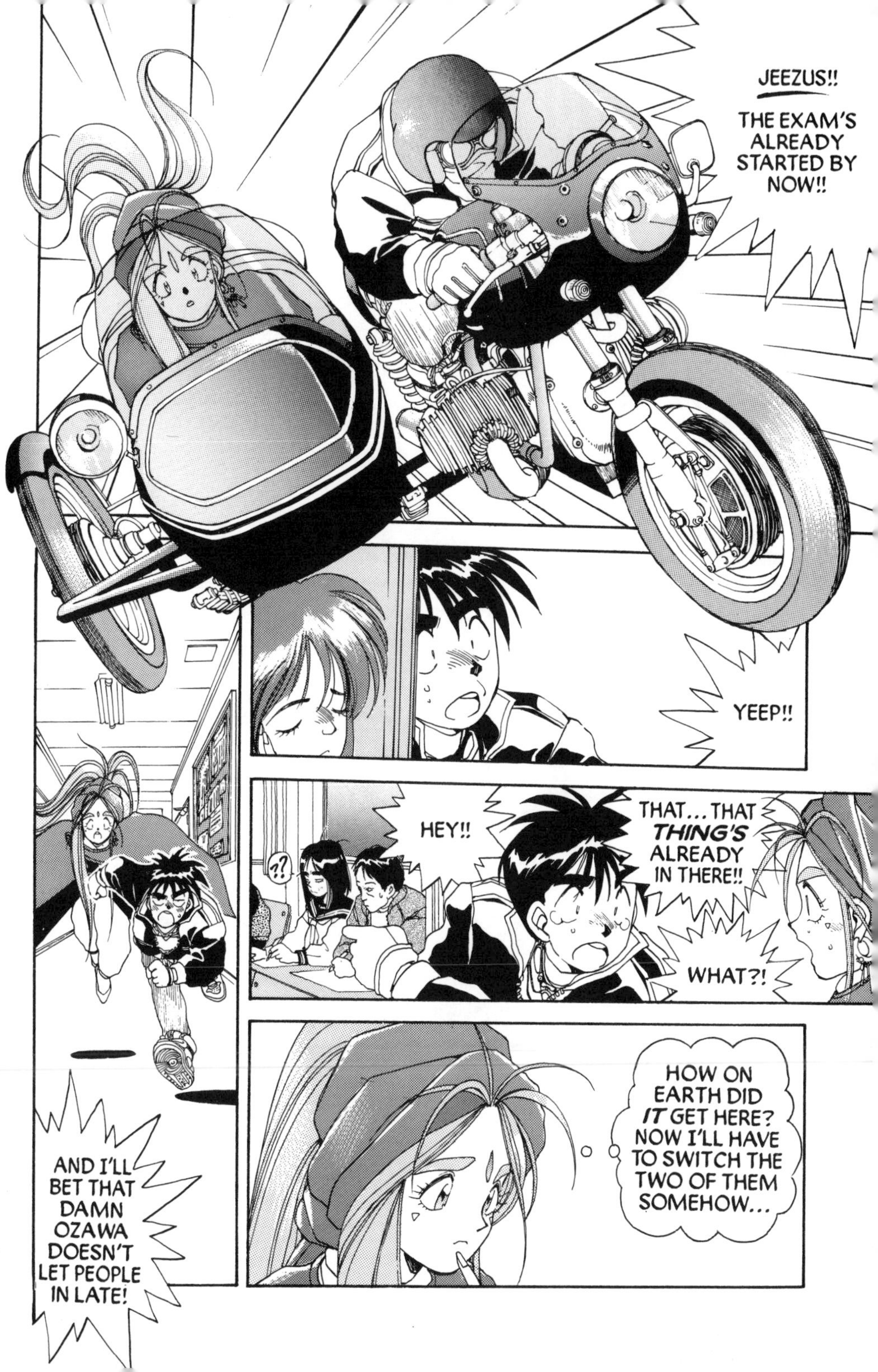
JEEZUS!!
THE EXAM'S ALREADY STARTED BY NOW!!
AND I'LL BET THAT DAMN OZAWA DOESN'T LET PEOPLE IN LATE!
YEEP!!
HEY!!
?!
THAT... THAT *THING'S* ALREADY IN THERE!!
WHAT?!
HOW ON EARTH DID *IT* GET HERE? NOW I'LL HAVE TO SWITCH THE TWO OF THEM SOMEHOW...

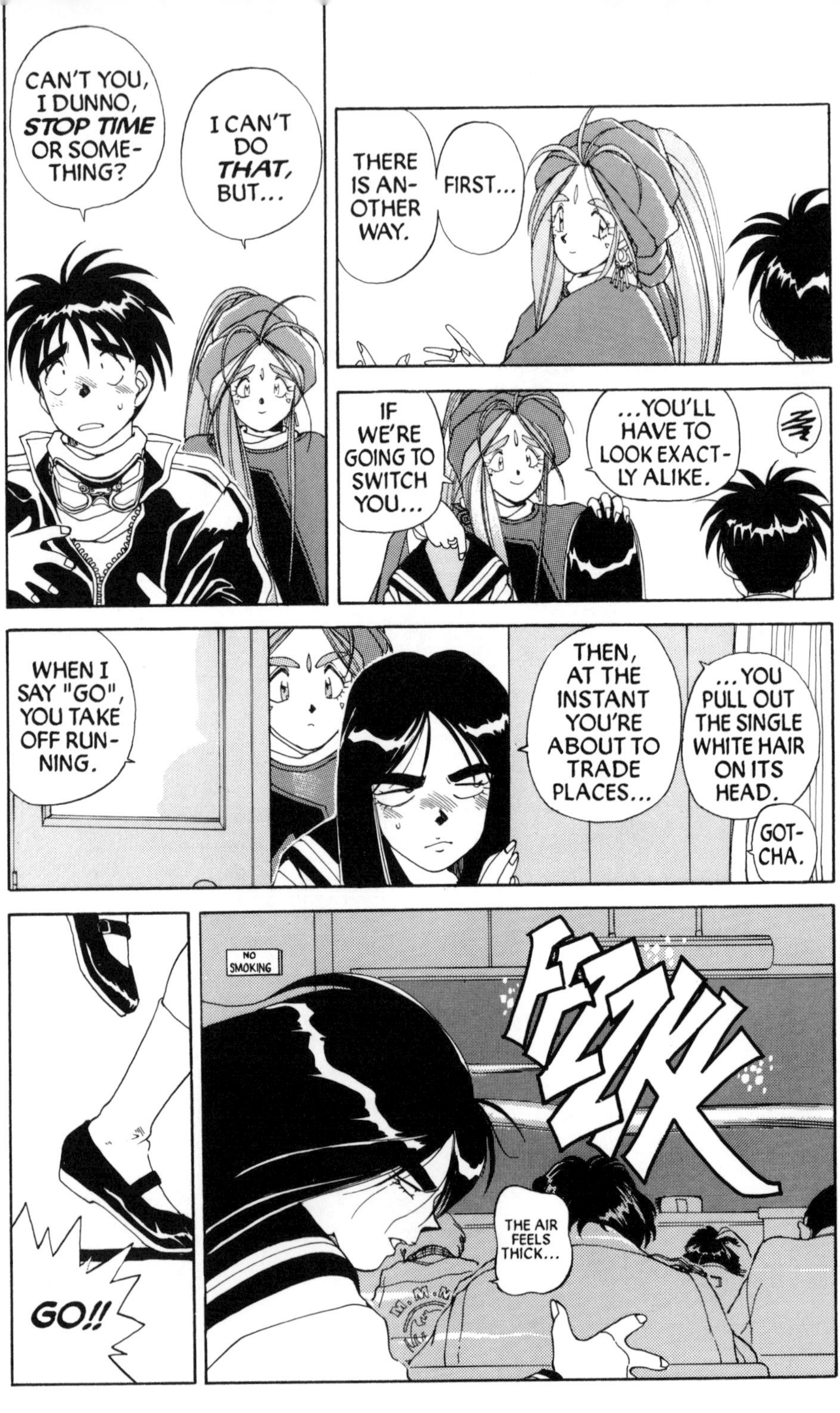
CAN'T YOU, I DUNNO, ***STOP TIME*** OR SOME-THING?
I CAN'T DO ***THAT,*** BUT...
THERE IS AN-OTHER WAY.
FIRST...
IF WE'RE GOING TO SWITCH YOU...
...YOU'LL HAVE TO LOOK EXACT-LY ALIKE.
WHEN I SAY "GO", YOU TAKE OFF RUN-NING.
THEN, AT THE INSTANT YOU'RE ABOUT TO TRADE PLACES...
...YOU PULL OUT THE SINGLE WHITE HAIR ON ITS HEAD.
GOT-CHA.
GO!!
NO SMOKING
FZZK
THE AIR FEELS THICK...

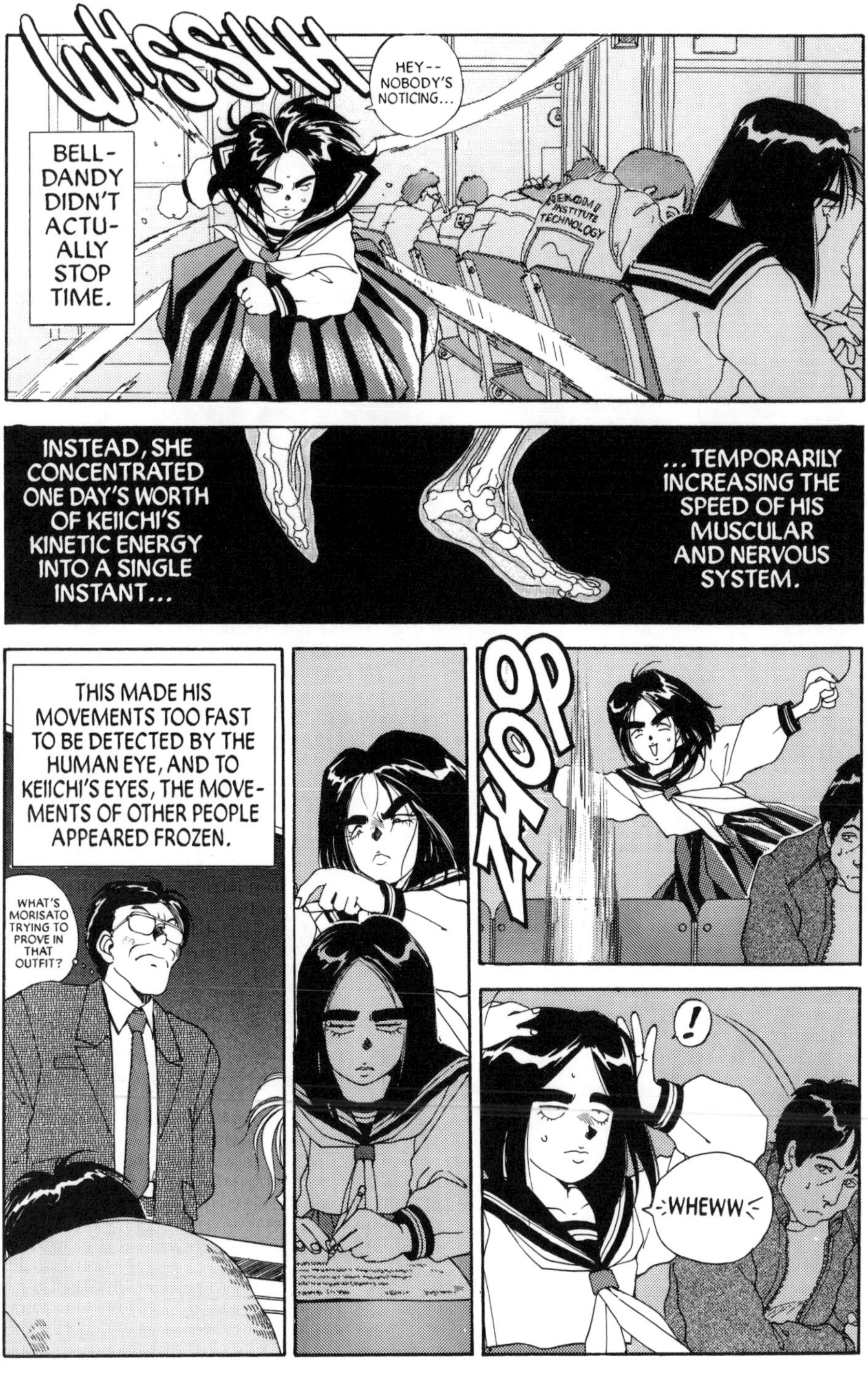
WHSSH
BELL-DANDY DIDN'T ACTU-ALLY STOP TIME.
HEY-- NOBODY'S NOTICING...
INSTEAD, SHE CONCENTRATED ONE DAY'S WORTH OF KEIICHI'S KINETIC ENERGY INTO A SINGLE INSTANT...
...TEMPORARILY INCREASING THE SPEED OF HIS MUSCULAR AND NERVOUS SYSTEM.
THIS MADE HIS MOVEMENTS TOO FAST TO BE DETECTED BY THE HUMAN EYE, AND TO KEIICHI'S EYES, THE MOVE-MENTS OF OTHER PEOPLE APPEARED FROZEN.
WHAT'S MORISATO TRYING TO PROVE IN THAT OUTFIT?
ZHOOP
!
WHEWW

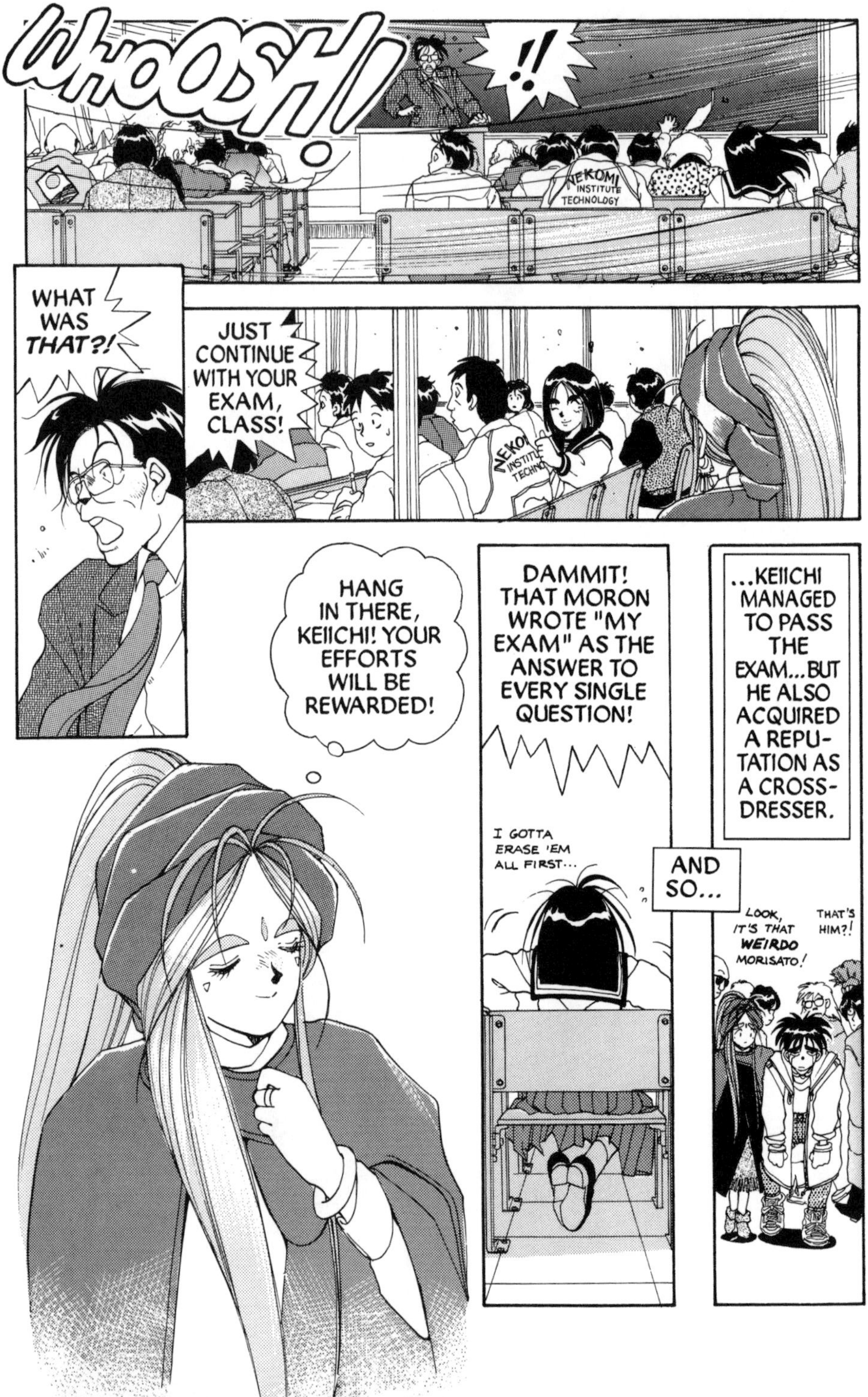
WHOOSH!
!!
WHAT WAS THAT?!
JUST CONTINUE WITH YOUR EXAM, CLASS!
NEKOMI INSTITUTE TECHNOLOGY
HANG IN THERE, KEIICHI! YOUR EFFORTS WILL BE REWARDED!
DAMMIT! THAT MORON WROTE "MY EXAM" AS THE ANSWER TO EVERY SINGLE QUESTION!
I GOTTA ERASE 'EM ALL FIRST...
AND SO...
...KEIICHI MANAGED TO PASS THE EXAM...BUT HE ALSO ACQUIRED A REPUTATION AS A CROSS-DRESSER.
LOOK, IT'S THAT WEIRDO MORISATO!
THAT'S HIM?!

BELLDANDY'S
NARROW ESCAPE

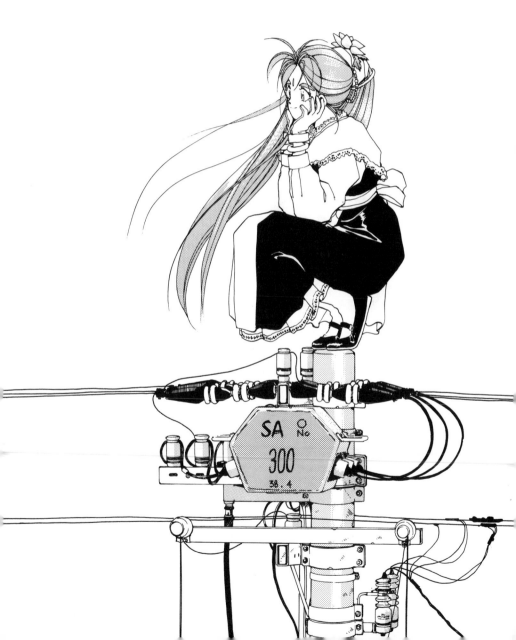

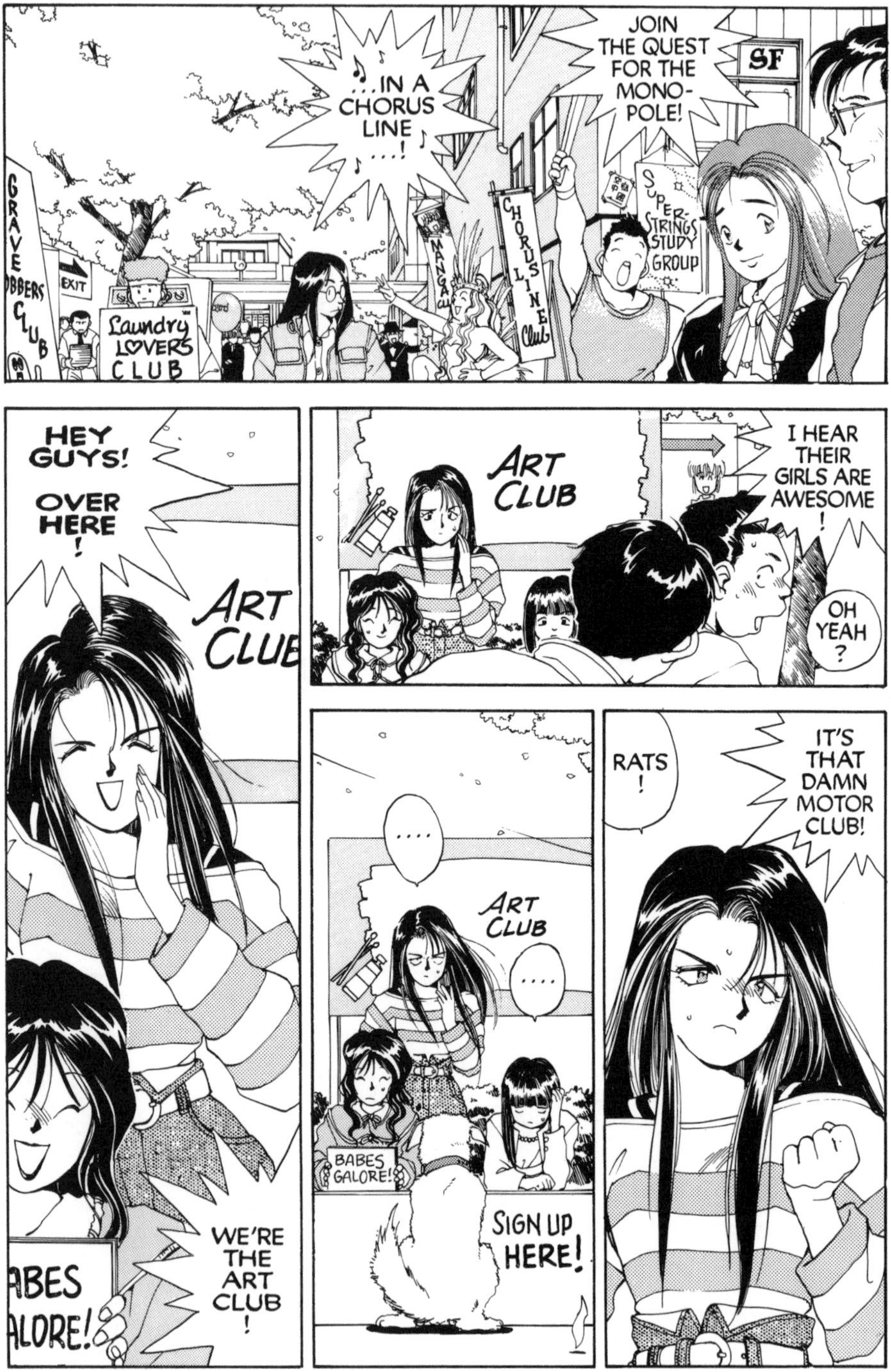
♪ ...IN A CHORUS LINE ....! ♪
JOIN THE QUEST FOR THE MONO-POLE!
SF
GRAVE OBBERS CLUB
EXIT
Laundry LOVERS CLUB
MANGA club
CHORUS LINE Club
SUPER-STRINGS STUDY GROUP
HEY GUYS! OVER HERE!
ART CLUB
WE'RE THE ART CLUB!
ABES ALORE!
ART CLUB
I HEAR THEIR GIRLS ARE AWESOME!
OH YEAH?
....
ART CLUB
....
BABES GALORE!
SIGN UP HERE!
RATS!
IT'S THAT DAMN MOTOR CLUB!

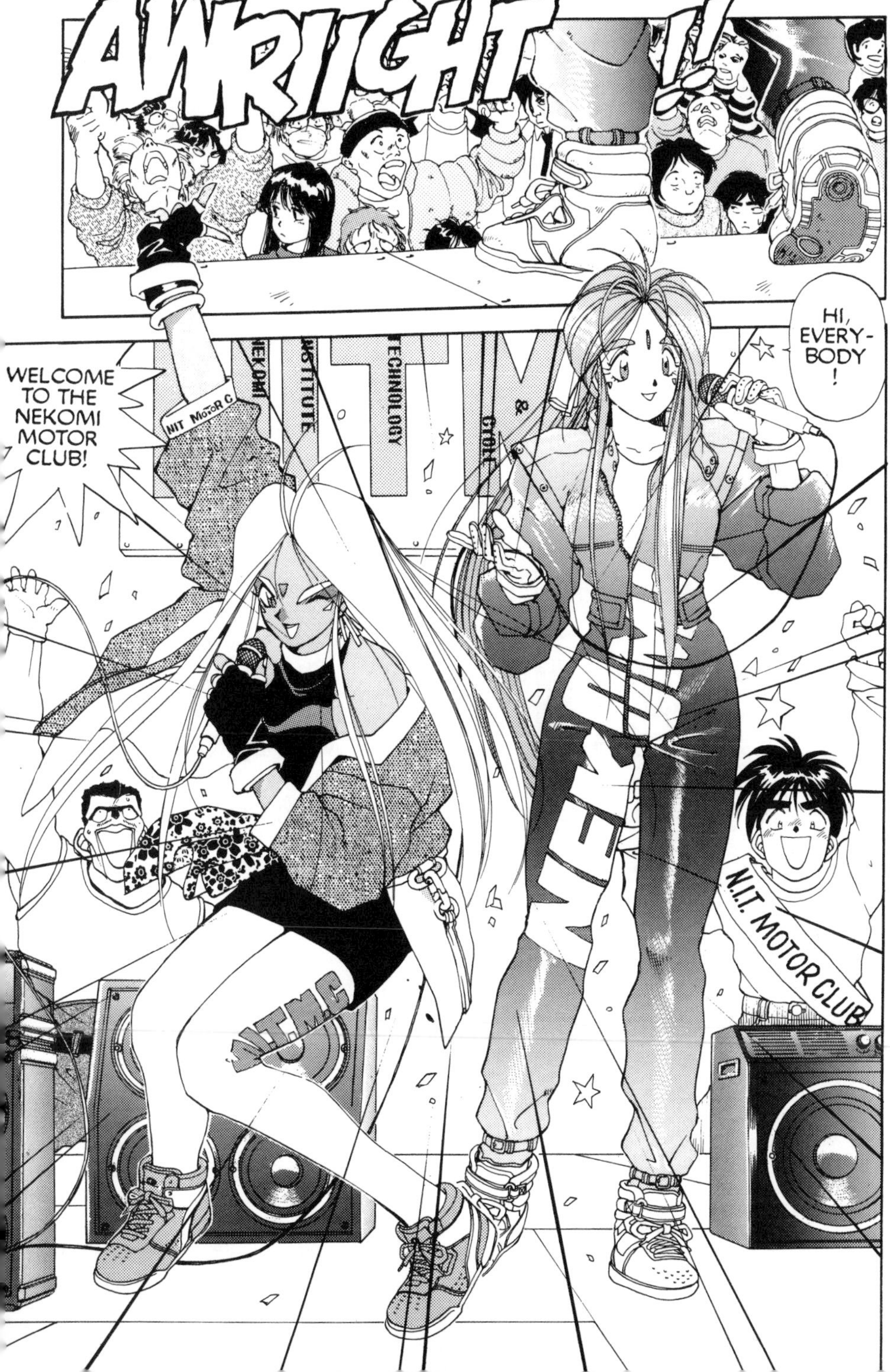
AWRIIGHT !!
WELCOME TO THE NEKOMI MOTOR CLUB!
HI, EVERY-BODY !
NEKOMI
INSTITUTE
TECHNOLOGY
CYCLE
NIT MOTOR C
N.I.T. MOTOR CLUB
N.I.T.M.C
NEK

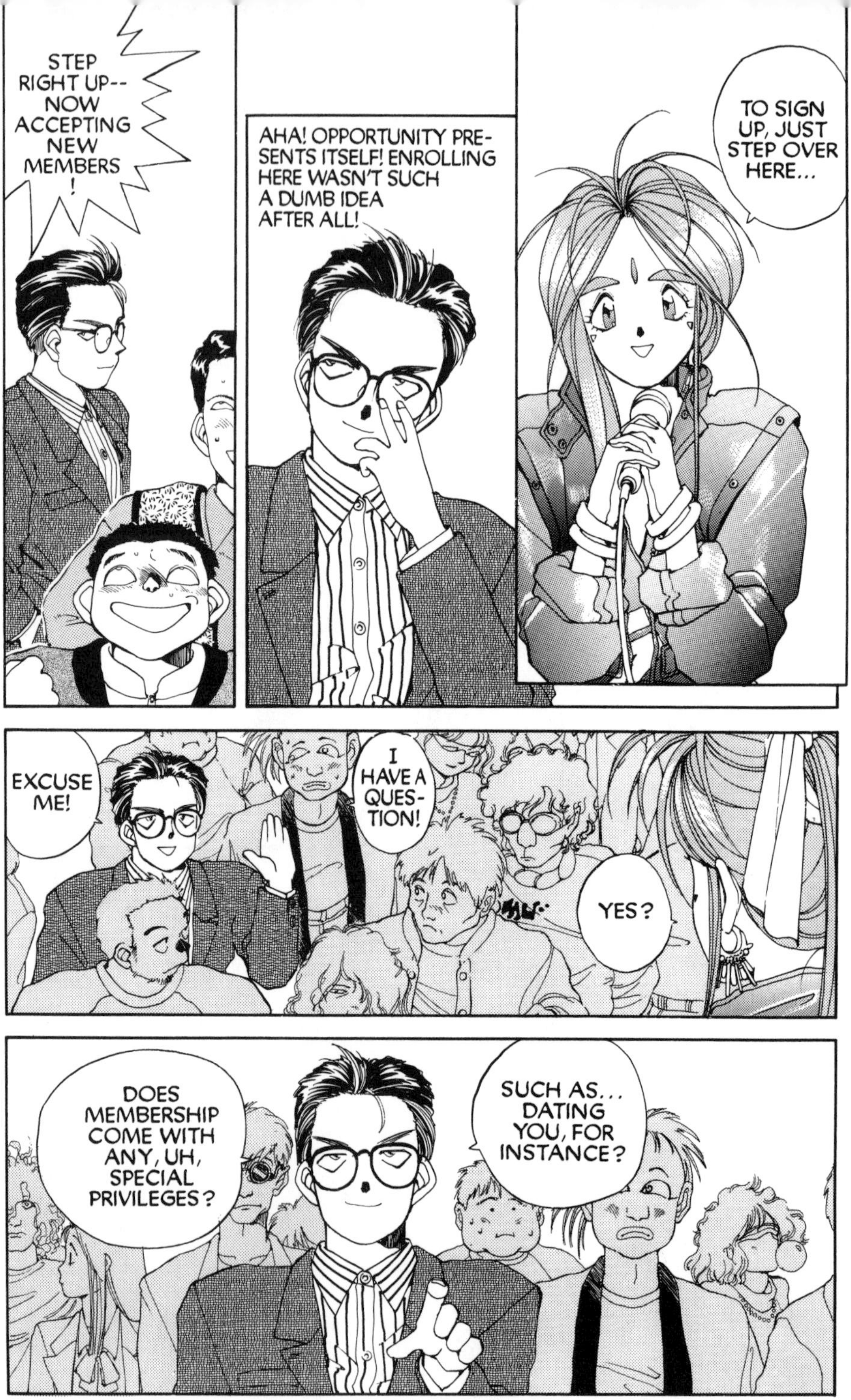
STEP RIGHT UP-- NOW ACCEPTING NEW MEMBERS !
AHA! OPPORTUNITY PRESENTS ITSELF! ENROLLING HERE WASN'T SUCH A DUMB IDEA AFTER ALL!
TO SIGN UP, JUST STEP OVER HERE...
EXCUSE ME!
I HAVE A QUESTION!
YES?
DOES MEMBERSHIP COME WITH ANY, UH, SPECIAL PRIVILEGES?
SUCH AS... DATING YOU, FOR INSTANCE?

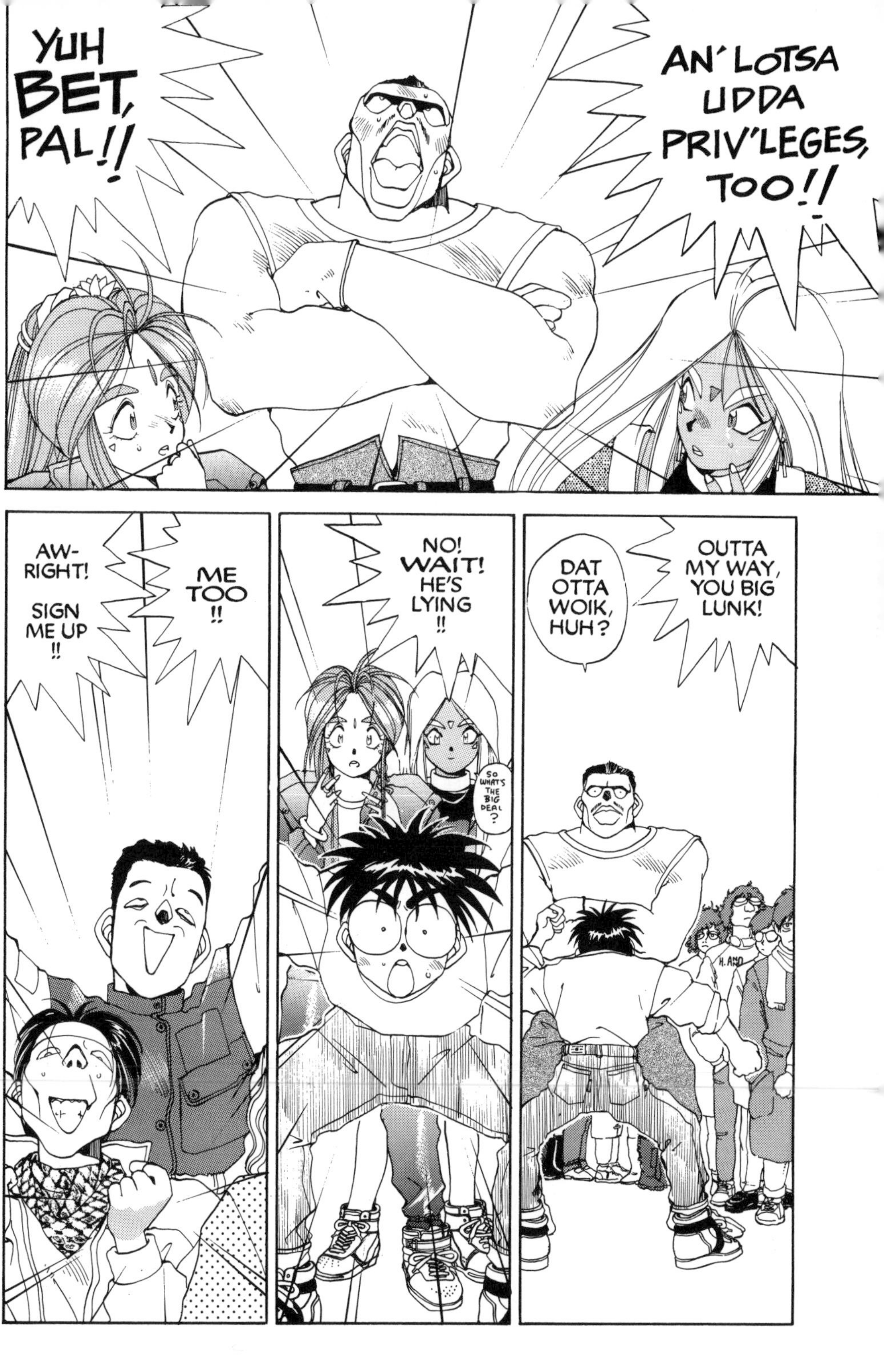
YUH BET, PAL!!
AN' LOTSA UDDA PRIV'LEGES, TOO!!
AW-RIGHT! SIGN ME UP!!
ME TOO!!
NO! WAIT! HE'S LYING!!
SO WHAT'S THE BIG DEAL?
DAT OTTA WOIK, HUH?
OUTTA MY WAY, YOU BIG LUNK!

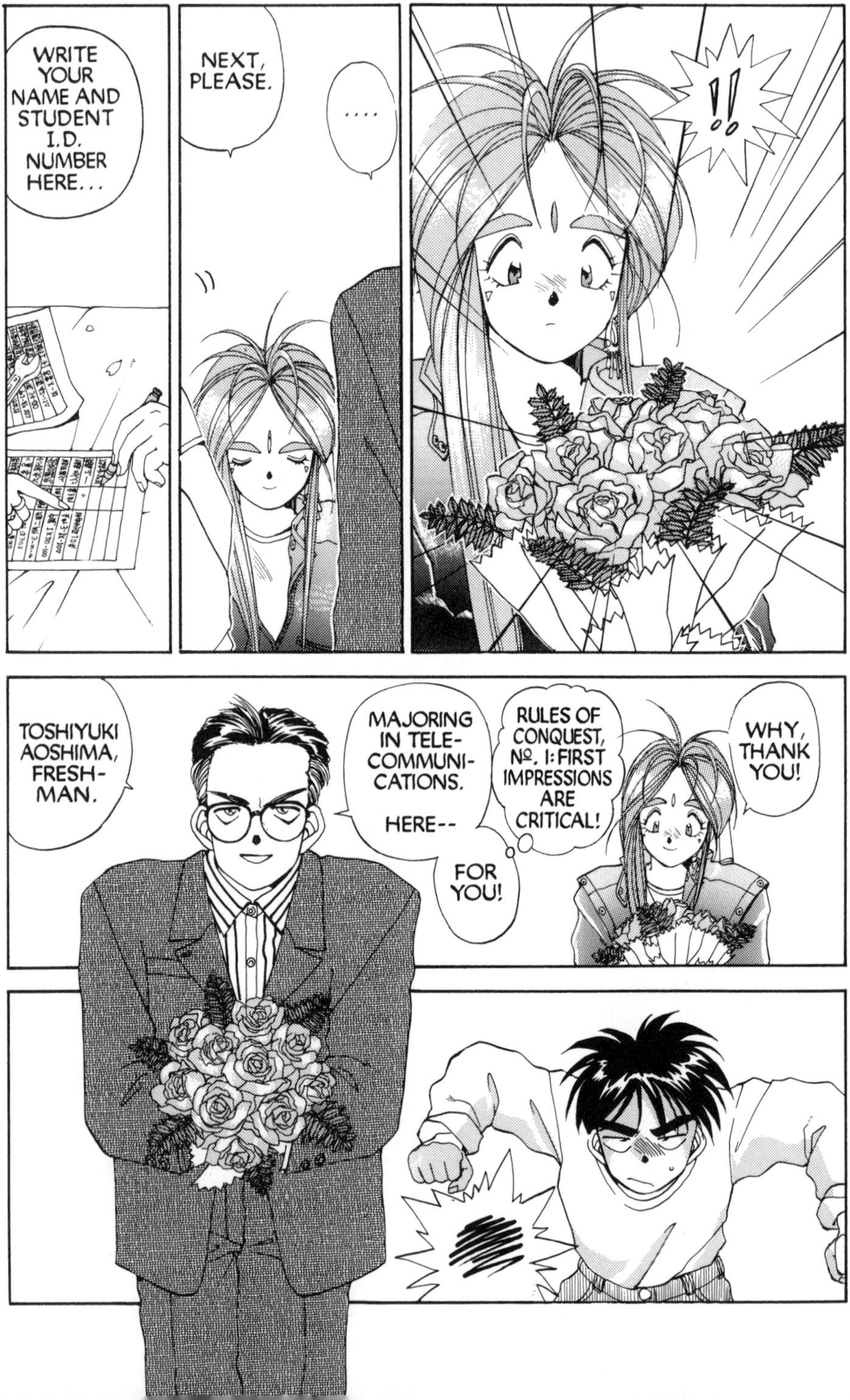
WRITE YOUR NAME AND STUDENT I.D. NUMBER HERE...
NEXT, PLEASE.
....
!!
TOSHIYUKI AOSHIMA, FRESH-MAN.
MAJORING IN TELE-COMMUNI-CATIONS.
HERE--
FOR YOU!
RULES OF CONQUEST, №. 1: FIRST IMPRESSIONS ARE CRITICAL!
WHY, THANK YOU!

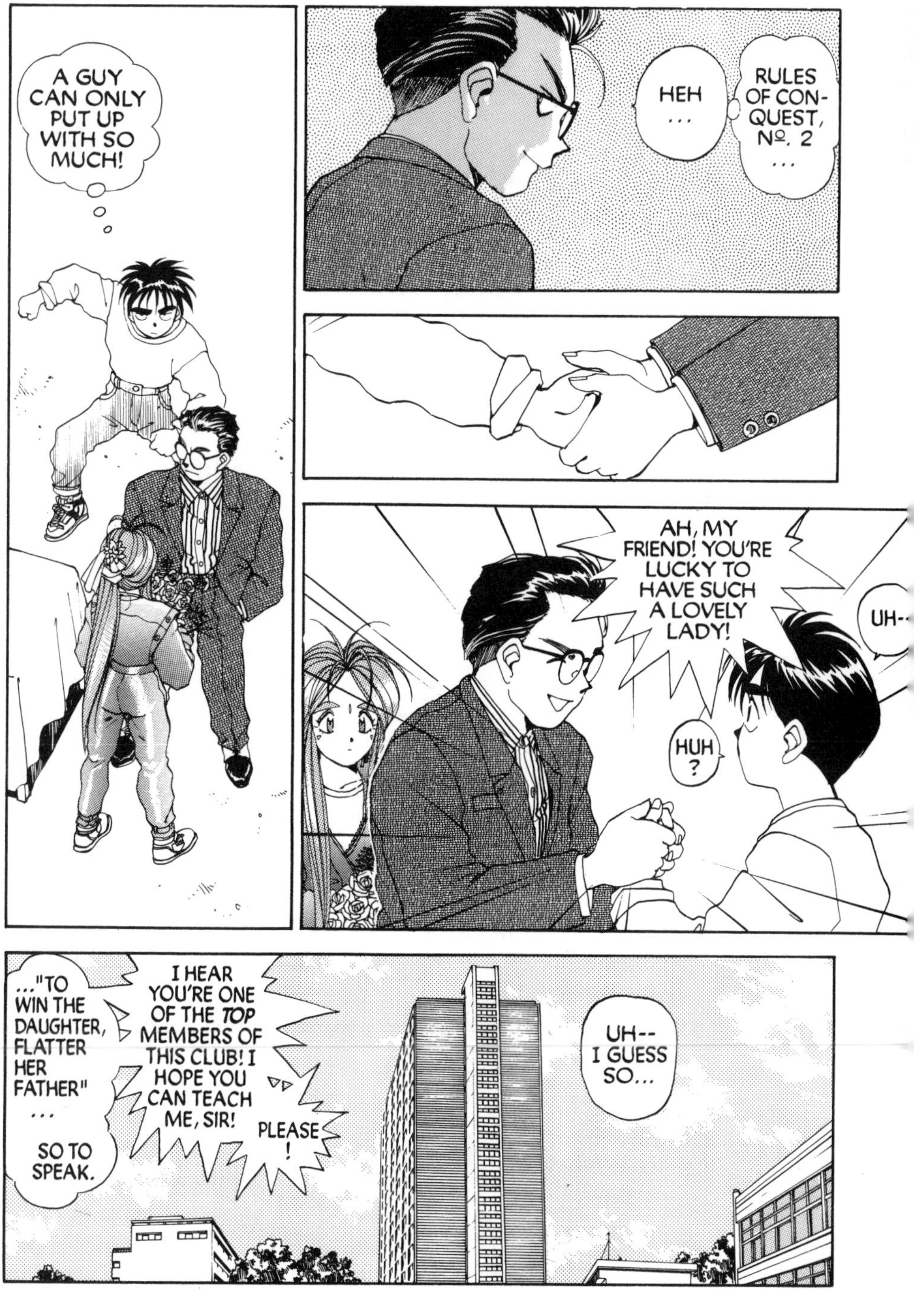
A GUY CAN ONLY PUT UP WITH SO MUCH!
HEH . . .
RULES OF CON- QUEST, Nº. 2 . . .
AH, MY FRIEND! YOU'RE LUCKY TO HAVE SUCH A LOVELY LADY!
UH--
HUH ?
..."TO WIN THE DAUGHTER, FLATTER HER FATHER" . . .
SO TO SPEAK.
I HEAR YOU'RE ONE OF THE *TOP* MEMBERS OF THIS CLUB! I HOPE YOU CAN TEACH ME, SIR!
PLEASE !
UH-- I GUESS SO...

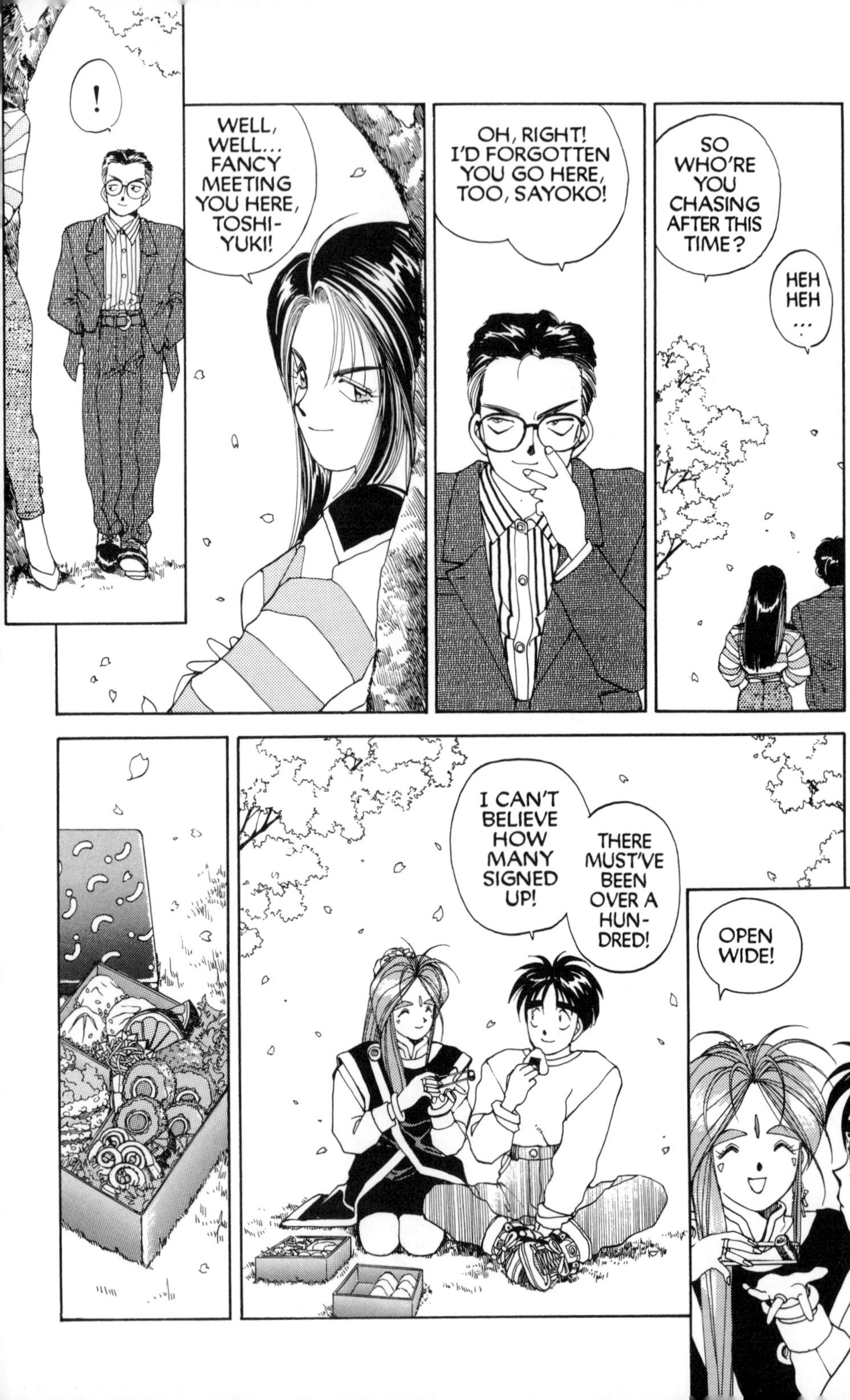
!
WELL, WELL... FANCY MEETING YOU HERE, TOSHI-YUKI!
OH, RIGHT! I'D FORGOTTEN YOU GO HERE, TOO, SAYOKO!
SO WHO'RE YOU CHASING AFTER THIS TIME?
HEH HEH ...
I CAN'T BELIEVE HOW MANY SIGNED UP!
THERE MUST'VE BEEN OVER A HUN-DRED!
OPEN WIDE!

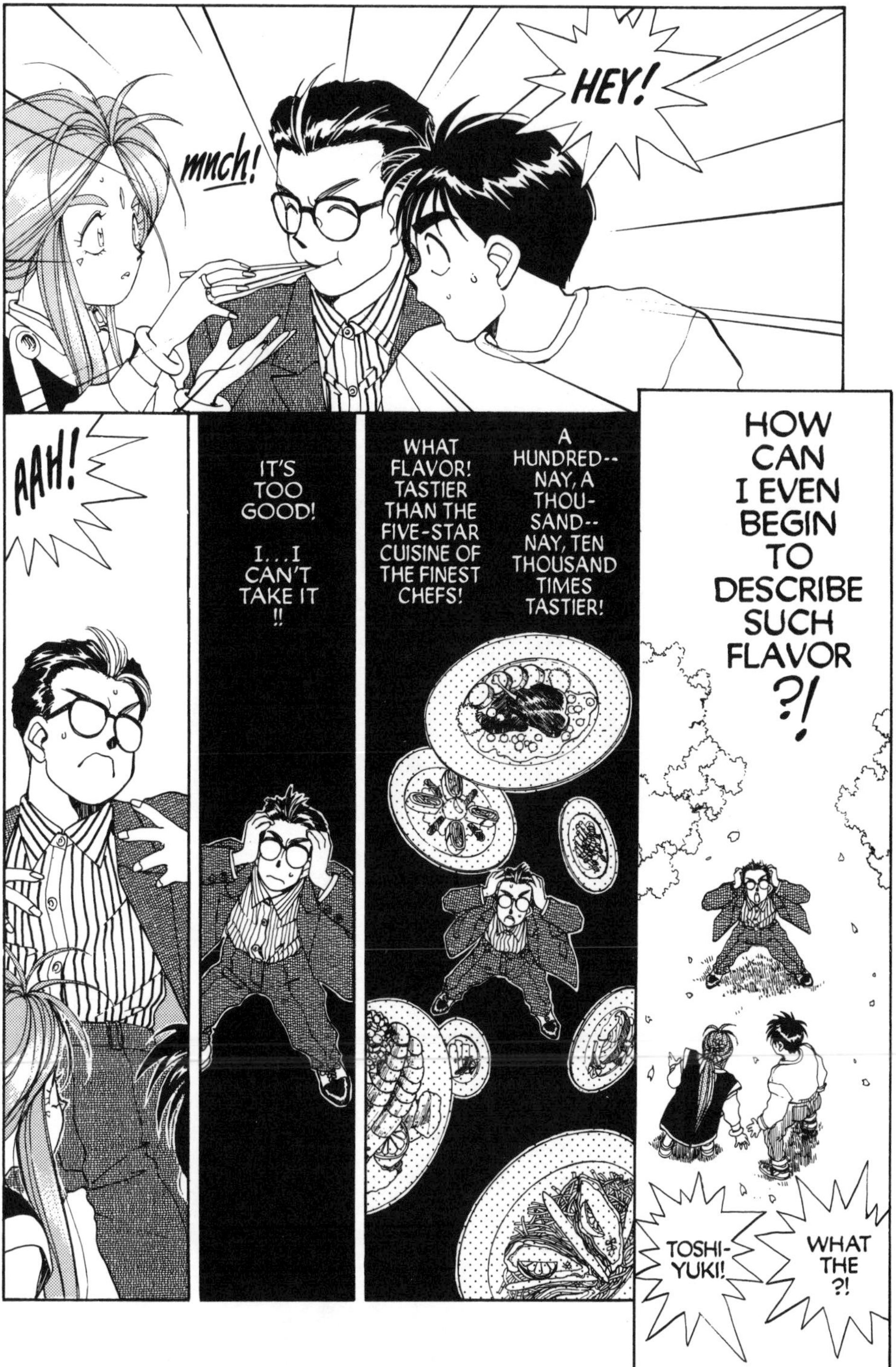

mnch!
HEY!
AAH!
IT'S TOO GOOD!
I...I CAN'T TAKE IT !!
WHAT FLAVOR! TASTIER THAN THE FIVE-STAR CUISINE OF THE FINEST CHEFS!
A HUNDRED-- NAY, A THOU-SAND-- NAY, TEN THOUSAND TIMES TASTIER!
HOW CAN I EVEN BEGIN TO DESCRIBE SUCH FLAVOR ?!
TOSHI-YUKI!
WHAT THE ?!

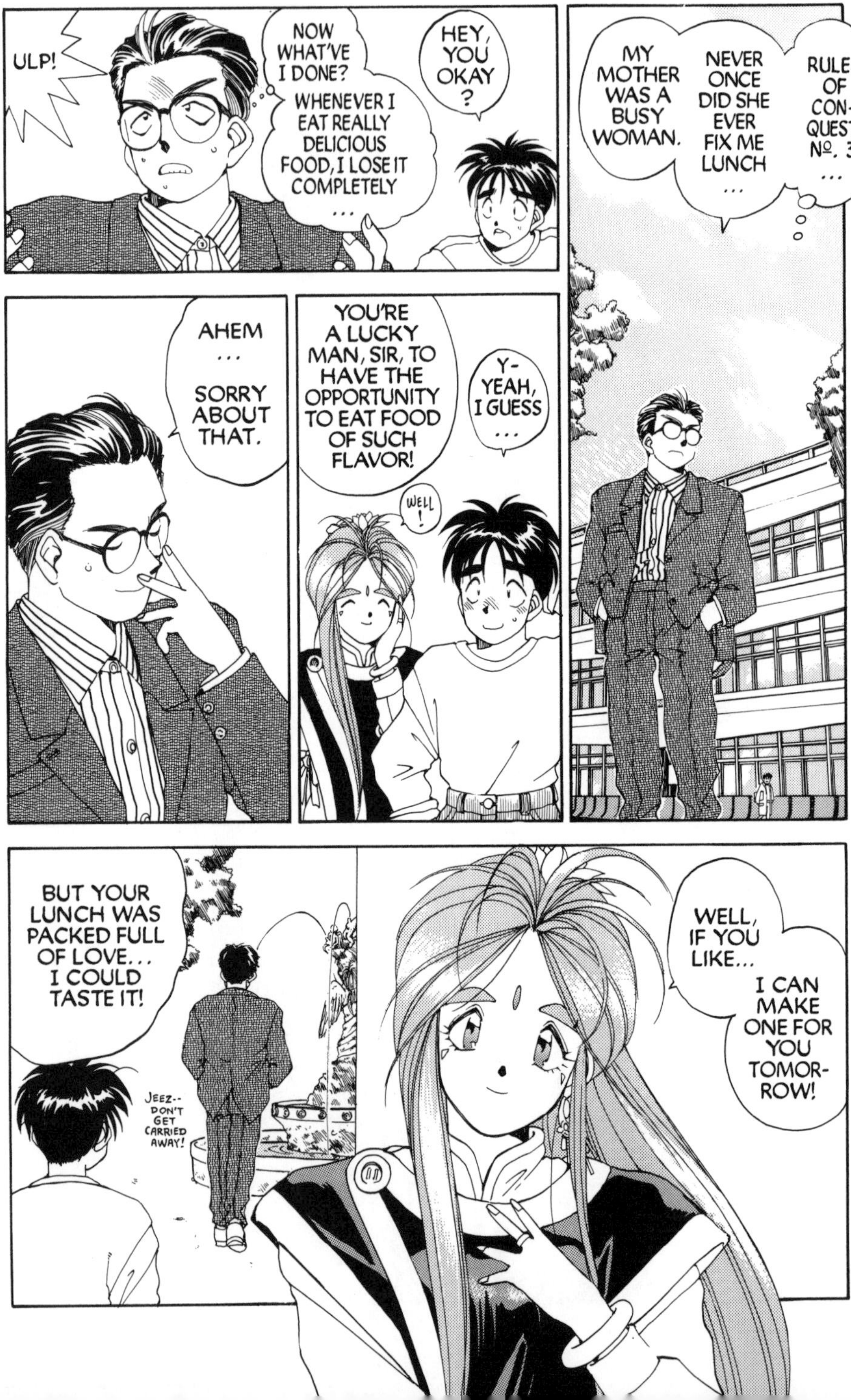
ULP!
NOW WHAT'VE I DONE?
WHENEVER I EAT REALLY DELICIOUS FOOD, I LOSE IT COMPLETELY...
HEY, YOU OKAY?
AHEM... SORRY ABOUT THAT.
YOU'RE A LUCKY MAN, SIR, TO HAVE THE OPPORTUNITY TO EAT FOOD OF SUCH FLAVOR!
Y-YEAH, I GUESS...
WELL!
MY MOTHER WAS A BUSY WOMAN.
NEVER ONCE DID SHE EVER FIX ME LUNCH...
RULES OF CON-QUEST, №. 3...
BUT YOUR LUNCH WAS PACKED FULL OF LOVE... I COULD TASTE IT!
JEEZ-- DON'T GET CARRIED AWAY!
WELL, IF YOU LIKE...
I CAN MAKE ONE FOR YOU TOMOR-ROW!

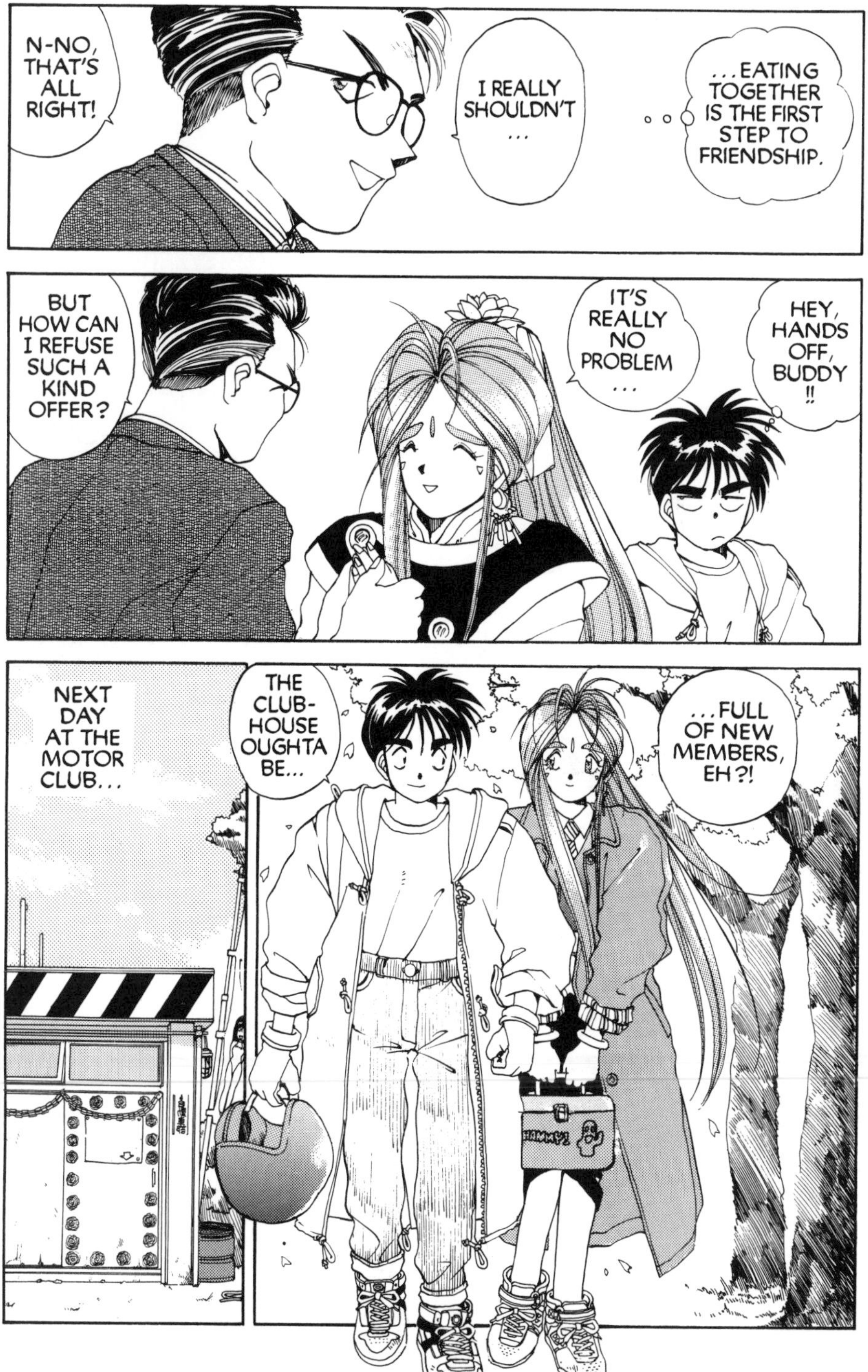
N-NO, THAT'S ALL RIGHT!
I REALLY SHOULDN'T ...
...EATING TOGETHER IS THE FIRST STEP TO FRIENDSHIP.
BUT HOW CAN I REFUSE SUCH A KIND OFFER?
IT'S REALLY NO PROBLEM ...
HEY, HANDS OFF, BUDDY !!
NEXT DAY AT THE MOTOR CLUB...
THE CLUB-HOUSE OUGHTA BE...
...FULL OF NEW MEMBERS, EH?!

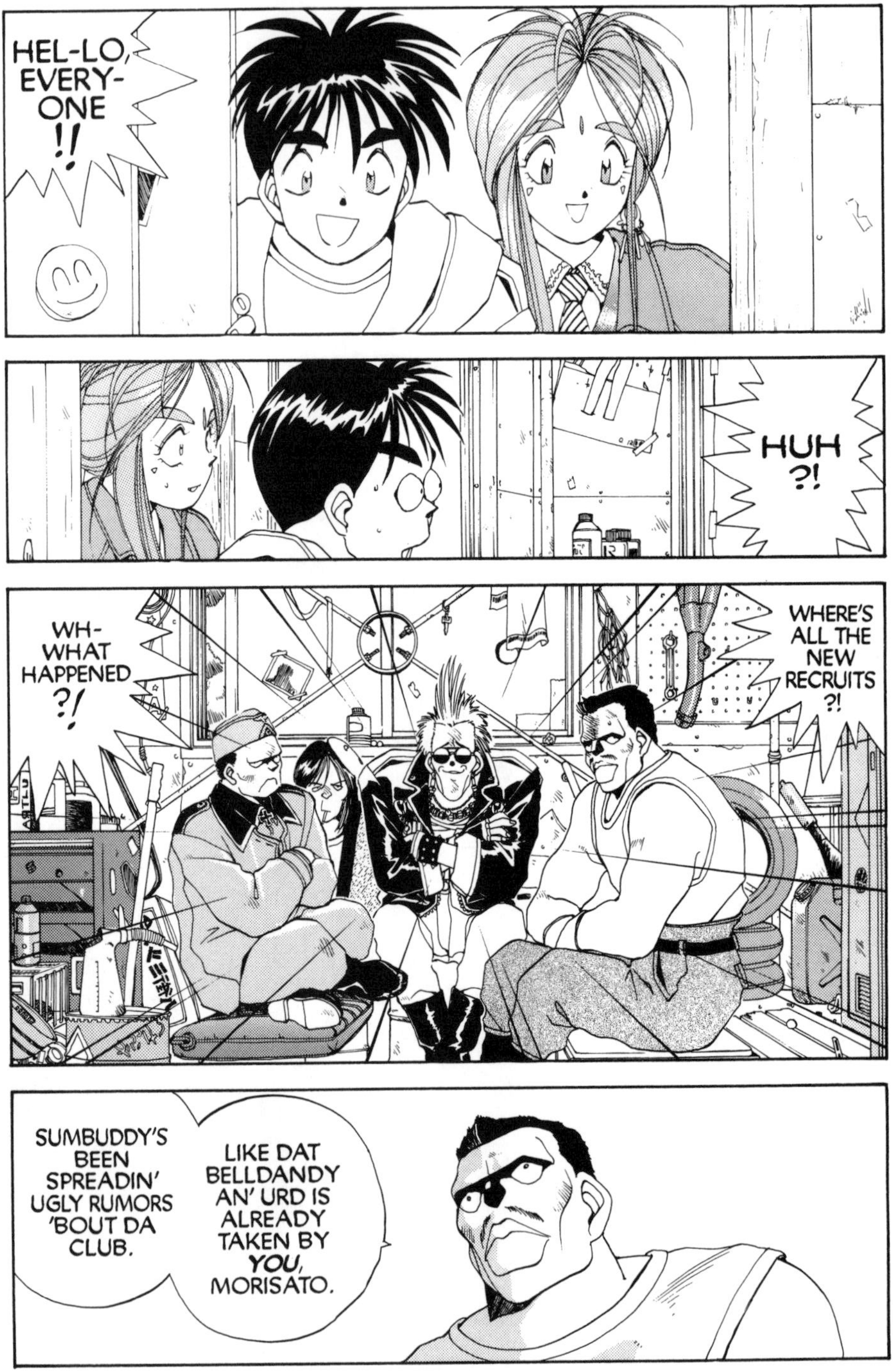
HEL-LO, EVERY-ONE!!
HUH?!
WH-WHAT HAPPENED?!
WHERE'S ALL THE NEW RECRUITS?!
SUMBUDDY'S BEEN SPREADIN' UGLY RUMORS 'BOUT DA CLUB.
LIKE DAT BELLDANDY AN' URD IS ALREADY TAKEN BY *YOU*, MORISATO.

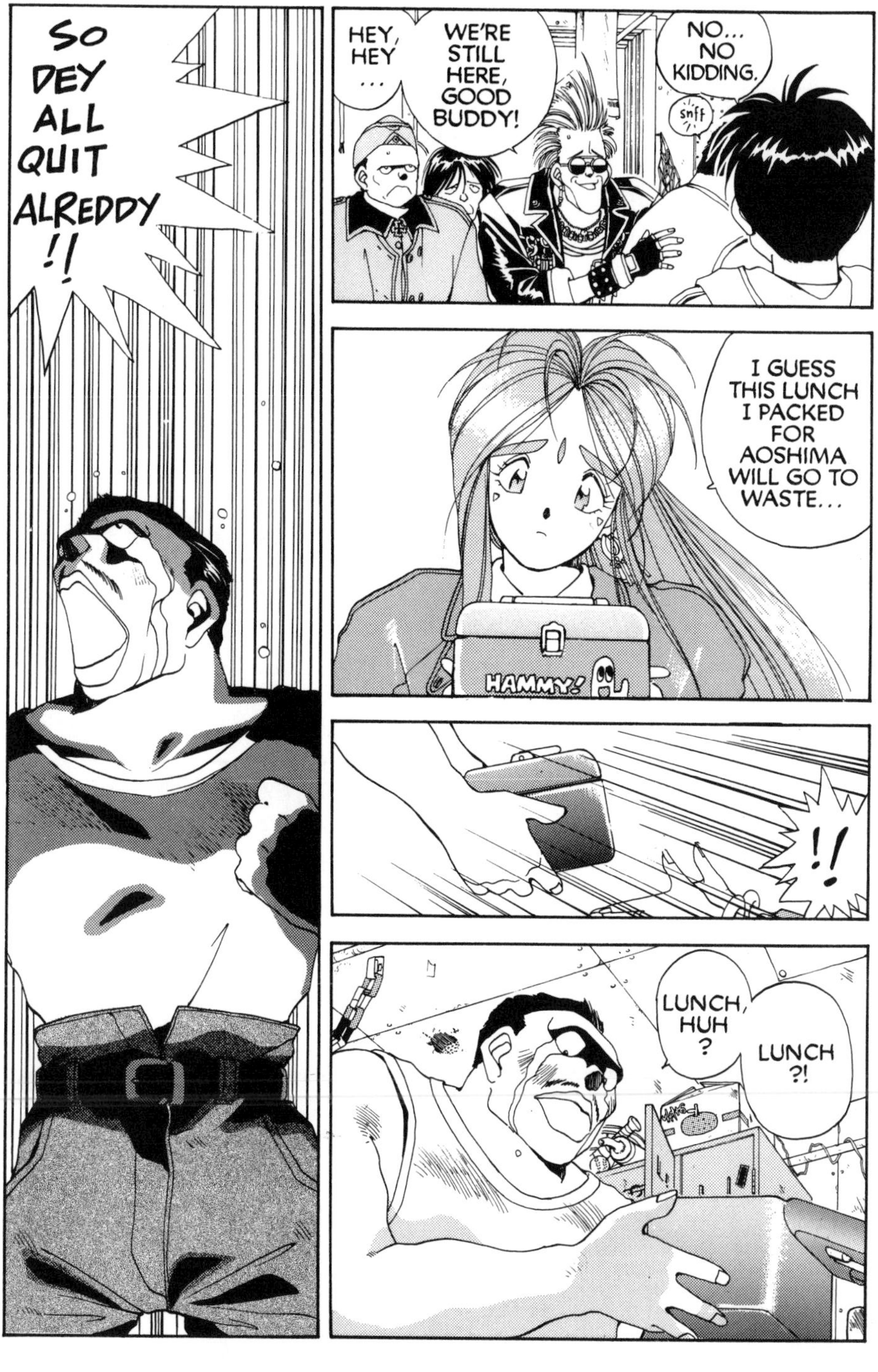
SO DEY ALL QUIT ALREDDY !!
HEY, HEY ...
WE'RE STILL HERE, GOOD BUDDY!
NO... NO KIDDING.
snff
I GUESS THIS LUNCH I PACKED FOR AOSHIMA WILL GO TO WASTE...
HAMMY!
!!
LUNCH, HUH ?
LUNCH ?!

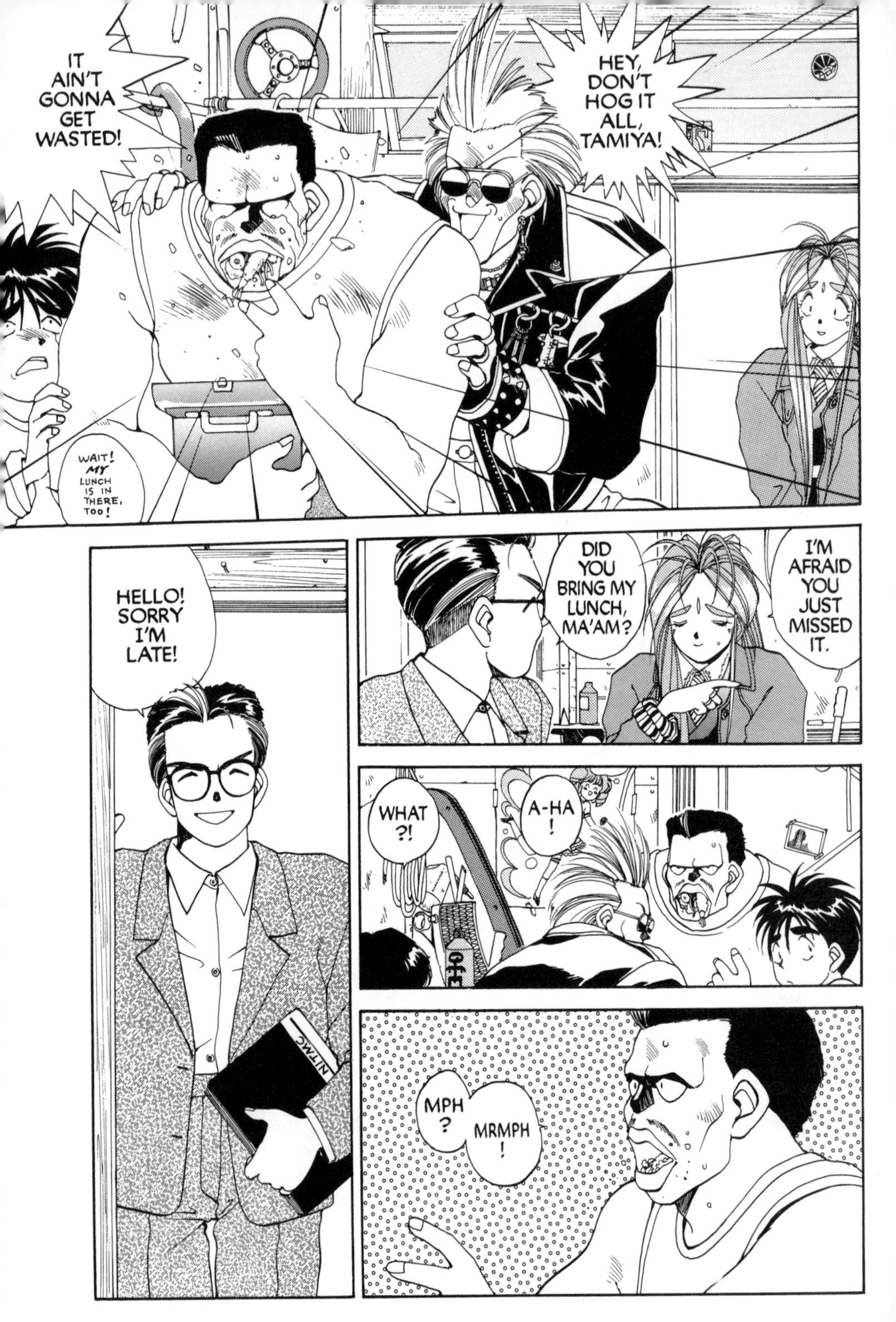
IT AIN'T GONNA GET WASTED!
HEY, DON'T HOG IT ALL, TAMIYA!
WAIT! MY LUNCH IS IN THERE, TOO!
HELLO! SORRY I'M LATE!
NITMC
DID YOU BRING MY LUNCH, MA'AM?
I'M AFRAID YOU JUST MISSED IT.
WHAT ?!
A-HA !
MPH ?
MRMPH !

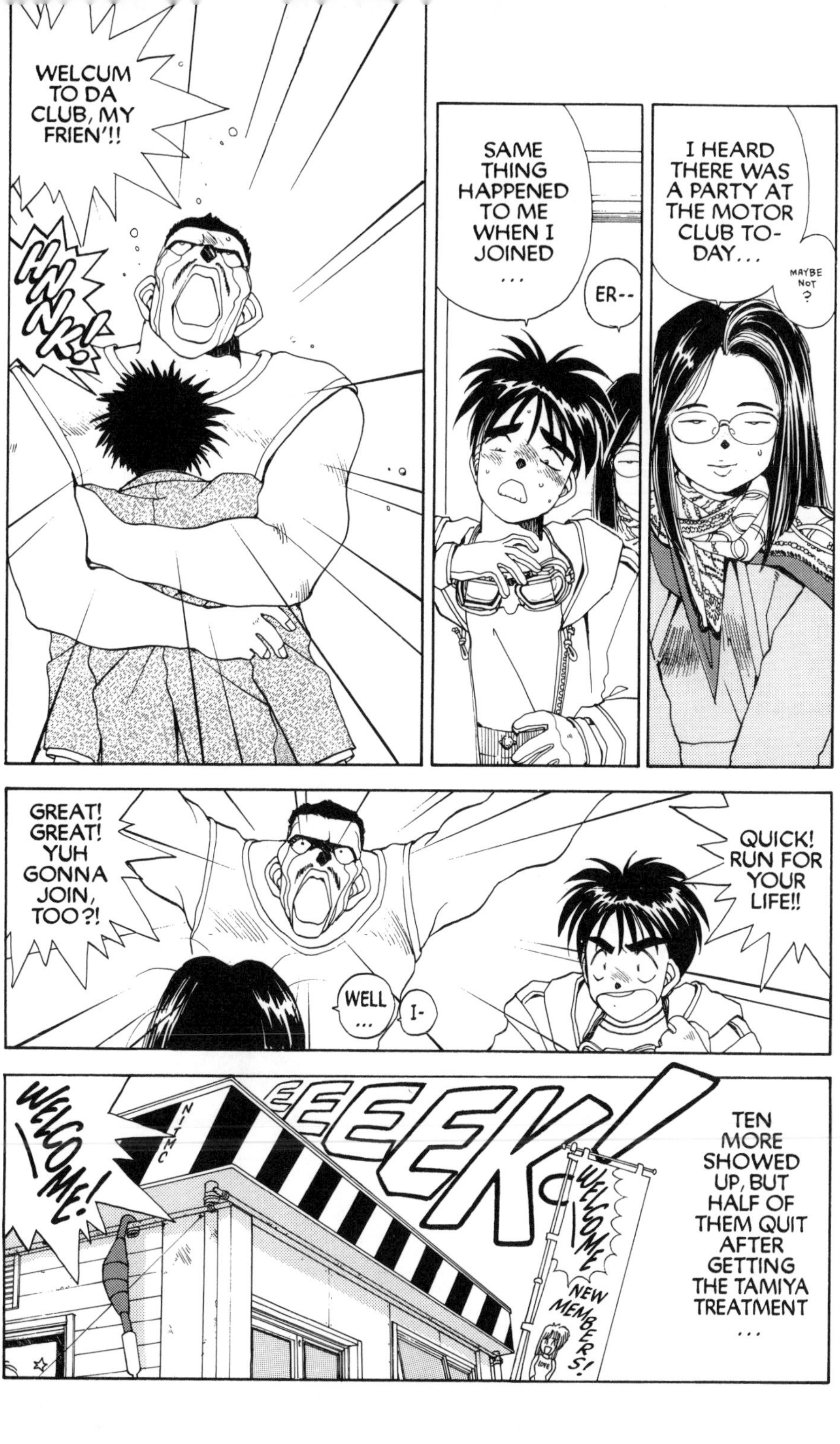
WELCUM TO DA CLUB, MY FRIEN'!!
HWNK!
SAME THING HAPPENED TO ME WHEN I JOINED . . .
ER--
I HEARD THERE WAS A PARTY AT THE MOTOR CLUB TO-DAY . . .
MAYBE NOT ?
GREAT! GREAT! YUH GONNA JOIN, TOO?!
WELL . . .
I-
QUICK! RUN FOR YOUR LIFE!!
WELCOME!
NITMC
EEEEK!
WELCOME NEW MEMBERS!
TEN MORE SHOWED UP, BUT HALF OF THEM QUIT AFTER GETTING THE TAMIYA TREATMENT . . .

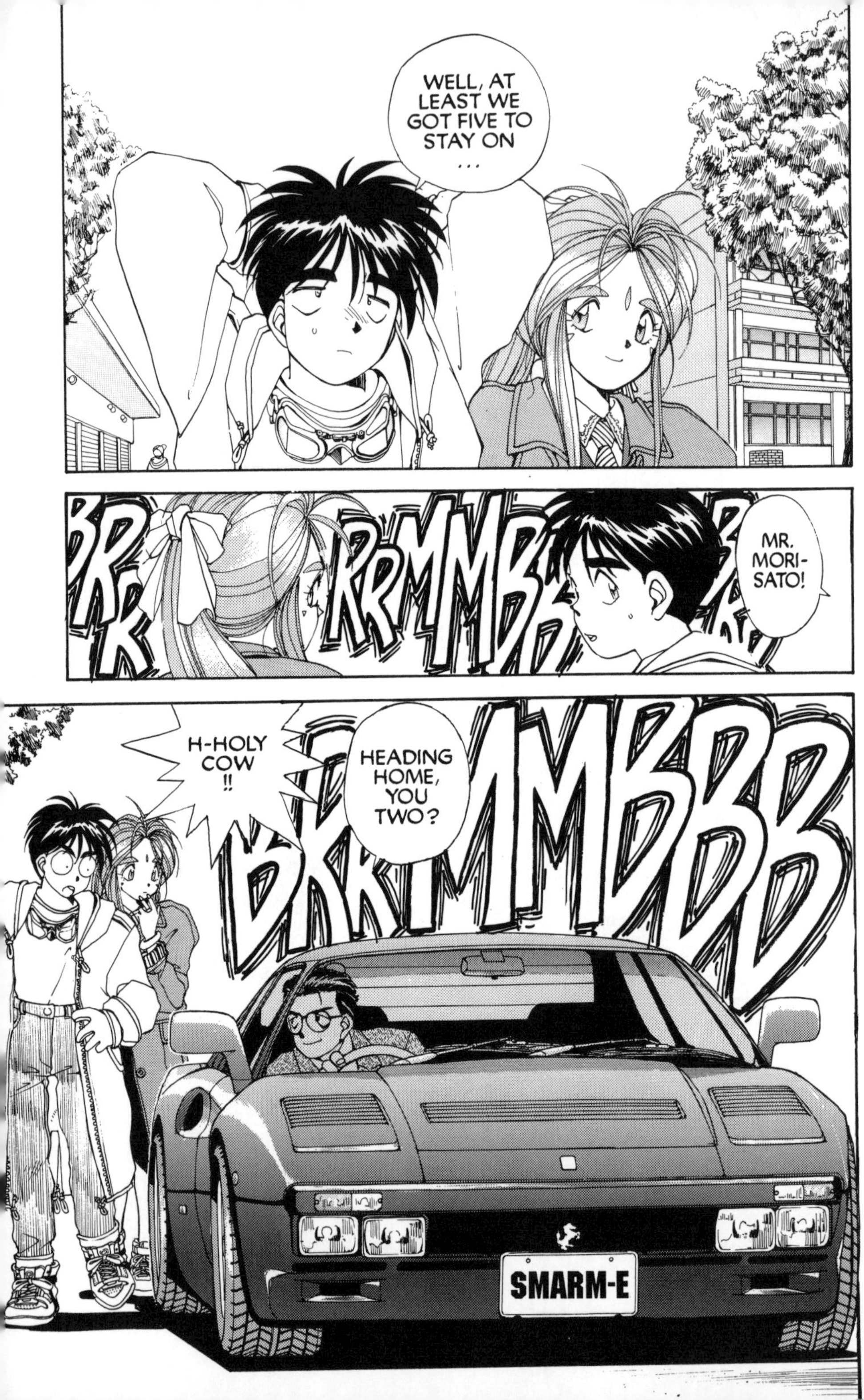

WELL, AT LEAST WE GOT FIVE TO STAY ON . . .
RRMMB
MR. MORI-SATO!
H-HOLY COW !!
HEADING HOME, YOU TWO?
BRRMMBBB
SMARM-E

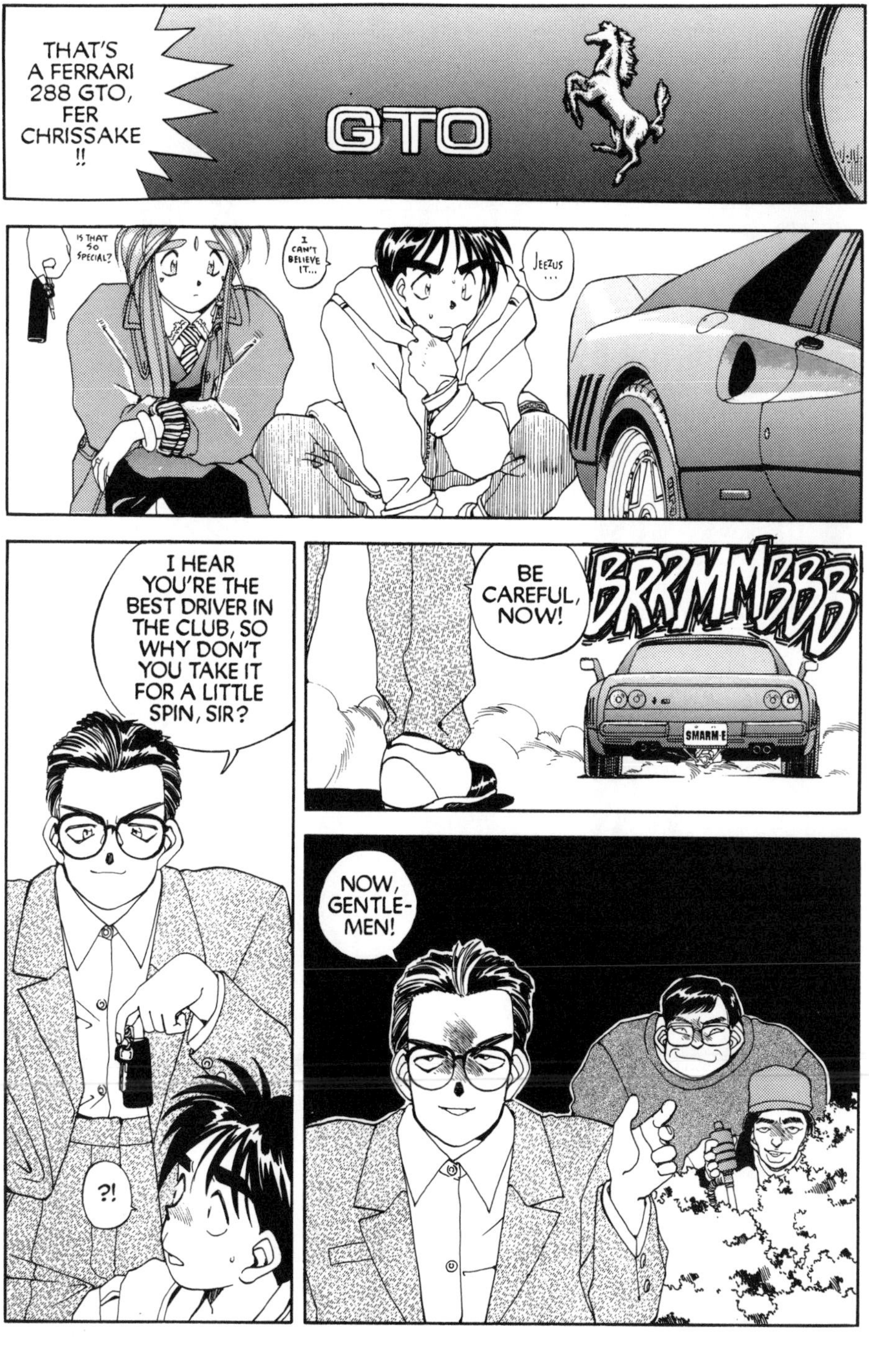
THAT'S A FERRARI 288 GTO, FER CHRISSAKE !!
GTO
IS THAT SO SPECIAL?
I CAN'T BELIEVE IT...
JEEZUS ...
I HEAR YOU'RE THE BEST DRIVER IN THE CLUB, SO WHY DON'T YOU TAKE IT FOR A LITTLE SPIN, SIR?
?!
BE CAREFUL, NOW!
BRRMMBBB
SMARM-E
NOW, GENTLE-MEN!

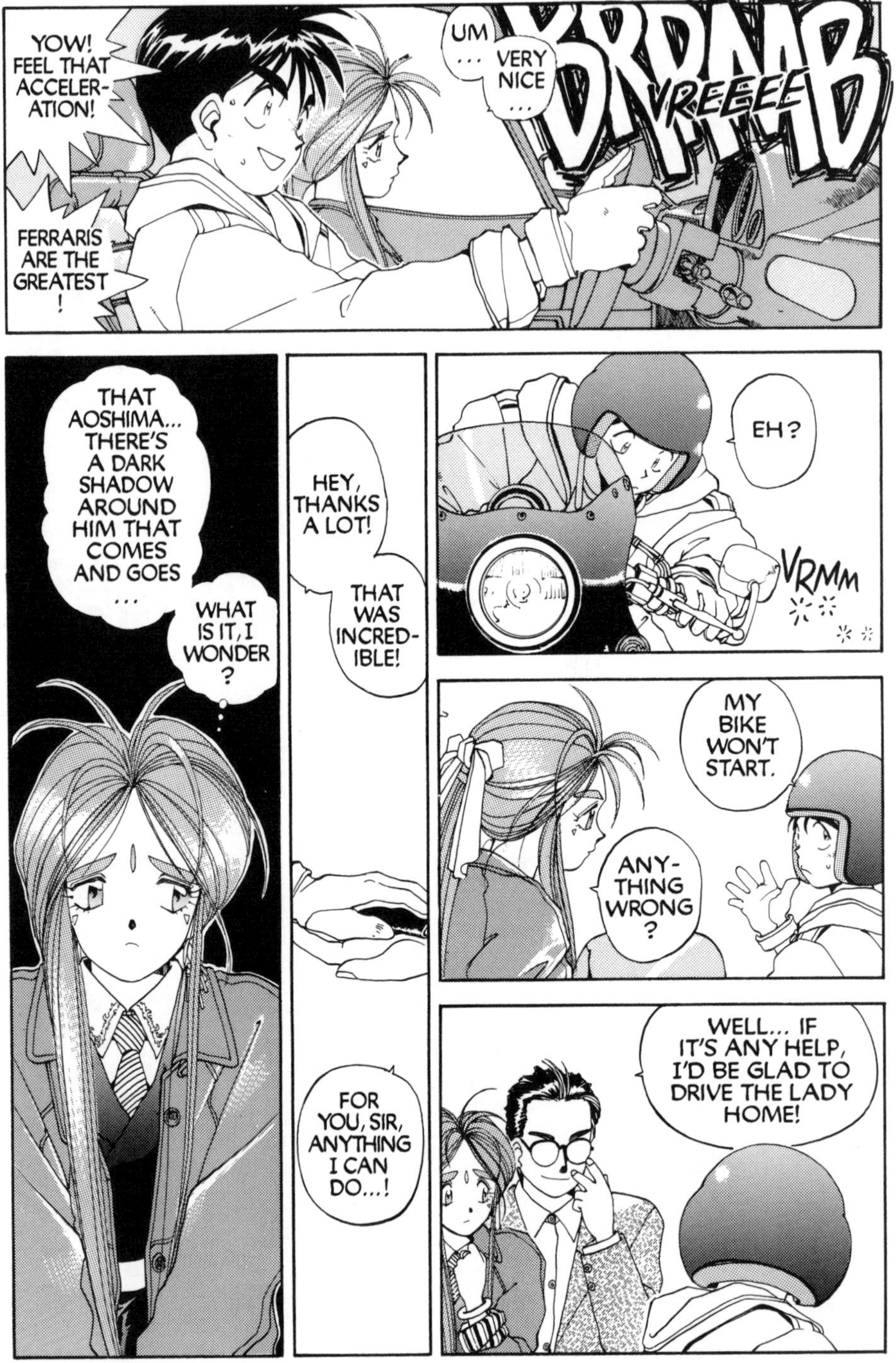
YOW! FEEL THAT ACCELER-ATION!
FERRARIS ARE THE GREATEST!
UM... VERY NICE...
BRDMMB VREEEEE
THAT AOSHIMA... THERE'S A DARK SHADOW AROUND HIM THAT COMES AND GOES...
WHAT IS IT, I WONDER?
HEY, THANKS A LOT!
THAT WAS INCRED-IBLE!
FOR YOU, SIR, ANYTHING I CAN DO...!
EH?
VRMM
MY BIKE WON'T START.
ANY-THING WRONG?
WELL... IF IT'S ANY HELP, I'D BE GLAD TO DRIVE THE LADY HOME!

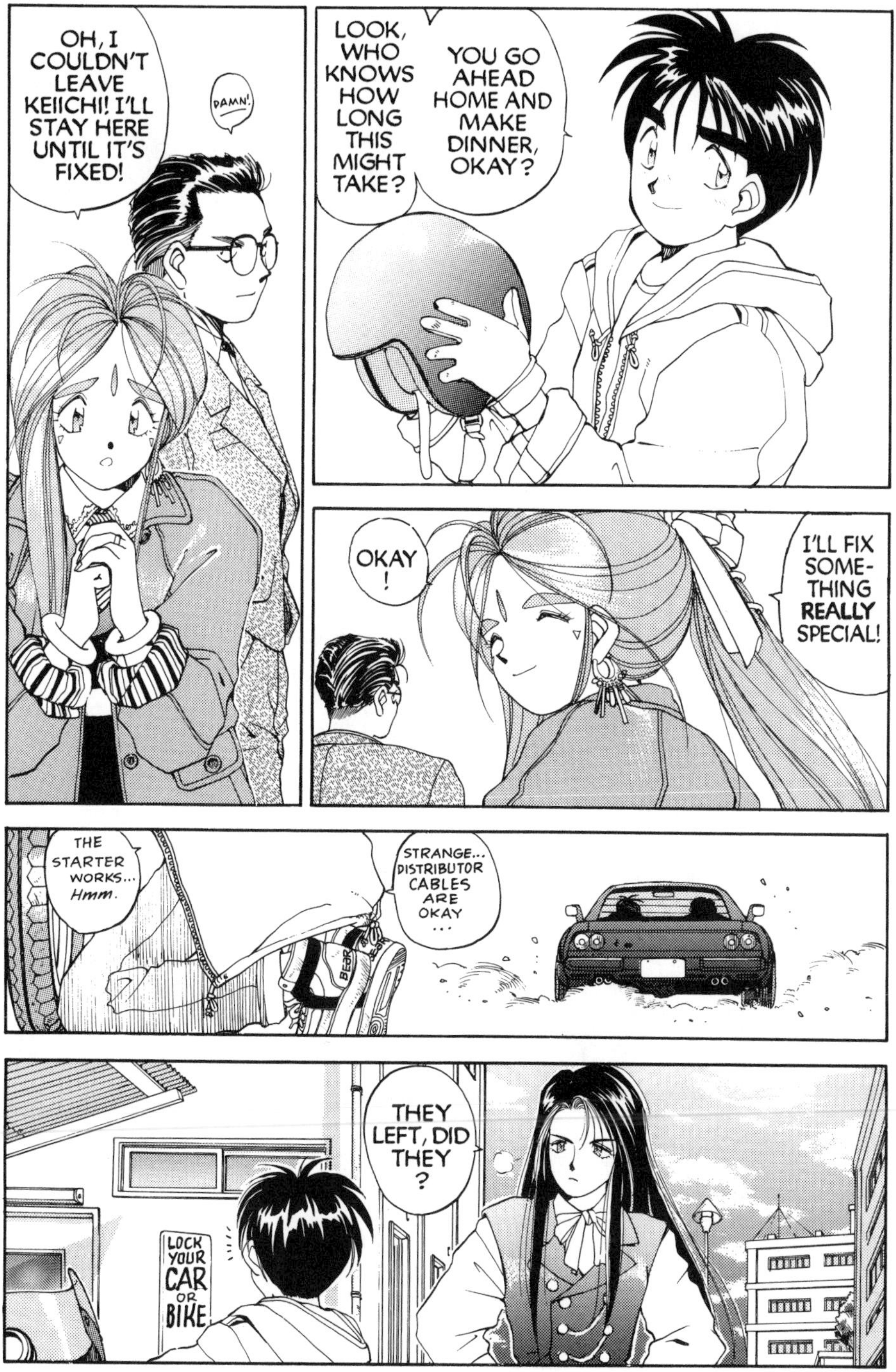
OH, I COULDN'T LEAVE KEIICHI! I'LL STAY HERE UNTIL IT'S FIXED!
DAMN!
LOOK, WHO KNOWS HOW LONG THIS MIGHT TAKE?
YOU GO AHEAD HOME AND MAKE DINNER, OKAY?
OKAY!
I'LL FIX SOMETHING REALLY SPECIAL!
THE STARTER WORKS... Hmm.
STRANGE... DISTRIBUTOR CABLES ARE OKAY...
LOCK YOUR CAR OR BIKE
THEY LEFT, DID THEY?

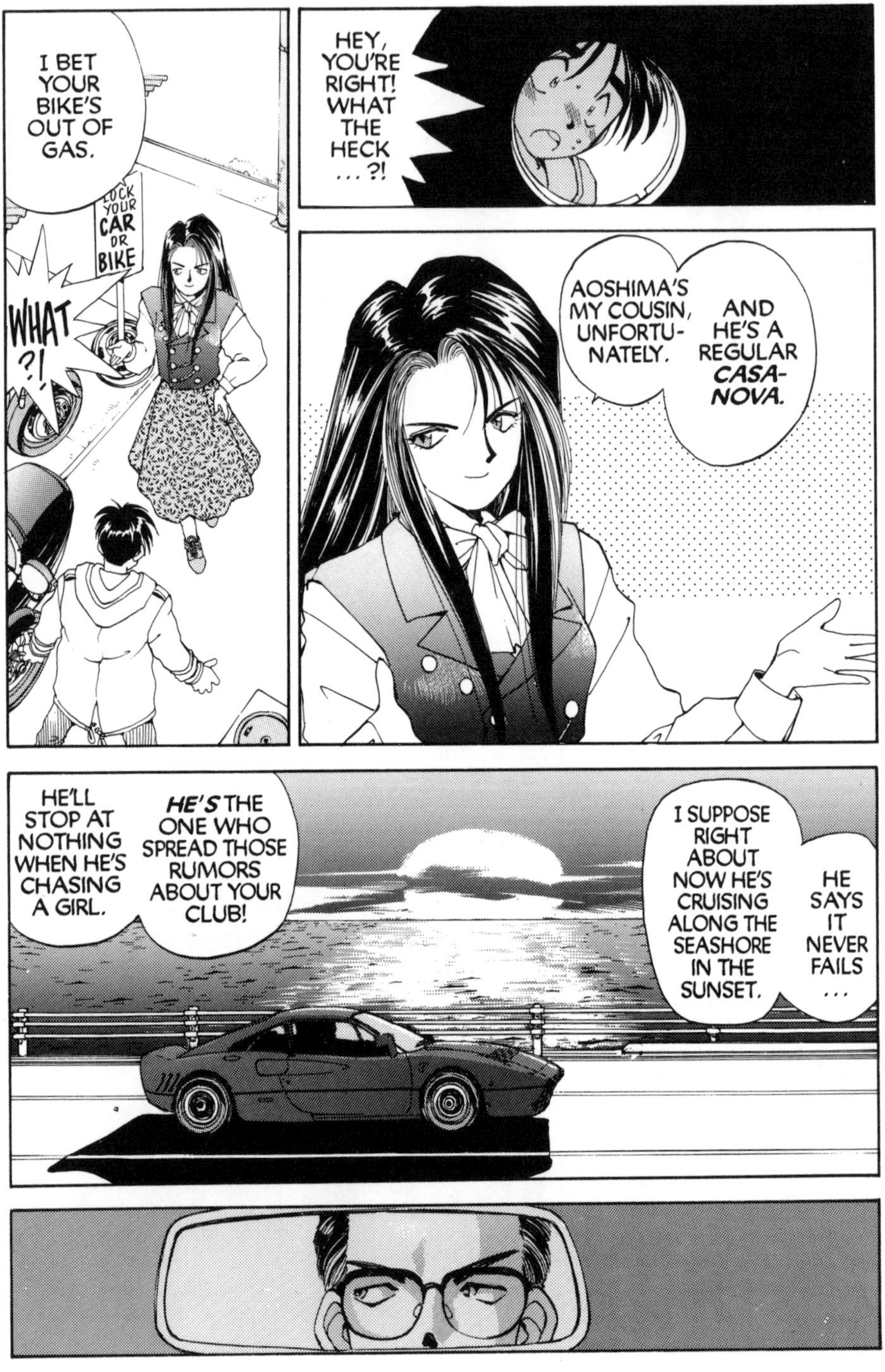
I BET YOUR BIKE'S OUT OF GAS.
LOCK YOUR CAR OR BIKE
WHAT ?!
HEY, YOU'RE RIGHT! WHAT THE HECK ...?!
AOSHIMA'S MY COUSIN, UNFORTUNATELY.
AND HE'S A REGULAR *CASANOVA*.
HE'LL STOP AT NOTHING WHEN HE'S CHASING A GIRL.
HE'S THE ONE WHO SPREAD THOSE RUMORS ABOUT YOUR CLUB!
I SUPPOSE RIGHT ABOUT NOW HE'S CRUISING ALONG THE SEASHORE IN THE SUNSET.
HE SAYS IT NEVER FAILS ...

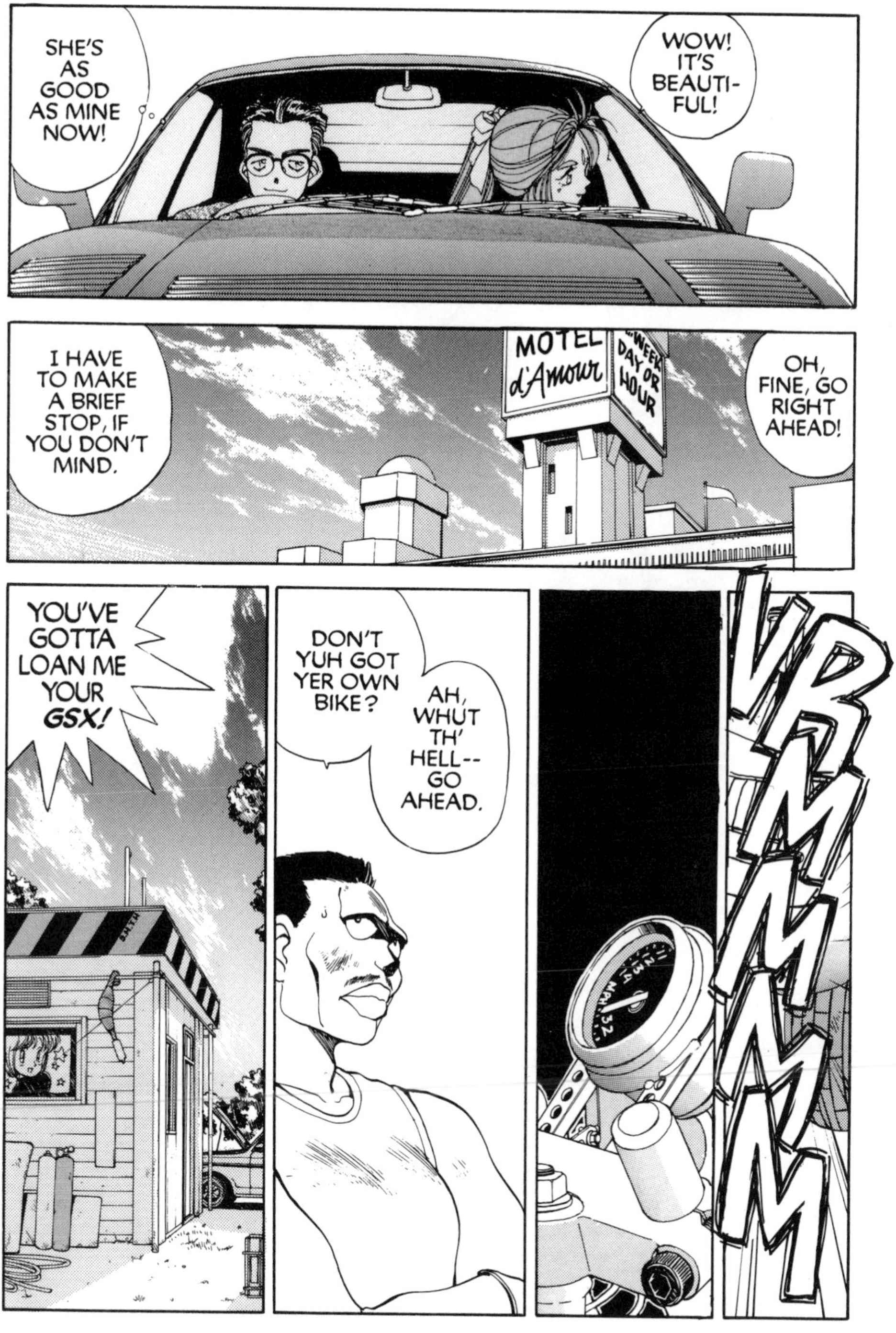
SHE'S AS GOOD AS MINE NOW!
WOW! IT'S BEAUTIFUL!
I HAVE TO MAKE A BRIEF STOP, IF YOU DON'T MIND.
MOTEL d'Amour
WEEK DAY OR HOUR
OH, FINE, GO RIGHT AHEAD!
YOU'VE GOTTA LOAN ME YOUR GSX!
DON'T YUH GOT YER OWN BIKE?
AH, WHUT TH' HELL-- GO AHEAD.
VRMMMMM

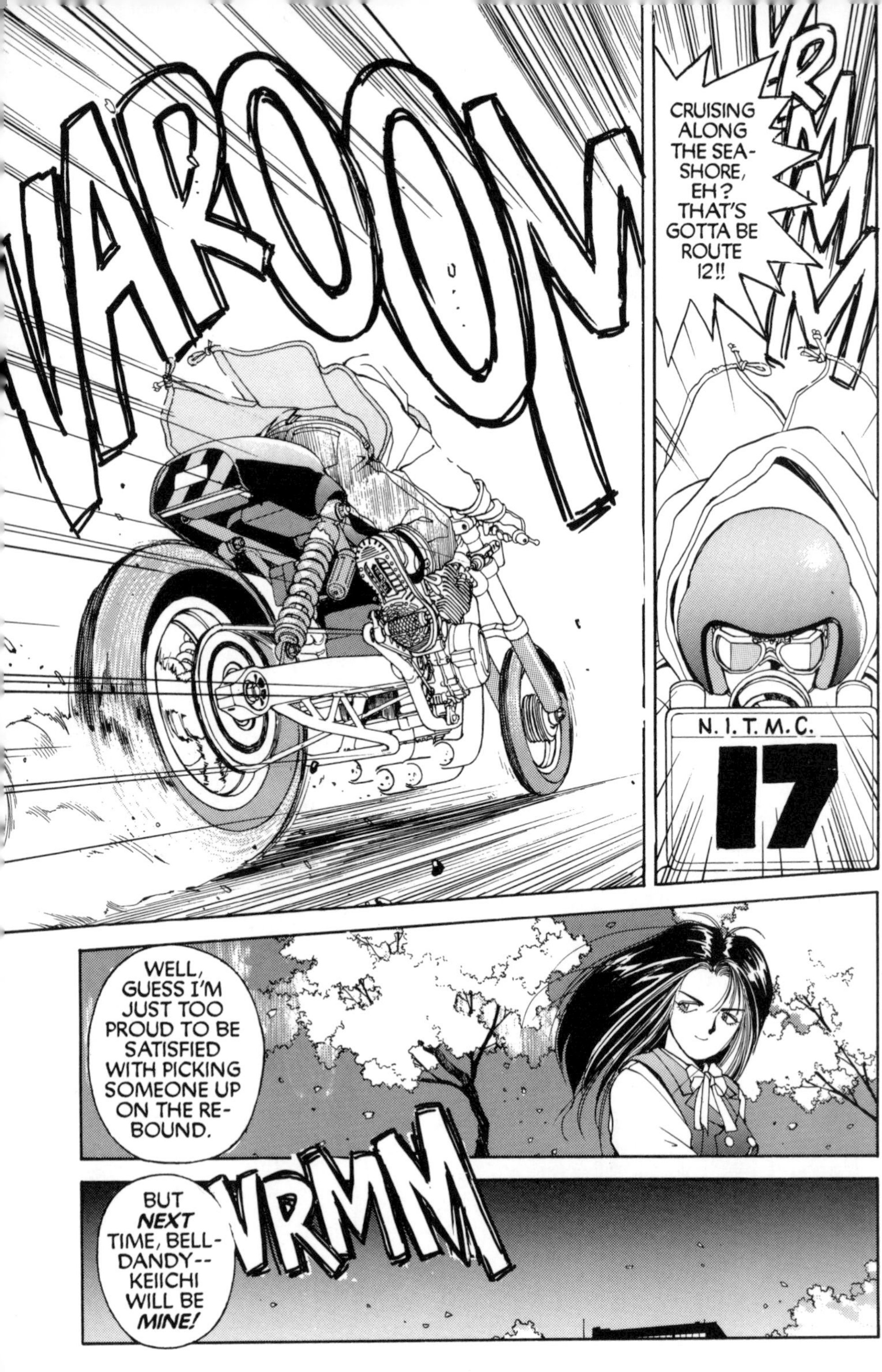
VAROOM
CRUISING ALONG THE SEA-SHORE, EH? THAT'S GOTTA BE ROUTE 12!!
N. I. T. M. C.
17
WELL, GUESS I'M JUST TOO PROUD TO BE SATISFIED WITH PICKING SOMEONE UP ON THE RE-BOUND.
VRMM
BUT *NEXT* TIME, BELL-DANDY-- KEIICHI WILL BE *MINE!*

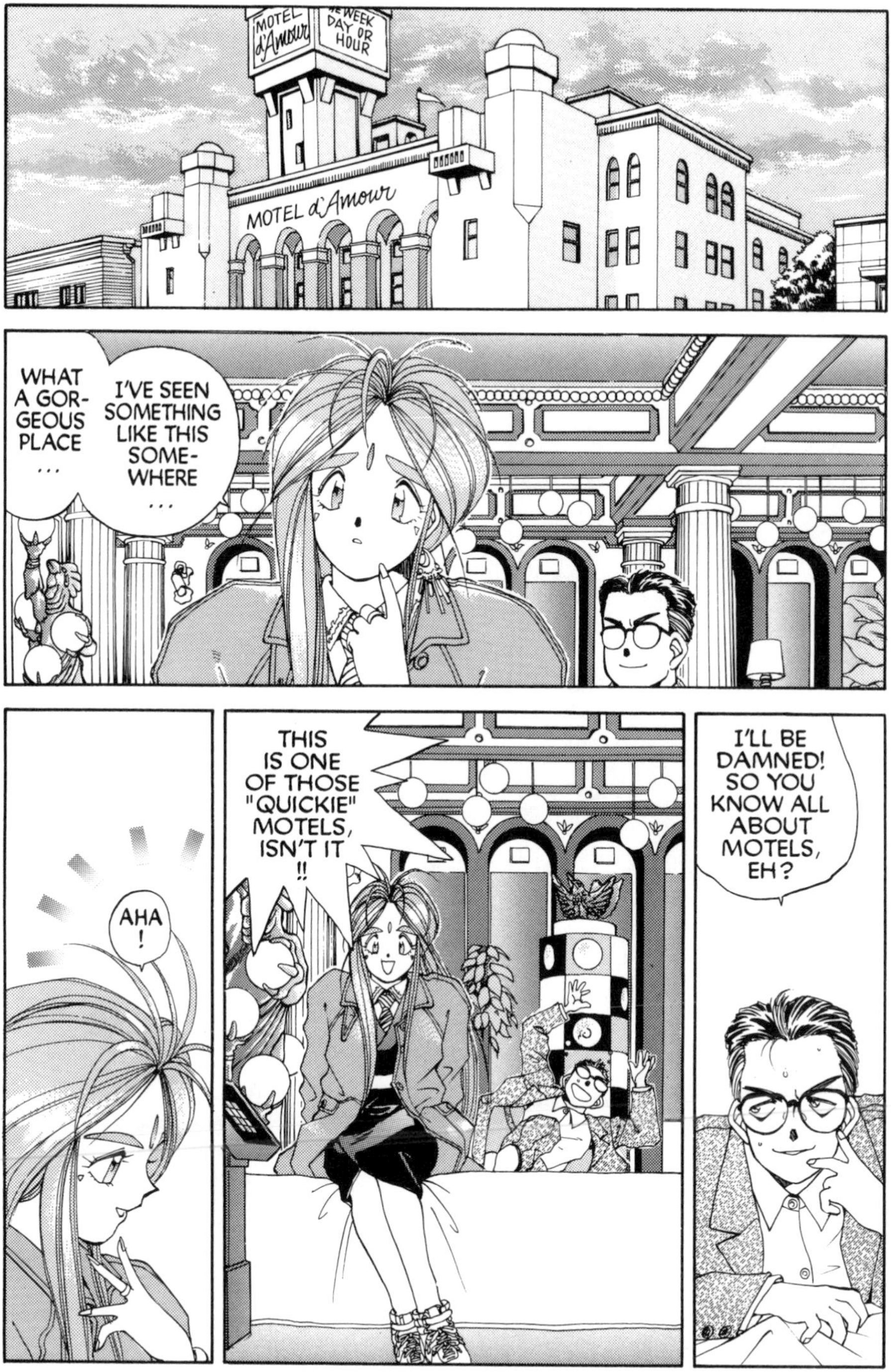
MOTEL d'Amour
WEEK DAY OR HOUR
MOTEL d'Amour
WHAT A GORGEOUS PLACE ...
I'VE SEEN SOMETHING LIKE THIS SOMEWHERE ...
AHA!
THIS IS ONE OF THOSE "QUICKIE" MOTELS, ISN'T IT!!
I'LL BE DAMNED! SO YOU KNOW ALL ABOUT MOTELS, EH?

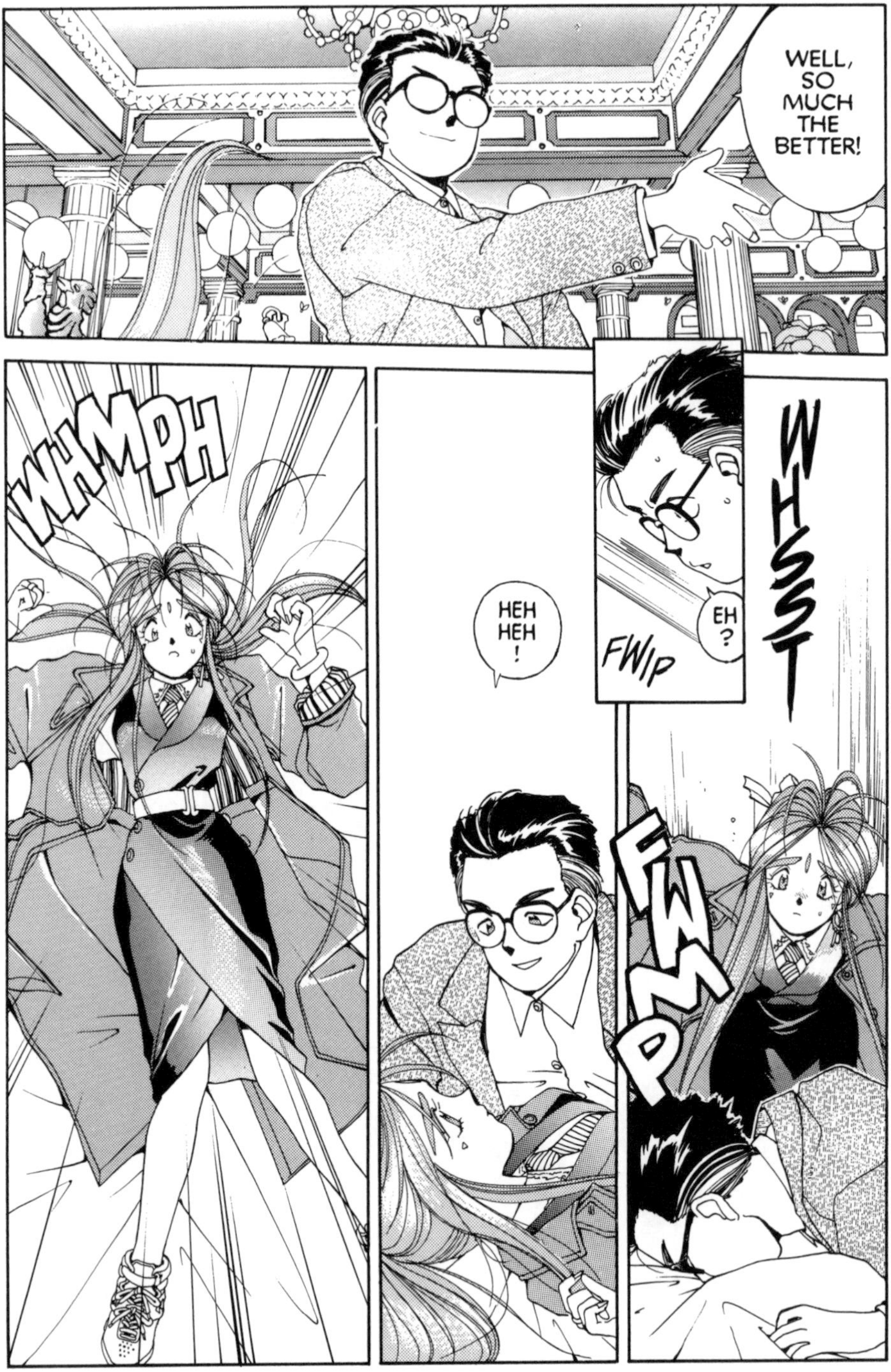
WELL, SO MUCH THE BETTER!
WHMPH
HEH HEH!
FWIP
EH?
WHSST
FWMP

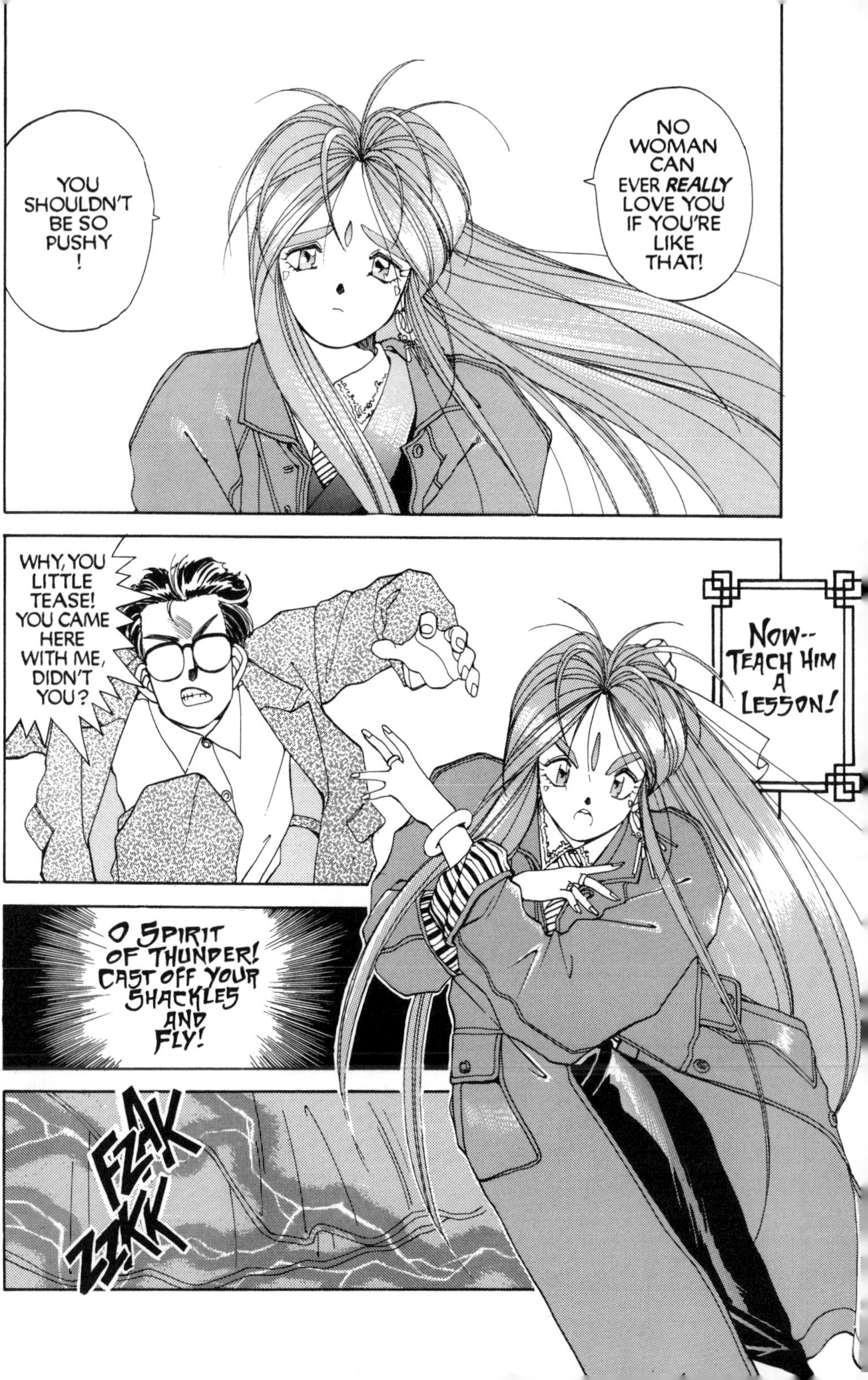
YOU SHOULDN'T BE SO PUSHY!
NO WOMAN CAN EVER *REALLY* LOVE YOU IF YOU'RE LIKE THAT!
WHY, YOU LITTLE TEASE! YOU CAME HERE WITH ME, DIDN'T YOU?
NOW-- TEACH HIM A LESSON!
O SPIRIT OF THUNDER! CAST OFF YOUR SHACKLES AND FLY!
FZAK ZZKK

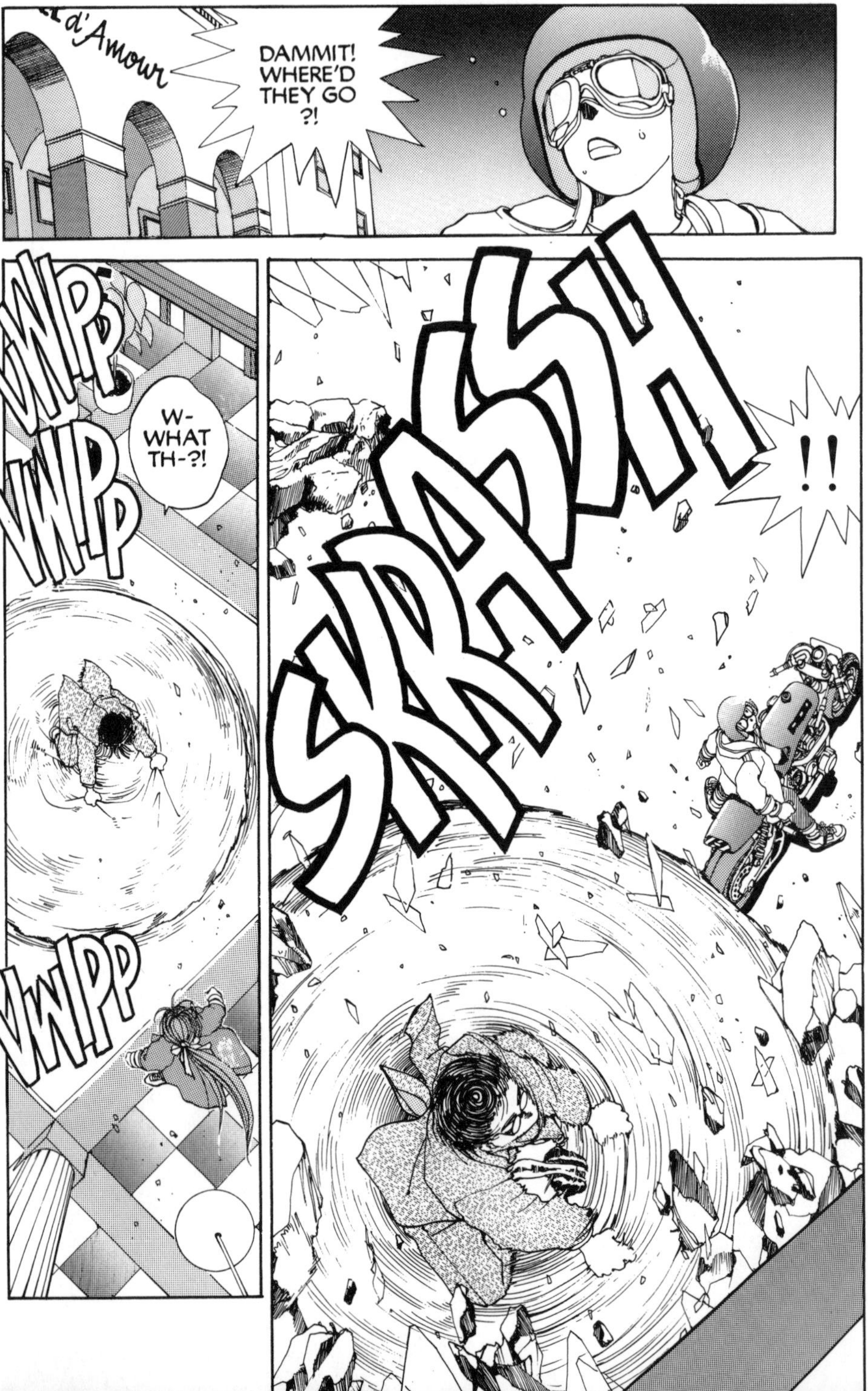
d'Amour
DAMMIT! WHERE'D THEY GO ?!
VWIPP
VWIPP
W-WHAT TH-?!
VWIPP
SKRASH
!!

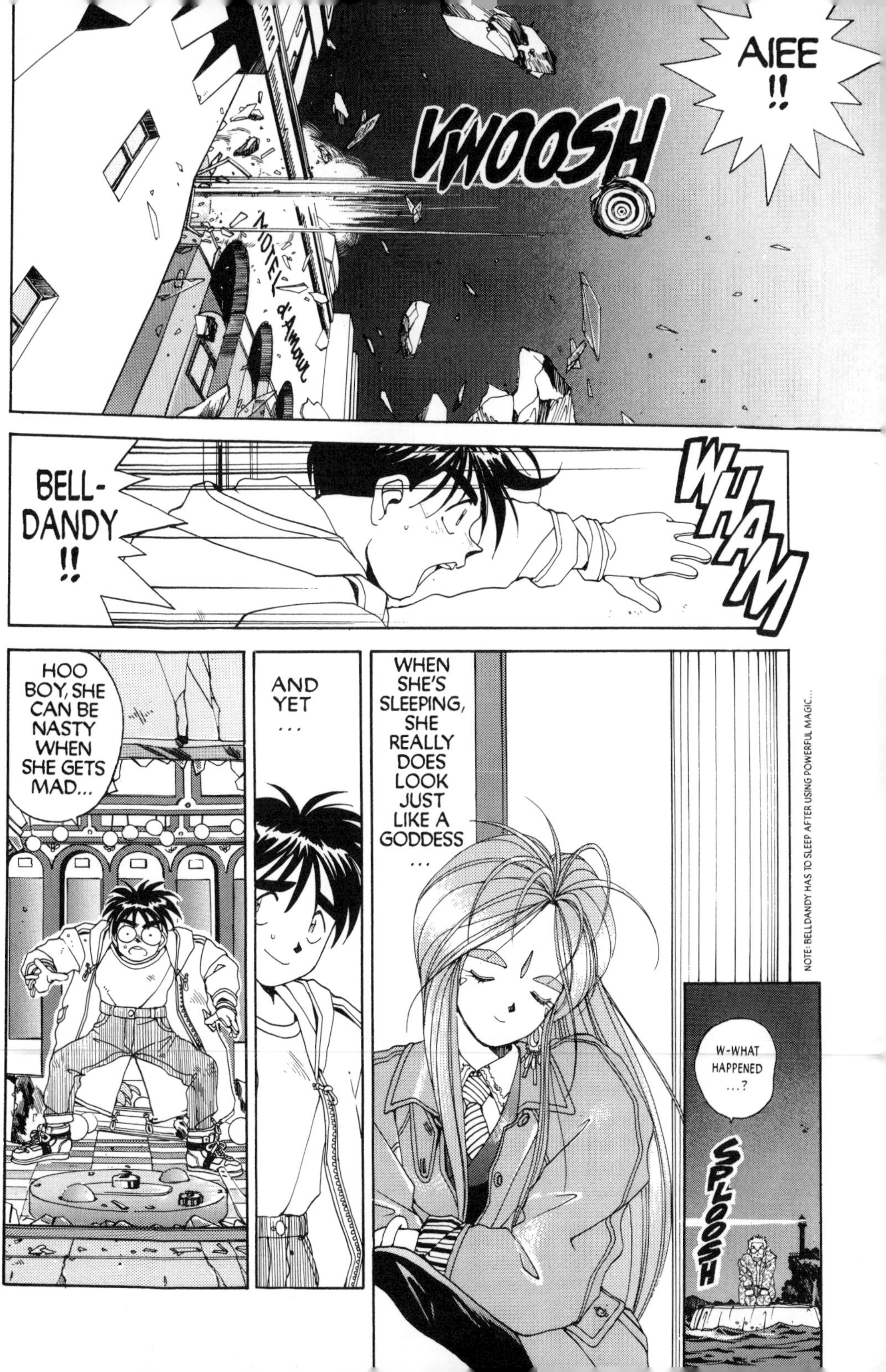
VWOOSH
AIEE !!
MOTEL d'Amour
BELL-DANDY !!
WHAM
HOO BOY, SHE CAN BE NASTY WHEN SHE GETS MAD...
AND YET ...
WHEN SHE'S SLEEPING, SHE REALLY DOES LOOK JUST LIKE A GODDESS ...
NOTE: BELLDANDY HAS TO SLEEP AFTER USING POWERFUL MAGIC...
W-WHAT HAPPENED ...?
SPLOOSH

Dark Horse Comics: **Mike Richardson** *publisher* • **Neil Hankerson** *executive vice president* • **Andy Karabatsos** *vice president of finance* • **Randy Stradley** *vice president of publishing* • **Chris Warner** *senior editor* • **Michael Martens** *vice president of marketing* • **Anita Nelson** *vice president of sales & licensing* • **David Scroggy** *vice president of product development* • **Mark Cox** *art director* • **Dale LaFountain** *vice president of information technology* • **Kim Haines** *director of human resources* • **Darlene Vogel** *director of purchasing* • **Ken Lizzi** • *general counsel*